CAMBRIDGE STUDIES IN FRENCH 63

GENDER, RHETORIC, AND PRINT CULTURE
IN FRENCH RENAISSANCE WRITING

Recent titles in the series include

ELIZA ADAMOWICZ
Surrealist Collage in Text and Image: Dissecting the Exquisite Corpse

NICHOLAS WHITE
The Family in Crisis in Late Nineteenth-Century French Fiction

PAUL GIFFORD AND BRIAN STIMPSON
Reading Paul Valéry: Universe in Mind

MICHAEL R. FINN
Proust, the Body and Literary Form

JULIE CANDLER HAYES
Reading the French Enlightenment: System and Subversion

URSULA TIDD
Simone de Beauvoir, Gender and Testimony

ANN JEFFERSON
Nathalie Sarraute, Fiction and Theory: Questions of Difference

A complete list of books in the series is given at the end of the volume.

In this book Floyd Gray explores how the treatment of controversial subjects in French Renaissance writing was affected both by rhetorical conventions and by the commercial requirements of an expanding publishing industry. Focusing on a wide range of discourses on gender issues – misogynist, feminist, autobiographical, homosexual, and medical – Gray reveals the extent to which these marginalized texts reflect literary concerns rather than social reality. He then moves from a close analysis of the rhetorical factor in the *Querelle des femmes* to consider ways in which writing, as a textual phenomenon, inscribes its own, sometimes ambiguous, meaning. Gray offers richly detailed readings of writings by Rabelais, Jeanne Flore, Montaigne, Louise Labé, Pernette du Guillet, and Marie de Gournay among others, challenging the inherent anachronism of those forms of criticism that fail to take account of the rhetorical and cultural conditions of the period.

FLOYD GRAY is Professor of French at the University of Michigan. He is a leading figure in French Renaissance studies, well known for his many books on Montaigne and Rabelais. His recent books include critical editions of Rabelais's *Gargantua* (1995) and *Pantagruel* (1997), *Rabelais et le comique du discontinu* (1994), and *Montaigne bilingue: le latin des Essais* (1991).

GENDER, RHETORIC, AND PRINT CULTURE IN FRENCH RENAISSANCE WRITING

FLOYD GRAY

CAMBRIDGE
UNIVERSITY PRESS

CAMBRIDGE UNIVERSITY PRESS
Cambridge, New York, Melbourne, Madrid, Cape Town, Singapore, São Paulo

Cambridge University Press
The Edinburgh Building, Cambridge CB2 2RU, UK

Published in the United States of America by Cambridge University Press, New York

www.cambridge.org
Information on this title: www.cambridge.org/9780521773270

First published 2000
This digitally printed first paperback version 2006

A catalogue record for this publication is available from the British Library

Library of Congress Cataloguing in Publication data
Gray, Floyd, 1926–
Gender, rhetoric, and print culture in French Renaissance writing / Floyd Gray.
p. cm. – (Cambridge studies in French: 63)
Includes bibliographical references and index.
ISBN 0 521 77327 X (hb.)
1. French literature – 16th century – History and criticism.
2. French literature – 17th century – History and criticism.
3. Sex in literature. 4. Gender identity in literature.
I. Title. II. Series.
PQ239.G73 2000
840.9′003–dc21 99–45327 CIP

ISBN-13 978-0-521-77327-0 hardback
ISBN-10 0-521-77327-X hardback

ISBN-13 978-0-521-02487-7 paperback
ISBN-10 0-521-02487-0 paperback

Contents

Introduction   *Page* 1

1   Discourses of misogyny   6
    The rule of rhetoric   7
    The *Querelle des femmes*: rhetoric or reality?   11
    Antifeminism and marriage in Rabelais's *Tiers Livre*   21

2   Irony and the sexual other   30
    Jeanne Flore and erotic desire: feminism or male fantasy?   31
    Reading and writing in the tenth story of the *Heptaméron*   47

3   Anonymity and the poetics of regendering   62
    The "I" as another   63
    Pernette du Guillet's Platonism   77
    Louise Labé's Petrarchism   86

4   The women in Montaigne's life   107
    Montaigne's women   108
    Marie de Gournay's Montaigne   121

5   Sexual marginality   133
    Reading homosexuality   134
    Cross-dressing   144
    The androgyne myth   149
    Brantôme, medical discourse, and the makings of pornography   156

Conclusion   164

Notes   169
Bibliography   209
Index   224

vii

Introduction

One of the principal themes running through this study is that of the implications of the use of rhetorical strategies in the articulation of marginal discourses. The question variously raised is to what extent and in what ways the peculiar expression of the place and presence of women, sexual difference, auctorial identity, is a reflection of literary rather than social reality. Another, corollary theme is that of the contribution of print and printers to the shape of vernacular writing and the subjects it privileges.

The gradual acceptance of French as a language of literature and science is mirrored in the printing of French, regularly by the middle of the sixteenth century, in the roman and italic formerly reserved for Latin texts. Printing and the printing trade redefined in profound ways the context of editor–author and author–reader interaction, encouraging the introduction and exploitation of commercially motivated materials and techniques, while compounding the problem of how and what to read. Given the formal rhetorical training Renaissance writers and readers alike received, and the fact that rhetoric is essentially the means by which writers contrive to rival with and reorganize reality, it is hardly surprising that topical and linguistic play is one of the factors at work in the literature of the day, or that the reading public was adequately prepared to anticipate and appreciate both its performative and its provisional qualities.

From an analysis of the rhetorical factor in the *Querelle des femmes*, this study moves to a consideration of the ways in which writing, viewed as a textual phenomenon, inscribes its own, sometimes ambiguous, meaning. Centered on women writing and writing about women, this is essentially a work on interrelated themes and topics. It does not pretend to afford a history of gender or of print culture in the Renaissance. Rather, it is intended primarily to provide an understanding of the manner in which texts were conceived and

I

written at the time and, therefore, of the way they might best be read today.

Various critical approaches to writing practices and print culture are examined, not only because examples are drawn from different contexts and genres and observed, consequently, from different angles, but also because of their particular relevance to the reading of the texts in question. Finally, one of the crucial themes of this work is that of the inherent anachronism of certain methods of assigning meaning to Renaissance texts, namely those which avoid the cultural reality or blur the rhetorical conditions in which they were written.

The separate chapters of this study are focused successively on a number of marginal or marginalizing discourses – misogynist, feminist,[1] autobiographical, homosexual, medical – considered in their thematic and rhetorical configurations. Together, they are intended to provide a series of readings, through the example of representative authors, on the interaction between rhetoric and subject matter in French Renaissance texts. An underlying premise is the idea that much that is current or contemporary in the cultural context of these works is due, partially at least, to printing, or, more particularly, to the realities of the printing trade – to those *libraires-imprimeurs* who, subscribing to the interests of a wider and more curious reading public, are prompted to promote controversial, and therefore commercially viable, subjects and authors.

It must be emphasized that the treatment of these topics is selective. Thus, certain authors and texts have been given priority in an attempt to illustrate the different ways in which language is meant to mean in early modern texts. Further, the theoretical and historical questions of marginality and print culture are frequently more implicit than explicit. Nevertheless, the line of argument, being accumulative, is constantly reinforced. Revolving around the relationship of rhetoric with writing about women and women writing, this study begins with a review of the rhetorical training the Renaissance writer and reader would have received, and proceeds with an analysis of a number of instances or cases of rhetoric in action, ranging from the *Querelle des femmes* and Rabelais to Jeanne Flore and Marguerite de Navarre. Following a review of the place of the masculine "I" in the poetry at the beginning of the century, the question of the appearance of its feminine equivalent in the works of Pernette du Guillet and Louise Labé is taken up. The penultimate chapter deals with referential rhetoric, first in Montaigne, then in Marie de Gournay, whereas the last one is concerned with sexual and medical discourse in the vernacular. These concluding pages raise the broader question of the final, perhaps inevitable, effect of printing on marginal discourses, when misogyny and sexuality become increasingly tinged with pornography.

Most of the works addressed here open up onto the problematic world of print culture and the multiple questions it raises. Why, for example, were certain books published rather than others? What was the intended audience of writings for or against women and on the sexual mores of the Court? What was the relationship between printers, book-sellers, and authors, and to what extent were the former influential in the choice of subjects treated by the latter? When and under what circumstances were writers authorized to enter into the public area of the text? What was the impact of economic factors on the newly established trade? In what ways did printing influence reading? These are difficult questions, with no easy nor definitive answers. Just asking them may be enough, especially if they turn out to be some of the right questions. Right or wrong, however, they will have provided the framework for further questions, which is one of the aims and purposes of any critical study.

Although the invention of printing revolutionized the manner of reproduction of classical texts, most of the prestigious material humanists recovered and presses turned out was limited to a relatively small and learned Latin reading public. In order to offset the expense of such publications, printers had recourse to works in the vernacular, which, if we are to believe Rabelais's claim in the prologue to *Pantagruel*, were likely to sell more copies in two months than the Bible in nine years. Thus Marot was stimulated to prepare a modernized edition of Villon's works, "à l'instigation, priere et requeste de honnorable personne Galiot du Pré, libraire marchant juré en l'université de Paris, qui nouvellement l'a faict imprimer après avoir veu sa correction,"[2] and similar prodding from his printers may help to account for Rabelais's spectacular conversion from humanist editor to author of works of fiction.

Generally speaking, sixteenth-century writers were influenced less perhaps by the advent of printing than by the commercial instincts of printers whose interest it was to remain responsive to the evolving demands of the reading public. First the great works of Antiquity –

Latin, then Greek – were put into print to satisfy the demands of a relatively homogenous group of literate, humanist readers. Next came works of piety, pedagogy, and neo-Latin poetry. As the market for these works became saturated and the reading public more varied and broader, printers turned to writings designed to appeal to Court circles, merchant and legal classes, as well as women. Thus Jean de Tournes, humanist publisher of the first generation of printers in France, installed his press at Lyons at the same time as Claude Nourry, Estienne Dolet, and François Juste. He made it a center for translations, not only from Greek and Latin, but also, Italian and Spanish. At the same time, he was the printer for a group of local poets: Maurice Scève, Louise Labé, and Pernette du Guillet, authors whose works were innovative in genre, language, or gender, hence their potential appeal to printers and readers alike.

First, therefore, publishers printed works which were already popular in manuscript form and for which there was a continuing demand. Gradually, however, they turned to new authors and original works, in an effort to maintain and expand their market. Print culture, in this context, is not basically a condition resulting from the ready propagation of new literature through the medium of the printed book; it defines rather the peculiar place and meaning this new literature came to acquire through the management, even the manipulation, of printers. Their interests had an impact on writers and what they wrote, helping to form what we now perceive to be the shape of early modern culture. When, for example, literary history instructs us that authors with a misogynist bias are regularly offset by authors with a profeminist slant, it is useful to remember that this exchange is at once rhetorically and commercially motivated. This is equally true of the displacement of courtly or epic themes and values by popular scenes and situations, or the translation of scientific, especially sexual, information into the vernacular.

Thus, another of the main concerns of the present study is the effect of printing on the reading public; but it is concerned as well with the way in which printing was affected by the expansion and changing demands of the reading public. With the advent of print, books rapidly become more readily available and cheaper to purchase and own. This fact, in conjunction with the extension of public education, brought about a wider and more varied audience, with different reading habits and expectations. Whereas Renaissance readers were prepared to recognize the play of rhetorically structured texts and to appreciate them accordingly, they were soon confronted with writings of a different cast and purpose, which took their rhetoric more seriously. As writers and readers were led to view words more as purveyors of things, the literary tended to become proportionately more literal. Therefore when historical and medical discourses, presumably devoid of rhetorical intent, take up much of the same material as the *Querelle des femmes* towards the close of the century, printing and pornography begin to come together. Print culture, in this perspective, is the culture which printing brings about, and which, in its way with words, results in the conflation, even the confusion, of meaning with meaningfulness. Writers are suddenly held accountable for their words, become responsible for their intentions, implied or expressed, and the rule of rhetoric is over.

Throughout then, this study is concerned with the relationship between writing and "reality," whether that reality is experiential or refracted through ideological constraints. No text is without context, but when context is made to include any and everything which lies outside and beyond the text, it tends to lose critical pertinence as well as referential usefulness. Moreover, context is not only cultural or political; it is also and essentially textual. Writing, in short, creates its own context, producing contingencies whereby words are joined together to constitute meaning.[3] In this sense, contextualization implies that discourse, instead of imitating life or replicating thoughts, constructs and mediates both in very complex, displaced ways. For this reason, literary realities affecting linguistic conduct enter inevitably into play, and print culture as well as rhetoric have a prominent, even a determining, place among these realities.

CHAPTER I

Discourses of misogyny

A substantial number of early modern French texts display a troubling preoccupation with questions relating to the proper place of women in literature and society.[1] While this particular subject has been studied rather extensively in recent years, it has been most usually in conjunction with the development of contemporary feminism, and therefore within the parameters of an ideologically charged context. Consequently, the part that rhetoric and print culture have played in informing the language of misogyny in Renaissance French texts has not always been properly recognized nor sufficiently appreciated. In many instances, unfamiliarity with the right reading of early modern literary works has resulted in the conflation of the dynamics of persuasion with the prejudices of gender, making discrimination between them problematic as well as indispensable.

Historians have tended to lose themselves in the structural and semantic intricacies of early modern writing, confusing the rhetorical protocol of antifeminist discourse with social or personal reality. Women, of course, had long been the focus, both negative and positive, of masculine writing. Praised as noble and pure or reviled as evil and corrupt, their respective virtues or vices form the topoi of countless medieval works.[2] This tendency to define female difference in contradictory terms was reinforced and readily propagated by the proliferation, through the recent invention of printing, of additional writings from classical Antiquity. Thus, while the arguments of medieval misogyny were revived and renewed in the Renaissance through reference to the authority of Greco-Roman literature and medical science, their implications were inflected by the rules and principles governing rhetoric as well as by the changing context and conditions of the writing and reading public.

6

THE RULE OF RHETORIC

The history of rhetoric is largely that of the development of a traditional body of theory, to which many philosophers and pedagogues have contributed. Classical rhetoric prescribed certain conventions for addressing a large assembly in a public forum or for pleading a case in a court of law, but it provided few or no rules of writing for a large group of people widely scattered in time and place, a phenomenon which was to occur with the inception of printing. Whereas texts in manuscript form were read aloud and reception was restricted to a small and homogeneous group of listeners, printing occasioned the emergence of an expanding body of solitary and anonymous readers. This new reality was experienced and exploited in different ways by different writers in their attempt both to manipulate the critical distance between reader and text and to adapt classical rhetorical strategies to literature in print.[3] Not unexpectedly, then, Renaissance authors tend to measure their relationship with their public more carefully and to a greater degree perhaps than those of any other period, especially in their presentation of new or controversial materials.[4]

Renaissance rhetorical theory and practice privileged the recovery and appropriation of antecedent models and motifs of expression, so that intertextual recuperation became a fundamental condition of prose and poetry.[5] In fact, *mimesis* or imitation was such a major concern of humanist pedagogy that it tended to dominate the discipline. Thus, given a subject to advance or an argument to develop, students were required to locate and analyze prior examples from their readings, together with appropriate figures of thought (*figurae sententiae*) and speech (*figurae verborum*). Personal copybooks provided supporting documentation, including, *inter alia*, quotations, references, adages, and set-pieces, all conveniently categorized and catalogued under various, more or less standardized rubrics, making relevant material readily available. Essentially, every speaker or writer was expected to make a proposition coherent and convincing, adducing suitable arguments in a pleasing form, in order to obtain and retain the attention of the intended audience.[6]

The distinction between rhetoric and dialectic has never been clear-cut or absolute: both are regarded traditionally as an aspect of "logic" in the literal sense of the term, that is, the science of words; each reflects a different manner of treating one and the same subject, rhetoric being intent upon rendering it convincing as well as pleasing, dialectic focusing on the appropriate procedures of critical reasoning; but their association has always been somewhat uneasy.[7] Thus Plato made a clear distinction between dialectic, the question and answer method of obtaining truth, and rhetoric which, he argued, was less concerned with the universal validity of the answer than with its momentary persuasiveness; whereas Aristotle, in the opening paragraph of his *Rhetoric*, claims a close relationship between them.

For their part, Renaissance humanists, whether upholding a theoretical division between dialectic and rhetoric or declaring one to be an aspect of the other, increasingly advocated that the two disciplines be combined in practice.[8] Accordingly, in handbooks and texts, dialectic and rhetoric commonly work together to articulate and enhance received ideas, interrelating modes of investigation and means of expression. In short, whereas dialectic is the *science* of investigative and systematic reasoning, it becomes the *art* of persuasion when combined with rhetoric. Works operating under this double franchise should not be confused with arguments of personal belief or conviction; on the contrary, they are intended primarily to demonstrate a proposition, to convince others of the logic and sincerity of a topic or position, introduced and supported according to the rules and practices of the three kinds of public discourse, deliberative, judicial, and epideictic, regardless of the author's own views or preferences on the subject.[9]

In classical as well as Renaissance treatises of rhetoric, the first and usually the longest section is on invention, that is, the technique of locating, identifying, organizing, and deploying *loci* or *sedes*, the "places" or "seats" of arguments designed to persuade or to influence the public. These places are also called "topics" (from the Greek *topos*), and the places or topics applicable to all sorts of situations are called "common topics" or "commonplaces" – allegations of facts admitted, of demonstrations already made, which the speaker or writer is charged with developing both elegantly and convincingly.[10] Commonplaces provide not only the material with which dialectic forms arguments, but also rhetoric which, according to some theoreticians, is a kind of dialectic applied to public, then literary, discourse.

For the theory of rhetoric, the sixteenth century looked to Aristotle, Cicero, and more especially to Quintilian's *Institutio oratoria*, recently rediscovered and first printed in 1470. Since none of these works was arranged to serve as a manual for classroom use, with illustrative models for students to imitate in their own compositions, Renaissance schoolmasters turned to the more suitable treatises of two late Greek rhetoricians, Hermogenes (second century) and Aphthonius (fourth century). Priscian's Latin version of Hermogenes, made about 500 AD,[11] had been the more popular of the two in the Middle Ages, but Aphthonius' *Progymnasmata* or "preliminary exercises," translated and edited with commentaries by numerous medieval and Renaissance scholars, became the most widely used textbook of Latin composition in the sixteenth century, serving to initiate schoolboys into both logic and rhetoric, while providing models for practice in formulating and debating various themes and theses.[12] They provided instruction in writing and speaking prose themes, beginning with narrative exercises in retelling fables and tales from poetry and history. These exercises introduced stock topics or commonplaces in support of an allegation. The matter at issue (*quaestio*) is the first of the argumentative exercises.[13] The thesis (*quaestio infinita*) occupies the field of general debate without reference to a particular person or circumstance, such as the advisability of marriage, whereas the hypothesis or cause (*quaestio finita*) deals with a particular person or subject, such as whether or not Cato should marry.

Humanist pedagogy encouraged the compiling and composing, according to set patterns, of topics and elegant phrases assembled from one's readings, combining ideally in a single process the parallel procedures of literary criticism and creative writing a process which could be categorized as a kind of *bricolage* and which, at times, bordered on parroting (as in *centones*) or parody (not always intentional). Training in the speaking and writing of Latin carried over quite naturally into the speaking and writing of French, so that instructional methods which encouraged the practice of remembering topics and appropriate patterns of expression tended to color, even compromise, the acknowledged primacy of thought over words.

Cicero and Quintilian distinguish between *res*, which implies subject matter, and *verbum*, which include tropes and other verbal figures.[14] *Res* is not to be confused with truth; it includes the possible and the probable, which *verba* are charged with presenting in an appropriate manner. Although the priority of *res* is recognized, it is never opposed to *verbum*. On the contrary, *verba* materialize and authorize *res*, obviating *loquacitas* or prolixity. *Words* remain subsidiary to *things*, consequently, but things are organized, mediated, and realized by words.[15] *Res*, finally, are inherent in the categories of thought stored in the memory, and rhetoric is the discipline which teaches how to retrieve (*inventio*) and arrange (*dispositio*) them appealingly and persuasively through the intermediary of words (*elocutio*).

In a logocentric, essentially medieval perspective, words are considered to be the reflection of thought, and writing coincides ideally with meaning. Renaissance writers, on the other hand, remembered and played out the Cratylic distinction between their natural and their conventional meaning. Thus, whereas humanist philology was posited on the notion that words have a definite, even an inherent meaning, authenticated by the prerogatives of etymology,[16] poets and prose authors alike, beginning with the Rhétoriqueurs, tended to multiply and manipulate words at will, encouraging them to determine their own meaning in contingent competition with one another, frequently as rhyme and word-play dictated. Language, as Du Bellay's echoing of Hermogenes' position explains, has its source and origin in the "fantasie des hommes."[17] Words consequently, as Pantagruel reminds Panurge, have no natural meaning, coincidental with their form or sound, but only conventional meaning, operative when agreed to by speaker and listener alike.[18] If, therefore, meaning is not in words but in the way they are perceived and received, then writers no longer have full authority over what they write, making textual transparency both illusory and impossible.

Although words tend to have a way of their own, writing can be said nevertheless to confer a semblance of semantic stability. In humanist works, present meaning is filtered through past works and words, sometimes improvisationally, but more frequently in a process of deliberate, self-conscious imitation and emulation, endowing it with remembered prestige. Writing then falls within the purview of reading, and the art of rhetoric, knowledge of which is at the core of Renaissance pedagogy, is designed to provide proper access to both. Children educated according to its methods inevitably absorbed certain mental attitudes and habits which continued to influence their literary expectations for the rest of their lives, making them conscious and appreciative of writing as performance and persuasion.

Humanist pedagogy exploited a whole collection of traditional subjects, designed to be demonstrated and varied according to individual abilities and intentions. Misogyny and misogamy were among the most commonly treated both in Antiquity and the Middle Ages, and centuries of clerical and courtly dissertations, in Latin or French, developed their respective discourses both copiously and conventionally. Moreover, the almost exclusive male monopoly on literacy restricted the production and reception of most writing to Europe's Latin-reading public, and therefore to an audience with similar cultural and educational backgrounds. Thus, in the early modern period, the nature of literature concerning women and marriage continued to be shaped by both the rhetorical formation of the writer and the anticipated expectations of the reader. Even in vernacular literature, antifeminism fell quite naturally into the same easy masculine pattern, provoking Christine de Pisan to radicalize what, until then, had been more or less a clerical exercise, discussing and questioning its premises for the first time along clearly gendered lines.

THE *QUERELLE DES FEMMES*: RHETORIC OR REALITY?

When defamatory literature against women, long the prerogative of the male-dominated Church, became secularized in the late Middle Ages with the publication of the second part of the *Roman de la rose*, it prompted a protracted and polarized debate between male and female factions on the nature and status of women, which developed eventually from a *Querelle de la Rose* into the so-called *Querelle des femmes*.[19] From the outset, the works which fall under these separate rubrics, whether in prose or verse, vied with one another in arguing their competing ideologies. A standard repertory of themes and examples quickly came into being, which successive writers exploited perfunctorily, to the eventual weakening of their social or cultural content.[20]

In fact, despite the incredible number of early modern authors dealing directly or indirectly with women and marriage, all of their misogynistic writings are similar in language and method. Unfailingly, each relies on a common store of examples and arguments, rehearsing the raw materials of a discourse which, in its history and articulation, is both derivative and redundant.[21] First written *by* men and *for* men, most of these works were drafted originally as display pieces, eloquent demonstrations of the author's deliberative skills.

Ultimately and perhaps inevitably, women came to read them otherwise, interpreting them as programmed attacks on their intellectual and personal integrity – especially those women who set out resolutely to defend the worth and rights of their own gender and works.

Medieval antifeminism is not the only subject whose aim and intent are difficult to assess. There is a parallel tradition of antimatrimonial literature in Latin and French which pictures husbands as long-suffering victims of their deceitful and contentious wives. Some works denigrating women and marriage also contain defenses of either or both. Arguments in favor can be as problematic as those against, since it is difficult to measure the degree to which either reflects public opinion or personal prejudice. While much of this writing was clerical or courtly in origin and audience, Renaissance authors adapt it for a wider, more general reading public, sometimes with polemic or satiric intent, but almost always in conformity with the rules of rhetorical argumentation.[22]

In a very real sense, all of these works, whether for or against women, are paradoxical, in that they tend to develop the logic of their argument exhaustively, almost to the point of absurdity.[23] Generally speaking, their strategy was less to pursue a consistent line of argument than to assemble all possible arguments in support of the case at hand. On the profeminist side of the ledger, Henri Cornelius Agrippa of Nettesheim's *De nobilitate et praecellentia foeminei sexus declamatio* (1529) falls within this purview insofar as it presents an amalgam of arguments against the prevailing current of misogynistic and misogamic ideology. As if to signal its paradoxical bent, Agrippa qualifies his work both as "trifles of his youth" ("pueritatae meae nugis") and as a "thesis" based on "reason, authority, examples, and evidence drawn from Holy Scripture and both civil and canon law" ("quam rem ipsam ratione, authoritate, exemplis, ipsisque sacrarum litterarum, et vtriumque iuris testimoniis commonstrare").[24]

Although Agrippa stresses that he has not sacrificed facts to praise and that his treatise is a serious argumentation based on relevant examples, the status of the work as a humanist declamation made it difficult for the reader to determine to what extent it was also a rhetorical exercise. When, therefore, he formally set out to prove that women were superior to men, quoting classical and scriptural sources to offset philosophical, theological, legal, and medical arguments to the contrary, many, probably mostly male, Renaissance readers would have been amused by his clever handling of a thesis which, in the cultural context of the *Querelle des femmes*, would have seemed provocative and paradoxical.

Paradox is never far from parody. But while parody operates in relation to a prior text or system of inscribed values, paradox tends to alternate between concepts and categories, underscoring and undermining their structures and pretensions. In this sense, all of the writings which fall under the *Querelle des femmes* rubric, organized along the lines of traditional *encomia* in praise or dispraise of an unexpected or unworthy subject and designed, as *epideixis*, to demonstrate the skill of an orator and provoke the admiration of the audience, are paradoxical in both matter and method.[25]

If, then, both feminist and antifeminist arguments are equally paradoxical, it is partially because of the pervasive influence of the lessons of humanist education on the selection and structuring of appropriate topics. Rhetorical training, as we have seen, taught how to argue both sides of a question, and one of the set subjects of declamatory exercises, already traditional in classical rhetoric, was whether or not a man should marry. What is particularly revealing in this respect is the fact that arguments advanced on either side tended to be extreme, with absolutely no attempt to examine the middle ground or to arrive at any kind of understanding or reconciliation, attesting once again to the inability of the authors of these treatises to break out of the mold imposed by tradition and view women otherwise than in opposition to men. There is, in a word, little discussion, little true evaluation or impartial examination of the question; the only position taken is for or against, or, at times, both.[26]

This is already true in Rabelais, who exploits antifeminist and antimatrimonial discourses for comic effect; but also in Montaigne, who is more concerned ultimately with weighing their opposing positions. Yet both Rabelais and Montaigne are ideologically and thematically ubiquitous, exploring and reviewing what others have thought and written, frequently as illustrations of the logical or linguistic idiosyncrasies of the human mind. Thus it is difficult to locate or position them precisely in relation to a particular subject they treat. Furthermore, when medieval misogyny acquires a Renaissance configuration, it asserts itself with new authority, but with the same tired premises and foregone conclusions.

Most of the texts associated with the *Querelle des femmes* were short-lived, disappearing from sight long before the end of the sixteenth century. Revived in scholarly circles by Abel Lefranc's and Emile Telle's pioneering and influential studies (the first on Rabelais, the second, Marguerite de Navarre),[27] they finally acquired notoriety when the twentieth-century feminist movement began to be interested in its own prehistory. In fact, recent scholarship on the *Querelle des femmes* has broadened the scope of its investigation to include Renaissance texts in medicine, law, and politics, providing a more comprehensive understanding of its appropriate cultural context, but not always with an equivalent appreciation of discursive practices.[28] Thus historians have conducted a detailed survey of the history of the *Querelle* as political propaganda and sexist polemic, yet continue to neglect the principles of play and playfulness which configured its literary vocation and displaced its social relevance.

Undeniably, there is a confluence of texts dealing with the interrelated question of woman and marriage in the first half of the sixteenth century, some for and some against, with most rehashing traditional clerical or courtly arguments. Concurrently, moreover, in humanist and, more particularly, legal circles there is a series of learned publications on the subject, furnishing it with academic prominence and respectability. Thus, *inter alia*, André Tiraqueau's *De legibus connubialibus* (first published in 1515), Giovanni Nevizzano's *Sylvae nuptialis* (1521), and Gratian du Pont's *Controverses des sexes masculin et femenin* [*sic*] (1534), canvassed civil and canon law for arguments *pro* and *contra*, with the latter two giving equal weight to both sides of the question.[29] The clash of their indecisions and doubts provided Rabelais and his readers with a humanist context for situating and appreciating the comedy of Panurge's matrimonial dilemma. There is therefore a learned and a literary aspect of the *Querelle des femmes*, and both will concern us here.

The first point to be remembered is that as rhetorical exercises on a traditional subject, writings praising or defaming women are not necessarily feminist or antifeminist, even if, from a twentieth-century perspective, their consequences inevitably are. Thus the phenomenon historians have described as the *Querelle des femmes*, and which has long been interpreted as a polemic between feminist and antifeminist factions, needs to be reviewed in the context of humanist pedagogical methodologies concerning and regulating agonistic and encomiastic literature. For the most part, feminist and antifeminist writers do not *live* their rhetoric, they *practice* it, contriving arguments to convince their audience of a particular point of view. Ultimately, then, these writers rely on the strength and effect of words to convey, even manipulate, meaning, regardless of personal preference or prejudice.

Curiously enough, although there has been frequent, if cursory, reference to the *Querelle des femmes* in past histories of French literature and, more recently, in works dealing with the origin and development of contemporary feminism, it has never been the object of a comprehensive study.[30] Moreover, the term poses a problem in both terminology and chronology. Originally, it was meant to describe works which participated in the debate on the pros and cons of woman's estate during the late Middle Ages and, more particularly, the first part of the sixteenth century. Today the term is increasingly used in conjunction with any work which, because it treats women negatively or, less often, positively, is considered to afford yet another chapter in the continuing discussion of their role and place in literature and society. In other words, since feminist historians have extended the designation *Querelle des femmes* to the struggle for equality in general, it has lost some of the dialectical play and chronological specificity which formed integral parts of its original reality.

Misogyny of course, beginning with Adam, has always been with us. Classical Greek and Roman literature is replete with misogynistic and antimatrimonial propaganda. Christianity reinforced it with disdain from Paul, Jerome, and Tertullian, yet attenuated it considerably with *dulia* for Mary. Clerical literature appropriated and codified many of its stock features and stereotypes, defaming woman as impure, ignorant, and inconstant, whereas courtly texts, especially those with Neoplatonic tendencies, presented her as the spiritual means by which man could rise above the vice of the world and attain finally to the harmony and stability associated with virtue. Moreover, whether in praise or dispraise of women, these texts were written by men, and the *Querelle des femmes*, before Christine de Pisan's intervention, was never a quarrel between participants of opposite genders.

While the modern history of the *Querelle des femmes* can be said to originate with Abel Lefranc's study of Rabelais's *Tiers Livre*, its prehistory coincides with the beginnings of antifeminism itself, in the legal, medical, and philosophical writings of Greece and Rome. Spuriously scientific in Aristotle, Galen, or Hippocrates, and fundamentally satiric in Aristophanes, Plautus, or Juvenal, misogynistic discourse assumes a theological stance in early Christian writings.[31] Furthermore, in considering celibacy superior to marriage, St. Paul and the Church Fathers, notably Augustine and Tertullian, appended misogamy to misogyny. Marriage for them was a remedy, consigned to those who were too weak and undisciplined to overcome or restrain their concupiscence. In disparaging marriage, theologians usually disparaged women as well, and it is in their polemical writings that medieval and Renaissance antifeminists tend to locate authority for their own misogynistic and misogamic arguments.[32] What we need to ascertain, however, is how seriously these arguments would have been taken by authors and readers alike.

In the Middle Ages, the question whether a man should marry was usually answered in the negative, with reference to the depraved and quarrelsome nature of women, and many of these same dissuasive arguments reappear in a variety of early modern texts.[33] It is not always clear, once again, when and to what extent this representation of antimatrimonial and antifeminist bias is actually misogynistic rather than moral, but what is certain is that the texts in which it operates, and which were long thought to be transparent expressions of masculine prejudice, are informed in both structure and subject matter by the prescriptions of rhetorical *exercitationes*, formal exercises contrived by clerical and humanist pedagogy to teach and imprint the principles of persuasive argumentation. When, therefore, we are confronted with works, sometimes by the same authors, which praise or demean women and marriage, we need to take into account their rhetorical origin as well as their performative, even ludic dimension and ultimate purpose.[34]

A crucial work in the medieval debate about women was the *Roman de la rose*, begun by Guillaume de Lorris in the 1230s and completed by Jean de Meun in the 1270s. Some critics think that Guillaume's part was intended to be read ironically, but most believe that it was conceived as a serious courtly dream allegory or art of love. In Jean de Meun's continuation, Reason is rejected by Amant in favor of Ami's cynically antifeminist advice on the art of seducing women. Similarly, the Vieille guarding Bel Acueil suggests that women should use their charms to exploit men while they can, thus reinforcing the misogynistic design. Jean de Meun's typical woman was a wanton, deceitful, unscrupulous person, whose character was derived from Eve, the faithless and disobedient first woman. While he was no innovator in his antifeminism, the popularity of the *Roman de la rose* gave it enormous resonance. What is clear, however, is that medieval readers could not agree on Jean de Meun's attitude to the misogyny expressed by his characters. Conflicting views were expressed already in the late fourteenth century: detractors accused him of immorality; defenders claimed that the opinions of fictional characters should not be attributed to the author.[35]

The *Roman de la rose* is not the only work whose intentions are difficult to judge. There is a whole tradition of antimatrimonial literature in Latin and the vernacular which presents husbands as victims of their wives' insatiable sexual appetite and deceptions, but both pro and antifeminist works can be ironic or dialectically complementary. Thus in a Latin manuscript poem entitled "Liber lamentationum Matheoluli," Mathieu de Boulogne, also called Mathieu le Bigame, a cleric whose career was compromised because of his marriage to a widow in violation of the rules of canonical interdiction, complains bitterly about marriage and women. Written around the close of the thirteenth century, between 1295 and 1301, and translated into French in 1371 or 1372 by Jehan Le Fèvre as *Les Lamentations de Matheolus*, it quickly became one of the most seminal examples of medieval antifeminist and antimatrimonial discourse.[36] But Jehan Le Fèvre's position was far from unilateral. Thus, towards the end of 1373, he followed his translation of the *Lamentationes* with a palinodic *Livre de Leesce*, a systematic response to and rebuttal of Matheolus' antifeminist and antimatrimonial stance, also known by its more specific titles in its earliest printed versions as *Le Rebours de Matheolus* or *Le Resolu en mariage*.[37] In appropriating both sides of the question Jehan Le Fèvre confirms the rhetorical nature of his works, making it difficult to know where he really stood in relation to his subject or how his public would have appreciated his conflicting stance. On the other hand, his arguments and counter-arguments codified the canon for subsequent generations of defamers and defenders of women.

Both Jean de Meun's *Roman de la rose* and Jehan Le Fèvre's *Lamentations* were to be invoked, quoted, and, eventually, refuted: first of all and most notably, in the early years of the fifteenth century, by Christine de Pisan, who exchanged letters critical of their position with two royal secretaries, Jean de Montreuil and Gontier Col, as well as with Pierre Col, Gontier's brother. When their respective correspondences were made public, Jean Gerson, one of the leading theologians of the day, in siding with Christine de Pisan's defense of women and their right to public recognition, momentarily silenced the misogynistic faction.[38] Moreover, these two works clearly anticipate and inspire Christine de Pisan's *Cité des dames*, in which she takes it upon herself to refute the literature of secular and clerical misogyny.[39] In this sense, she can be said to renew the *Querelle des femmes*, in that, in writing as a woman, she speaks for their civil and literary rights, interjecting a feminine voice into a previously masculine context.

What is especially significant about Christine de Pisan's contribution is that she begins her apology for women by exploring the cultural and political causes of antifeminism, rather than merely rehearsing, in the usual manner, all of the various conventional topoi and arguments on the question. Thus she is original in making the point that learning Latin tends to induce misogynistic tendencies, arguing that the elementary school curriculum includes texts for study from Ovid as well as from other Roman writers who denigrated women. Moreover, since it was somewhat unusual for women to learn to read at all, and more especially to read Latin, they are justified, she feels, in resenting books they are unable to understand and arguments they are unable to counter. Ultimately, however, her dissenting voice was not widely heard, and the medieval controversy as to the worth and place of women continued more or less uninterruptedly, but without their further active participation. Consequently, it is not until the Renaissance that there are clear indications that a truly gendered quarrel was beginning to take shape, with a significant number of women authors finally taking part and taking their own part in what was to be the beginning of a long and prolonged debate.[40] And while men continued to rework traditional topoi more or less as rhetorical performances, women were intent upon confronting them with topoi of their own. Thus, while the question of female virtue, both physical and moral, remained at the center of the quarrel in its medieval stance, the political and intellectual capabilities of women, together with the legal and religious status of marriage, emerge during the Renaissance as important new themes of debate.

The final question concerns the fundamental character of the works associated with the *Querelle des femmes*. Although for or against women and marriage, it is not certain that they are necessarily expressive of gendered prejudices on the part of their authors, nor that we should categorize them as properly misogynistic or misogamic when, in fact, they are manifestly determined in their form and formulation by literary convention, and displaced in their strategy and specificity by the norms and prescriptions of suasive argumentation. Thus, whatever the orientation or provenance of their themes, the manner of their presentation is shaped inevitably by the topics and methodology of rhetoric, classical or scholastic, requiring the protagonists to argue indifferently for or against a particular thesis – sometimes for *and* against, taking one side after the other. But does the sum of these writings, the codes of which are so rigidly defined and which are in conformity with rhetorical canons, add up to a quarrel, especially one intent upon marginalizing women?

The first, somewhat rudimentary answer to this question is that the authors of these separate works were writing on a traditional subject in a traditional way, without any demonstrated realization that they were involved, except incidentally and peripherally, in anything other than an academic contest. Their exchange, as we know it, is less the realization of a purposeful commitment to an ideology or a political cause than the contrived conjunction of a number of writings for or against an established topic. In other words, the *Querelle des femmes* would seem to be more fiction than fact, a rhetorical happening rather than a historical reality. To put the matter otherwise, these texts are not truly polemical – if by polemic we understand, as etymology dictates, engaged in hostile confrontation – but, more properly, prescribed exercises on a set subject, designed to impress and divert contemporary readers, generally and almost exclusively masculine, with a learned display of the writer's skill in assembling topoi and manipulating arguments.[41]

It is certainly not incidental that the sudden popularity of pro-women literature coincides with the advent of printing, leading one to suspect that confrontation with misogynistic literature was encouraged, even exploited, for commercial purposes by the printers themselves. Judging from the number of new editions of the competing works of Martin Le Franc's *Champion des dames* and Cornelius Agrippa's *De praecellentia foeminei sexus*, La Broderie's *Amye de court*, and Antoine Héroët's *La Parfaicte Amye*, it would appear that the *Querelle des femmes* and, more or less concurrently, the *Querelle des amyes*, provided ready material for one of the first successful promotional events in the history of the printing trade in France, inspiring

Rabelais to exploit its notoriety in the consultation scenes of his *Tiers Livre*.

Already in the 1520s, the lines of the debate set by Guillaume de Lorris and Jean de Meun in the thirteenth and fourteenth centuries were being redefined in humanist circles frequented by Rabelais, and by the 1540s, the predominance of Petrarchist idealism both in prose and poetry afforded a ready pretext for as well as renewed impetus to a reaction to its precepts. Moreover, as Rabelais recognized, the various works participating in the debate on women are essentially sophistic. All present similar topoi and arguments, ranging from lessons to be derived from the story of Adam and Eve to physical differences and advantages, contributions to the reproductive process, intellectual inferiority or superiority, the education of women, and their place in the domestic hierarchy and economy. Whereas misogamic treatises, as he also realized, are conceived according to the rules governing dissuasive arguments, misogynistic ones are much more loosely structured, incorporating a mass of traditional material without much regard for logic, interpretation, or innovation.

Given the charged and complex nature of the subject, it is hardly surprising that the meaning attached to the term *Querelle des femmes* has tended to fluctuate depending on whether it has been viewed historically or transhistorically – referring either to the encounter, at a certain time and in a certain place, between feminist and antifeminist works, or, more generally, to any intervention by women writing in their own name in reply to attacks leveled against them by men. Broadly speaking, it is clear that misogyny has always been with us, and that, eventually, the literature it produced would bring about a reaction; and that this reaction was informed, during the Renaissance, by Platonism and Petrarchism as interpreted first by male, then by female writers. It is less clear, however, that there was a distinct and self-conscious *Querelle des femmes*, even during the Renaissance. On the other hand, thanks in great part to the invention of printing, a significant intensification in the production and dissemination of feminist and antifeminist literature occurred during the first half of the sixteenth century, and Rabelais participated in its popularity, exploiting its tenets in a work of fiction centered on the question whether or not Panurge should marry.

ANTIFEMINISM AND MARRIAGE IN RABELAIS'S *TIERS LIVRE*

As a genre, both feminist and antifeminist treatises lend themselves to parody, and Rabelais is a reader with an interest in the rewriting and reception of ancient and contemporary texts, an area covered by the discipline of rhetoric. Confronted by works in Latin as massive and erudite as André Tiraqueau's ever-expanding *De legibus connubialibus* or Giovanni Nevizzano's *Sylvae nuptialis*, both of which propose arguments for and against marriage – not to mention similar works in the vernacular, such as Gratien du Pont's *Controverses des sexes masculin et femenin* – he was quick to realize their comic potentiality. The subjects they treat ponderously he takes lightly, parodying the way they say what they say, privileging their logic and language to the profit and promotion of laughter. If this is so, why and when did Rabelais come to be considered a misogynist? Mostly because of Abel Lefranc, who placed him and his *Tiers Livre* in the antifeminist camp of the recently refocused *Querelle des femmes*, on the strength of observations in François de Billon's *Fort inexpugnable de l'honneur du sexe femenin*, published in Paris in 1555.[42] Now Billon was very much a profeminist participant in the debate on women, and as such took his rhetoric seriously. It may be for this reason that he fails to recognize, or at least to appreciate, Rabelais's playful attitude towards the arguments and literature of misogyny, especially in the Rondibilis episode; but then, he was not writing for the same kind of audience.

Later scholars, however, most notably Emile Telle, M. A. Screech, and Verdun L. Saulnier, have been less convinced of the centrality of the marital question in the *Tiers Livre* or even of Rabelais's misogyny, emphasizing rather his concern with more fundamental matters pertaining to human inadequacy and, more particularly, the pressing problem of clandestine marriage, that is, of unions contracted with the Church's blessing but without parental knowledge or consent. Their studies rightly point out that Panurge's doubts about whether or not to marry should be viewed against the background and in the context of the literature pouring from the presses of the day on both sides of the feminist question; but they fail to conclude that whereas the various participants in the *Querelle des femmes*, whether clerical, courtly, or legal, treat the subject seriously, Rabelais, using the same material, fictionalizes it, turning it into the comedy which his characters play out in the pages of the *Tiers Livre*.

Significantly, Rabelais chooses not to resolve the exegetic dilemma which results from the divination sequence, leaving Panurge and the reader with two parallel and contradictory interpretations of each prophetic text. The series of consultations which follow represent a turning from the mythical, intuitive, or otherwise eccentric margins of revelational knowledge to the rational wisdom of professionals: a doctor, a theologian, and a judge. The progression from one to the other might lead us to believe that Rabelais, in keeping with humanist values, intended to valorize one over the other. But the satiric, even parodic twist afforded the application of authoritative knowledge to the peculiarities of Panurge's idiosyncratic problem tends to undermine the reliability of their prescriptive languages. Rabelais, through Panurge, dramatizes both questions and answers, demonstrating the futility and inherent folly of a search for predictability, regardless of gendered considerations, where human nature and future conduct are concerned.

This is nowhere more evident than in the consultation with Dr. Rondibilis. In fact, the four chapters comprising this episode prompted Screech to provide a detailed reinterpretation of the relation of the *Tiers Livre* to the *Querelle des femmes*.[43] Although his reading is compelling and has been widely accepted, there remains some suspicion that it accounts only partially for what Rabelais actually does with antifeminist discourses in this particular episode. As Screech points out,[44] Rabelais treats the question of Panurge's marriage in the two standard ways prescribed by rhetorical practice: first as an "hypothesis," "Should Panurge take a wife?", then as a "thesis," "Should any man take a wife?"; but his reminder that these divisions into *hypothesis* and *thesis* are taken straight from Aphthonius who, in the penultimate exercise of the *Progymnasmata*, argues the case for and against marriage, requires explanation.

A *hypothesis*, quite obviously, is an assumption or concession made for the sake of argument, referring, in the present instance, to Panurge's particular case, whereas a *thesis* consists of a more general inquiry into both sides of a matter. In rhetorical schemata, it falls under the heading of deliberative or suasive oratory. As the pseudo-Ciceronian *Ad Herennium* specifies, deliberative discourses are "either of the kind in which the question concerns a choice between two courses of action, or of the kind in which a choice among several is considered."[45] Directions regarding the orderly development of a *thesis* are given in Quintilian and illustrated abundantly by Aphthonius as well as other elementary texts. Often it weighed the relative advantages of two states, such as urban and rural life, prosperity and adversity. A favorite subject was the question of the advisability of marriage, the treatment of which Aphthonius outlines at considerable length.[46] Richard Rainolde, in his adaptation of Aphthonius, remarks that the answer to this problem will "minister matter to declaime upon,"[47] and there is a vast body of literature, both in Antiquity and in the early modern period, to demonstrate the point.

In Book III of the *Institutio oratoria*, Quintilian states that there are two ways of considering the question: either indefinitely, "Should a man marry?" or definitely, "Should Cato marry?"[48] This distinction determined the two main currents of thought on marriage in Antiquity, one general and popular, the other particular and philosophical, with exercises called *suasoria* or *controversia* providing formal techniques for arguing either side of the question. In fact, the proposition whether or not a man should marry, from the Greeks to Quintilian to Erasmus and beyond, is the universal example of a thesis to be deliberated persuasively or dissuasively, using amplification. Thus Giovanni Nevizzano includes the question in the title of his 1521 *Sylvae nuptialis* (*Sylvae nuptialis libri sex . . . Quae omnia ex quaestione, an nubendum sit, vel non, desumpta sunt*) and Erasmus prescribes examples, authority, proverbs, wise sayings, comparisons, contrasts, and opposites as a means of enriching subject matter, combined in such a way that one moves from reason to comparison, from comparison to example, from example back to reason.[49]

To illustrate his rules on amplification, Erasmus presents an example of a letter to persuade a friend to marry. The original version of this letter, first entitled *Declamatio in genere suasorio de laude matrimonii*, then *Encomium matrimonii*, was published in 1516. This text, with considerable revision and additions, became part of his *De conscribendis epistolis* in 1522, appearing as another example of the *epistola suasoria*.[50] Whatever its title, the treatise was widely read and eventually was censured by theologians as an attack on ecclesiastical celibacy and monasticism.[51] Erasmus responded to these attacks with an *Apologia pro declamatione matrimonii*, arguing that his work was merely a rhetorical exercise, adding that he had also written an argument against matrimony, and that both should be read as examples of the principles governing the writing of a fictitious letter. Consequently, given the prominence which both the Ancients and contemporary humanists had afforded the question, Rabelais could rightfully suppose that his readers, with or without Aphthonius, would have no difficulty in recognizing its academic antecedents and exemplary character, nor in appreciating the rhetorical play of argument and counter-argument in the chapters in which Panurge pursues his matrimonial query.[52]

In the hands of Renaissance teachers, rhetoric amounted almost entirely to exercises in amplification, and the *Tiers Livre* illustrates this practice in that it brings out various aspects of Panurge's question, expanding it in relation to theology, with Hippothadée, and then to medicine, with Rondibilis. Obviously, the pertinent answer would depend logically upon a number of extenuating considerations and circumstances, but Hippothadée and Rondibilis show more interest in treating the topic abstractly and copiously, not only in their capacities as theologian and medical doctor, but also according to established rhetorical practices. Thus, instead of responding simply and directly, they embark on a display of self-indulgent eloquence, giving themselves and their science priority and prominence over Panurge's dilemma. Without actually changing the subject, they displace it effectively with another aspect of the subject, allowing a massive intrusion of extraneous considerations to divert and even obscure the question which brought it about.

The obvious effect of this irrelevant display of erudition is, first of all, to promote and ridicule both theologian and medical doctor in their own right, as characters who incorporate the various quirks and conventions of their respective professions; and secondly, to introduce a new and highly specialized context within which to examine and problematize Panurge's matrimonial quest. Confronted with the difficulty of situating and interpreting a language which is intended to reflect the thinking of contemporary theology and medicine on woman and sexual desire, the reader tends to forget Panurge momentarily and to react, positively or negatively, to Hippothadée and Rondibilis. Although their explanations are perfectly serious theologically and sound (for the time) scientifically, they distract the reader from the problem in hand. Digression here, as in the other consultations, is not a wandering away from the subject, but an acceptable rhetorical tactic for giving it space, providing a textual reality for Panurge's doubts to operate on.

Especially in the consultation with Rondibilis, Panurge is caught up in a scientific matter which transcends his immediate concerns and which, in comparison, makes them seem relatively trivial. While

Panurge has no interest in Galenic and Platonic gynecologies or feminist and antifeminist ideologies, they provide Rabelais with a complex medical intertext.[53] Clearly, the evident pleasure he takes in inflecting references to the sexual appetites of women, or the animality of the uterus and its power of self-movement or ability to distinguish between smells, is superior by far, discursively speaking, to hermeneutic or narrative logic. Without actually changing the subject, Rabelais distorts it significantly, privileging Rondibilis's self-contained world of science over the specific demands of Panurge's matrimonial doubts. In this instance, as in the other consultations, there is a pronounced disproportion between the prerequisites of story and the proliferation of discourse, the quest for an unambiguous answer, and the ambiguity such a requirement inevitably encourages.

Initially, then, in interpreting Panurge's question whether or not he should marry to mean that he must be tormented by lust, Rondibilis introduces a new line of inquiry, enumerating and commenting on five remedies for restraining "carnal concupiscence," namely, wine taken intemperately, certain drugs and plants, hard physical work (developed ironically at greater length than the first two), fervent study (developed at even greater length), and finally copulation.[54] This is the remedy Panurge (and the reader) was anticipating and which Rondibilis (and Rabelais), with perverse procrastination, leaves until last. Significantly moreover, this final remedy is allotted a scant paragraph, and deals less with sex than with Panurge's physical condition and psychological disposition towards marriage: "Je voy Panurge (dist Rondibilis) bien proportionné en ses membres, bien tempéré en ses humeurs, bien complexionné en ses espritz, en aage competent, en temps opportun, en vouloir equitable de soy marier."[55] If he meets an appropriate partner, let him marry, Rondibilis advises anticlimactically, for he is well suited to it.

This summary diagnosis of Panurge's concupiscence quickly gives way to a more sustained analysis of female lasciviousness. Following an erudite anatomical and physiological description of the uterus, Rondibilis proceeds to the conventionally farcical and even more problematic question of cuckoldry. At this point, he abandons medicine for syllogism, stating that since cuckoldry is, by definition, something that can beset a man only after marriage, then one can say of any married man that he is, was, will be, or may be cuckolded.

The *may be* with which he concludes his reasoning simply restores Panurge's problem to the realm of probability, reviving all of his former uncertainty and despair. Moreover, as a corollary to his contention that cuckoldry is the hypothetical complement of every marriage, Rondibilis proceeds to locate its cause in the inconstant nature of women, rehearsing in the process all of the most prominent antifeminist commonplaces: "Quand je diz femme, je diz un sexe tant fragil, tant variable, tant muable, tant inconstant et imperfaict que Nature me semble (parlant en tout honneur et reverence) s'estre esguarée de ce bon sens par lequel elle avait créé et formé toutes choses, quand elle a basty la femme . . ." (p. 539).

Finally, in his account of the origin and symptoms of cuckoldry, Rondibilis no longer relies on his medical knowledge. Rather, he turns to personal experience as well as lessons derived from a number of stories and anecdotes. Thus in an adaptation of a fable drawn from Plutarch, he tells how Jupiter at first forgot to assign a feast day to "that poor devil Cuckoldry," but then gave him a share of Jealousy's, explaining that to forbid a woman to do anything is, infallibly, to make her want to do it. This is further illustrated by the story of the box that Pope John XXII confided to the nuns of Coingaufond and the "morale comoedie" of the man whose wife was mute. The episode ends on a farcical note with Rondibilis pretending to refuse, yet careful to take, the money Panurge offers him as a fee for his consultation.

The central theme of this whole episode is that woman is inconstant, imperfect, and libidinous because she is governed by an *animal avidum generandi*. It may be true, as Screech has argued, that Rondibilis's five remedies and learned commentary on the animal nature of the uterus are based on serious classical authority, and that Rabelais shows himself through Rondibilis to be familiar with contemporary medical discourse; but it is equally true, and certainly more immediately pertinent, that all Rondibilis has to say on these matters is beside the point – which is precisely the point. Clearly, Rabelais's intent in these various consultations is to privilege digression, which, in the *Tiers Livre*, is more salient and substantive than narration, creating thereby a context in which to play out Panurge's doubts.[56] Thus Raminagrobis, Hippothadée, Trouillogan, and Rondibilis represent their respective disciplines with learned profuseness, but the prolixity of their answers is proportionately irrelevant in relation to the simplicity and directness of Panurge's questions.

While these specialists talk like books, Panurge expects them to talk like men, even man to man. Their respective discourses are replete with professional tics and clichés, all of which combine to mark them as characters, making their episodic appearance all the more memorable.

Literary historians have suggested that Rondibilis was inspired by a certain Guillaume Rondelet, a real doctor Rabelais knew at Montpellier, and this may be quite true. But does this mean that he intended to satirize him or the medical profession as a whole? If satire was intended, it is operative only in reference to facts outside and beyond the text, whereas comedy is a product of the text itself, defined here as the process whereby Panurge and his friends deflate Rondibilis's "docte discours" (p. 537), puncturing it repeatedly with mundane, even inane, remarks, thereby making a mockery of its pretentiousness. This tactic is dramatically confirmed by Panurge's one-line reduction of Rondibilis's eloquent dissertation to its simplest linguistic denominator: "Vos parolles, translatées de barragouin en françois, voulent dire que je me marie hardiement et que ne me soucie d'estre coqu" (p. 548). Rondibilis's advice is useless, and Panurge dismisses it as such, moving on at last to the next consultation.

What, then, does this crucial episode tell us about Rabelais's own attitude towards women? Screech contends that there is so little question of their place in the *Tiers Livre* that it must seriously be doubted whether the book is really closely connected with the *Querelle des femmes*, as such, at all. Rabelais, he maintains, is concerned essentially with the question of the desirability of getting married, and more especially with the question of Panurge's suitability for marriage. In any event, what Rabelais has to say about women through the intermediary of Panurge and those he consults, Screech concludes, shows him adopting a middle ground between the extremes of feminism and antifeminism. This analysis is undoubtedly true and, while not beside the point, it seems to miss it once again. More pertinently, in adopting the middle ground Rabelais positions himself strategically in relation to both feminist and antifeminist literature. This allows him to play one against the other, to manipulate their opposing discourses with purposeful intent. In short, Rabelais is much more an amused spectator than a partisan participant of the battle between the sexes; as such, he capitalizes on the popularity and notoriety of the literature of the

Querelle des femmes, parodying its language, trivializing its premises, prioritizing a highly charged courtly and humanist intertext for comic relief and, it was hoped, commercial success.

The interest of this long medical exposition is not that it expresses Rabelais's position in the *Querelle des femmes* (as Abel Lefranc thought), or his professional views on the female anatomy (as Screech concludes), but that in designating Rondibilis as a representative of medicine, it confronts Panurge with an authoritative view on women contrary to his matrimonial hopes and desires. Indirectly expressive of prejudice or not, Rondibilis's advice is largely contextual, and as such replies directly to Panurge's concerns. As a doctor himself, one might expect Rabelais to reflect his own medical opinions through his character; but if this is so, it is difficult to identify them in this repertory of traditional antifeminist arguments and anti-Galenic commonplaces. On the contrary, it is this material which provided him with a ready-made language, one he reproduces as an example of ready-made thinking. Repetition in itself is already a form of paradox, if by paradox we understand the introduction of play into an otherwise serious statement or situation; and Rabelais is quick to demolish the seriousness of any idea or person, no matter how solemn or sacred the origin, by emphasizing its mechanical representation.

Renaissance feminist and antifeminist literature makes little attempt to enlarge or deepen the common stock of examples and arguments from personal experience and observation. In the *Tiers Livre*, however, along with the incidental comedy derived from medieval *contes* and *fabliaux* there is, through Panurge, a privileging, with parodic effect, of the rhetoric of the *Querelle* itself, the language of its discourse and the sophistry of its logic. Rabelais experiences the material represented in the *Querelle des femmes* as an appropriate context in which to situate Panurge's questions, giving sense and structure to his repeated attempts to obtain unambiguous answers. Bewildered by Rondibilis's contrary advice, which is more or less a recapitulation of the positions adduced in antifeminist literature of the day, Panurge is left dangling between extremes, unable to decide one way or the other. His dilemma is Rabelais's, or that of any other reader confronted with the jumbled mass of conflicting opinions which the age of printing was beginning to proliferate.

As history, the *Querelle des femmes* may be little more than a construct; as rhetoric, it provides the topical pretext and discursive structure for the various consultations of the *Tiers Livre*. Without Panurge's participation, the learning displayed in the *Tiers Livre* would have neither structure nor necessity, yet his place remains minimal in relation to the erudition he is expected to contend with. He informs the plot, provides the pretext for the consultations, while they, in turn, play out his problem against a vast and perplexing world of peripheral disciplines and discourses.

What would have appeared comic to Rabelais's readers in this collection of tired arguments is not necessarily comic to readers today. Obviously, the reverse is equally true. We need to have a clearer idea of Renaisssance readerly and intellectual expectations in order to understand how and why a given reference, situation, or episode might have provoked laughter. Thus what we might find humorous or, contrariwise, reprehensible in the antifeminism of the *Tiers Livre* may not coincide – in fact cannot coincide, since the advent of modern feminism, with how the sixteenth-century reader would have received and perceived it. The cultural and deliberative context is simply not the same. Thus we need to compensate for a lack or loss of competency in our ability to decipher the rhetorical bias of Renaissance writing which enabled authors to argue indifferently for or against a controversial subject. Conversely, given the renewed popularity of a debate which already had the configuration of a literary phenomenon, Rabelais's public would have had little difficulty in situating his rhetorical ploy. Moreover, if we read the *Tiers Livre* with the background of the *Querelle des femmes* in mind, its tenets, especially in the Rondibilis episode, acquire a distinctly ludic cast.

Without these linguistic and ideological excursions, however, the *Tiers Livre*, reduced to its fundamental narrative denominator, would be of little interest or consequence. The consultants alone command our full attention; but their learning, because of Panurge, is decontextualized, creating a meaningful contrast between their world and his. In the *Tiers Livre* at least, the only women in Panurge's life are figments of their erudition and his imagination, allowing Rabelais to play one against the other. Although we know next to nothing about the women in Rabelais's own life, his *Tiers Livre* exploits misogynistic legends and literature with gleeful indifference. His female contemporaries, Marguerite de Navarre and Jeanne Flore, re-use much of the same material with more political purpose, motivated it would seem, partially at least, by their own reaction to the cultural climate of the day.

CHAPTER 2

Irony and the sexual other

Misogynistic discourse, as we have seen, assumed many different shapes and styles in Renaissance texts. A subject for polemics in the tracts and treatises of the *Querelle des femmes*, misogyny becomes the pretext around which Rabelais revolves the fiction of Panurge's matrimonial quest in the *Tiers Livre*. In both instances, the role of rhetoric is instrumental in initiating and articulating the topic of the nature of women and whether or not man should marry: either as a thesis for general debate, as in the *Querelle des femmes*, or as an hypothesis, dealing with a particular person in a particular circumstance, as in Rabelais. The doubts concerning the status of women and marriage, which fueled the dialectics of the *Querelle des femmes* and which Rabelais transposed into narrative theme, also pervade the fictions of Jeanne Flore and Marguerite de Navarre: more as experience, however, personally grounded perhaps, but portrayed ironically, as part and parcel of the female condition.

So far we have looked mostly at the way in which men write about women. Here we will examine more closely the way in which women write about women. First, we will be concerned with depictions of female sexuality in Jeanne Flore's *Comptes amoureux* and, more particularly, with the role of irony in the shaping of character identity and intended meaning; secondly, with women and the dramatic, sometimes tragic, inadequacy of their ability to communicate with men, as played out in the tenth story from Marguerite de Navarre's *Heptaméron*. The question of distance will be addressed finally, especially in regard to the manner in which female authors and their female characters portray and interpret the speech and conduct of their male counterparts.

JEANNE FLORE AND EROTIC DESIRE: FEMINISM OR
MALE FANTASY?

If the complete meaning of a story is not inherent in its structure or
words, then it may depend also on narrative strategy and reader
perception. Thus a story proclaiming and extolling feminine sexual
freedom would be read differently according as it was written by a
male or female author and directed towards a male or female
audience. If written by a male posing as a female, knowing that the
intended audience would be primarily masculine, then it would
acquire a radically new configuration, shaped by culturally programmed expectations and reactions.

While Jeanne Flore's *Comptes amoureux* have been attributed to a
woman and read both as an apology for women's sexual liberation
and as a condemnation of arranged marriages, there would seem to
be an element of play at work in the author's emphatic and
systematic reversal of previously gender-coded texts and situations,
adding a measure of parodic undecidability to their meaning.[1] Read
as self-conscious exercises in male fantasy in favor of men's sexuality
and to their inevitable advantage, these stories become a kind of in-
joke (orchestrated perhaps, as was probably Rabelais's *Pantagruel*, by
an editor's commercial instincts) which a sixteenth-century public,
essentially masculine, would have had no difficulty in recognizing
and appreciating as such. Rather than serious feminist statements
from a female author to a female audience, the *Comptes amoureux*
appear, from this particular vantage point, to be ludic rewritings by
a male author (or authors) of prevailing Platonic and Petrarchan
literary conventions appertaining to codes of feminine discourse,
dress, and conduct, addressed primarily to a male audience. This,
obviously, is a hypothetical reading, which an analysis of (1) the
fiction of the female narrator, (2) the rhetoric of the portrait and of
dress, (3) the dialectic of love, and finally (4) the displaced ideology of
the story of Echo and Narcissus may help to substantiate.

What is unclear either from available documentary evidence or
from reading Jeanne Flore's work is whether the person behind the
author's name is a man or a woman, and consequently whether the
text affords an example of a woman's looking at women or of a
man's looking at women.[2] Both perspectives seem possible, depending on whether or not the text is perceived as feminist, calling
for sexual and spousal freedom, or ironic, reversing and depreciating

contemporary discourses tending to idealize women and their relationship with men. Not to be excluded, moreover, is the possibility that the author is a man looking at women in the way he would want women to look at men, making the work reflective of the kind of disabused or realistic sexuality voiced later by Hircan or Saffredent in Marguerite de Navarre's *Heptaméron*.

Less elaborate as a frame-story than the *cornice* of Boccaccio's *Decameron* or the prologue that Marguerite de Navarre, taking Boccaccio as a model, imagined for the *Heptaméron*, Jeanne Flore's dedicatory epistle, addressed to a cousin, brings together, somewhat arbitrarily, a select group of ladies who had agreed to tell stories "à ces vendanges dernieres" (p. 97). In it, she recounts that she suddenly realized, as she was preparing to transcribe them for her cousin as promised, that it would be agreeable and pleasing to all young ladies in love, and who delight in reading such stories, if she were to have them printed, making them thereby more widely available.[3] Whereas the pretext advanced by Boccaccio's and Marguerite's group of noble ladies and gentlemen is more diversionary than exemplary, in that they resort to story-telling in order to pass the time of day, Jeanne Flore's is purposeful, since her group means to convince one of their own, Madame Cebille, of the dangers of disobeying Venus and manifesting hostility towards men.

Another significant departure from Boccaccio's or Marguerite's later model is that all of Jeanne Flore's story-tellers are women. There is some fluctuation, however, in their number and names. Eight are mentioned in the opening *Epistre*: Madame Melibée, Madame Cebille, Madame Hortence, Madame Lucienne, Madame Salphionne, Madame Sapho, Madame Andromeda, Madame Meduse; but the actual *devisantes* turn out to be called Melibée (1), Andromeda (2), Meduse (3), Minerve (4), Solphionne (5), Cassandre (6), Briolayne Fusque (7), while Madame Cebille remains a silent listener throughout.

Supposedly, they voice the conventional feminine point of view on love, marriage, and sexuality; but their declarations are somewhat perfunctory, even simplistic, reiterated rather than logically reinforced or developed, leading one to wonder if they are meant to represent a woman's viewpoint or to overstate it with parodic intentions, as is suggested by the emphatically erudite language and convoluted examples of the following typical passage:

Sçaches, cheres et amoureuse [*sic*] dames, que l'ire et corroux inevitable
d'Amour ou tost, ou tard a de coustume faire telles punitions: telles que
souffrit par son peché la nimphe Castalia du Dieu Apollo. Et par celle
mesme offense, la belle fille de Phorcus, laquelle de tout son povoir aspre et
incivile envers ceulx qui la vouloient aymer, luy furent par sa ferme rigueur
des celestes Dieux ses cheveux blondz et dorez muez en horribles et tortués
serpens: dont elles après desirant et l'amoureuse et contemnée compagnie
se retrouver, eulx espoventez du chef serpentin s'en fuyoient, et elle autant
embrasée de desirs libidineux que le mont de Vesuvio de ses flammes
sulphurines, de plus fort les desiroit et poursuyvoit. (p. 163)

Some of the uncertainty as to the authorship and focus of the
collection arises quite obviously from the seemingly truncated state
in which sixteenth-century editions have transmitted it. There is
internal evidence which suggests that we have neither a complete
text nor the original order of the stories. Moreover, those we have
are strikingly unequal in length, erudition, and presentation. Some
are more fully developed, carefully written, and structured than
others, displaying a sure sense of narrative economy and development as well as a wide knowledge and appropriate use of classical
antecedents. On the other hand, the order in which they appear
seems arbitrary, even confused. Thus the work opens with a
reference to two stories which have already been recounted, one by
Madame Salphionne, the hostess of the group, and one by Madame
Lucienne, but which are not included in the published collection,
making the transition to the extant first story both awkward and
abrupt.[4] Moreover, at the end of the fifth story, once the gentlemen
from Lyons have been invited to join the women for the evening's
celebration, Madame Salphionne expresses both her disappointment
that they have not been present these past ten days to hear the
stories, and her pleasure that they have arrived in time to hear the
last one, implying that there were originally ten stories in all, and
that what is now the sixth was once probably the tenth.

Furthermore, not all of the *devisantes* named initially actually
participate in the story-telling, whereas others, not previously mentioned, unaccountably do, thereby confirming the suspicion that the
work as we know it is not only defective but also, as variations in
style and standpoint would seem to indicate, the product of several
different authors, male or female.[5] If female, the work is radical,
even revolutionary, in its call for the recognition and legitimization
of female sexuality. If male, its ideology is expressed tongue-in-

cheek, putting into the mouths of women what was already in the minds of men, reversing in a sense the roles Floride and Amadour will play in the tenth story of the *Heptaméron*.

Already in her lifetime, little more was known about Jeanne Flore than that a collection of seven *Comptes amoureux* appeared under her name in an undated edition, published around 1537, and that the volume continued to be printed until 1574, when the last edition was published at Lyons. Several unsuccessful attempts have been made to discover who Jeanne Flore really was, but her identity is less crucial finally to the meaning of the work than the function of the female narrator, whether the real author be male or female, for it is this primary fiction which establishes the context in which the stories are told as well as the way in which they are to be read, shaping both our perception of the intended relationship between writer and reader and our reception of the stories themselves.

In the introductory "Epistre" to "Madame Minerve sa chiere Cousine," Jeanne Flore acknowledges that her style is less polished than that of a male author,[6] a disclaimer which, judging from a similar profession of humility Marguerite de Navarre addressed to the readers of her *Miroir de l'âme pécheresse*, was already a topos in female writing of the day;[7] but her learned allusions, and her latinized language and syntax, belie the statement, showing her to be highly skilled in the art and artifice of rhetoric – which is quite unusual, generally speaking, for women of the day.

What is even more unexpected, especially given the restrictions which contemporary social and religious codes placed on women's sexuality, is that each story defends the rights and prerogatives of *fol'amor* and calls for the punishment of all who refuse to submit to its authority, as the programmatic title clearly indicates: *Comptes amoureux par Madame Jeanne Flore, touchant la punition que faict Venus de ceulx qui contemnent et mesprisent le vray Amour*. Initially, the author plays with the ambivalence inherent in the proposition that men and women, being sexually equal, have an equal right to sexual satisfaction, adopting a strategy which makes it possible, even necessary, for men and women to read and receive these stories differently, each according to his or her own prejudices and fantasies.

Much of Jeanne Flore's apology for sexual freedom would seem to be ironic, intended to ridicule coded discourses of female behavior, whether marital or courtly. What one needs to ask is to what purpose and to whose advantage. Is she taking an extreme position for the purpose of creating irony or is she representing uncritically and straightforwardly an extreme position which only appears ironic when viewed from a masculine, or maybe a Renaissance, standpoint? In any event, there is frequently a rhetorical playfulness in her arguments as well as in her examples, which needs to be addressed.

Marguerite de Navarre writes *nouvelles*, stories which, as the word itself indicates, are *new*, founded on contemporary events rather than inspired by literary models, events either experienced by her *devisants* or related to them by someone who had. Jeanne Flore, on the other hand, is an author of *comptes*, stories which, if not mythical or legendary, are old and immemorial, as if the past were a source and guarantee of truth.[8] Thus writing for her is first of all reading, or rather rereading and therefore rewriting, classical or canonical authors, most prominently, perhaps, Virgil, Ovid, and Jean Lemaire de Belges. Not only does she appropriate allusions and situations from the *Aeneid*, the *Metamorphoses*, and the *Illustrations de Gaule et Singularitez de Troie*, but she regenders them frequently as well, interpreting classical mythology and literature with a feminine bias, transforming men into women and women into men. Thus in the second of the seven stories, related by Andromeda, Pyrance's final, fatal monologue, and the expression of public consternation upon learning of his death, recall Dido's last words and the subsequent panic Rumor spread in Carthage. Meridienne's "laniation," in the same story, is reminiscent of the demise of Orpheus who, disdaining the love of the women of Thrace, is torn asunder by the Maenads. Juno takes pity on Dido in the *Aeneid* (IV 688–92), but Venus takes pity on Pyrance in the *Comptes*, and Meridienne replaces Aeneas in the comparison with an oak tree (*Aeneid* IV 445–6).

Moreover, the story of Meridienne, as told by Andromeda, is a rewriting of the story of the mythological Andromeda. According to legend, Cassiopeia, Andromeda's mother, angered Poseidon by saying that her daughter (or possibly herself) was more beautiful than the Nereids. To avenge himself of this insult, Poseidon sent a sea monster to lay waste to the country and was appeased only by the sacrifice of Andromeda. Chained to a rock by the shore, she was rescued by Perseus, who killed the monster, fell in love with her and, later, married her. Meridienne's story, contrary to Andromeda's, is not a love story but a revenge story, the tale of a woman punished by Venus, not for her beauty, but because she misuses her beauty and rejects the love of another for love of self.

Significantly, the order of physical description in the *Comptes* is structured as well as gendered by the model and rhetoric of the *blasons du corps féminin*. Thus all of the heroines are young and beautiful. Their dress and physical attributes are amply, even sensually, described, with details eroticized in keeping with a masculine rather than a feminine perspective. In the first story, Rosemonde, rescued by her lover, is presented

> simplement vestue d'une robbe faicte d'ung blanc taffetas armoisi, dont les bords estoient de passemans d'or: par dessoubs, la deliée chemise joignoit à sa chair blanche et ferme: si que quant le doulx vent Zephirus venoit à entresoufler parmy ses habillemens, ores il demonstroit à qui le voulait veoir, la composition de la cuisse, ores du ventre, et ores de sa jambe longuette et bien faicte.[9] (p. 122)

And in the bedchamber scene, her lover contemplates her sensuously, lingering on "la blancheur delicieuse de sa gorge," "la rondeur des petitz tetons," "le ventre uny et dur," "les cuisses bien tournées." Such erotic insistence upon a woman's physical charms seems incongruous and unlikely from a Renaissance woman's viewpoint or pen.

Their male counterparts, equally young and handsome, are presented much more succinctly, as would undoubtedly be the case if the narrator were a man, with emphasis placed on their strength and stamina. Pyrance, the man who loves Meridienne, is summarily described as "jeune, beau, riche et gracieux" (p. 140). Jeanne Flore does not look at him, however, only at her and at her cruel pleasure in his surrender to the seductive power of her eyes: "Subtilement s'en apperceut la cruelle Meridienne, et estoit fort joyeuse et contente de veoir ainsi l'imprudent jeune homme se perdre en la lueur de ses beaulx yeux, resemblante au serpent appellé Basilique, qui occit quiconque il aura attainct de son regard venimeux" (p. 140). Finally, women are depicted as sexually deprived, but the young lover is praised for his ardor, which is how a male author might imagine him:

> La belle Dame, qui auparavant se mouroit entre les impotens et sans chaleur accollemens de Pyralius, maintenant s'esjoyt de manier les membres refaictz et en bon poinct de son nouvel amy, et de veoir sa belle et bien colourée face: ses vers yeulx: sa blonde barbe: sa poictrine forte, et plaine de chaleur: ses bracs non rudes au delicieux exercisses d'amours.[10] (p. 125)

Husbands, on the other hand, most of whom are old, ugly, and impotent, are the true villains, and not men in general, especially not young men. Their portraits are compilations of grotesque details. Thus Pyralius, Rosemonde's husband, in the first story, is characteristically repulsive:

il eust la teste grosse et lourde, herissée de rude et aspre chevelure, jà envieillie et grise, le front ridé, les soucils gros et espaix, les yeulx tous chassieux et enfoncez en la teste . . . De l'estomach luy issoit une espaisse et fetide haleyne à travers une puante, noyre et baveuse bouche . . .[11] (p. 103)

Everything in this portrait seems to point to the rhetoric of *enargeia*, the art of presenting a vivid picture, reinforced here by an accumulation of increasingly negative details. These are not, of course, real persons, but rather characters, even caricatures, composed of a series of qualities belonging to the conventions of the topos in question, piled up with comic emphasis by a hand intent upon portraying sexual incompatibility.

This kind of descriptive accumulation, as Apollo's portrait of those who remain loveless in Louise Labé's *Débat de Folie et d'Amour* clearly shows, could easily express feminine disgust with loathsome husbands. It could also translate into a feature of masculine rhetoric designed not only to denigrate troublesome and impotent husbands, but also, and more pertinently, to praise the vigor of young love and lovers. Thus the following passage could easily be dictated from the standpoint of masculine self-interest:

Par laquelle cause, cheres compaignes, povez considerer en quelle melancolie estoit la dolente espousée: laquelle estant totalement frustrée de son intention, ne luy peult oncques, tant sceut elle bien user des actes que font les amoureuses couchées avec leurs jeunes amys, exciter les membres prosternez et endormis de sa vieillesse enorme et sans vigueur. (p. 162)

It seems obvious, despite what Pérouse and others have claimed, that the *Comptes amoureux* are not the work of a young author; or if they are, then of a young author who has read well and widely, and whose prose is replete with references to classical authors and, more directly perhaps, reminiscences of Rhétoriqueur prose. In any event, one of the most significant characteristics of the *Comptes amoureux* is the pronounced disproportion between personal and derivative discourse. Jeanne Flore has little to say on her own; both her stories and language are borrowed, and what is properly hers is limited to exercises in imitation and rhetorical amplification.[12]

In imitation there is always an element of parody, if by parody one understands, as etymology dictates, a *second singing*. Because of the double meaning of the preposition *para*, "against" and "beside" or "along with," this second singing can be opposed to the first or complete it. In a sense, parody is akin to irony, which, according to rhetorical treatises, is a trope by which one says one thing while meaning another.[13] The interest of parody as, moreover, of irony, lies therefore in the difference, the hiatus between two texts, rather than in their similarity, and it is in this critical space between the two that the author has room to manipulate writing, displace reading, and display originality.

Through parody, Jeanne Flore's stories acquire a double dimension, coexist in the past as well as in the present. There is a constant play of text and intertext, the distinct action of two discourses, side by side on the same page. Thus in the second story, Lemaire de Belges's authoritative depiction of Venus's seductive costume is grafted onto Jeanne Flore's depiction of Meridienne's dress, setting up reverberations between the two, awakening literary memory on the one hand and stimulating the reader's imagination on the other.[14] In this particular context, intertextuality is a form of parody: neither repetition or imitation, nor the absorption and transformation of other texts, but the ironic rewriting of a prior and commonly recognizable text.

The most striking feature of irony is the peculiar relation it creates between author and reader. In incorporating another text within the text, the author invites the reader to correlate them, less perhaps in an attempt to provide a criterion of relevance than to encourage recognition of critical difference. Distanced from the reader, as the reconstruction of a world in which the masculine past and the feminine present are juxtaposed and coexist, the text seems to aspire towards a rereading of literature itself, or, perhaps more accurately, towards a playful readjustment of its themes and conventions.

Generally speaking, Jeanne Flore's prose is disconcerting in its accumulation of erudition. At every step there is a name, an allusion or a detail which diverts the narrative present to the literary or mythological past. Thus Meridienne's arrival in public is conflated with Venus' departure for Mount Pelion:

Donc après les aultres plusieurs ceremonies feminines, et qu'elle eust prins conseil de son mirouer trois et quattre fois, la voicy apparoistre en la presence de ceulx qui l'attendoient: et à l'yssue de son palais resembla la grande Venus, laquelle partoit de l'isle de Chippre pour tirer droit au mont

Pellion à l'assemblée des nopces du Roy Pelleus et de Thetis: puis de là en Phrigie à la contention des beaultéz, montée sur son doré chariot trainé par douze colombes blanches comme laict. (p. 138)

And the description of the effect of her beauty calls up reference in quick succession to Juno, Phebe, Cleopatra, Cupid, Aeneas, Carthage, Mars, Adonis, Ganymede, and Psyche, creating a significant textual disproportion between the arts of telling and remembering.

What is more significant perhaps is the fact that Jeanne Flore's references to figures or events are frequently allusive or periphrastic, indicating that she expects her public to have read the same books she has. Her language requires cross-reading, which alone would seem to limit the intended public considerably. In fact, it is not everyone who would have read widely enough in Roman history or literature to understand this reference to Cleopatra: "Et pas n'eust sceu à mon advis, la femme de Marc Anthoine lorsqu'elle desploya les forces de son parler pour à soy rendre captif qui venoit pour la subjuguer soubz l'empire Romain, la surpasser d'eloquence et bien dire" (p. 137). Familiarity with classical mythology is taken for granted, as in this indirect reference to the peacock: "Aultres jectans l'oeil sur la chevelure blonde et desliée à l'entour du large front moderement undoiante, et de beaucoup meilleure grace que n'espand pas sa queüe l'oiseau de la Déesse Juno" (p. 138). Either Jeanne Flore was writing for a humanist audience, which means an essentially masculine one, or there was at Lyons at the time a group of women sufficiently educated to be able to understand and appreciate the subtleties of her language, as well as numerous enough to make the publication of successive editions of the *Comptes* commercially worthwhile.

What the author of these stories has assembled is a collection of the conventional situations and clichés of earlier romances concerning rejected suitors. In this sense the work is also metafictional, commenting or reflecting upon other texts in a way which allows the reader to recognize the irony inherent in their rewriting and regendering. In any event, appropriation in the *Comptes* has a twofold dimension in that it introduces a semantic intention that is different from the original text. Sexual comportment for Jeanne Flore, contrary to Platonic or Petrarchan conventions, is dictated by nature rather than by social or cultural codes. Thus she recognizes and promotes the imperatives of female sexuality, without always recog-

nizing the necessity of taking masculine reciprocity into consideration. Rather than degendering sexuality, she regenders it from a
different perspective. Although her language reflects the influence of
the courtly love tradition, the game aspect it supposes, with intricate
steps and rules to follow, is largely absent.[15] Sexual union is quite
clearly the immediate goal of the lovers in the first story (Rosemonde
and Jean Andro) and the sixth (Theodore and Daurine), but also of
the anonymous lady of the third.

The *Comptes amoureux* privilege female eroticism over male eroticism, but is this because their author is a woman or a man? To be
sure, Jeanne Flore's men are generally loathsome, especially husbands too old to be capable of sexual arousal, whereas her women
are always young and beautiful: either filled with love and unsatisfied
by their husbands, or filled with hate and causing the despair and
death of their lovers. In either case, it is the woman's sexuality or
lack of it which determines the happiness or misery of the men in
her life. Moreover, female sexuality is depicted as natural and not to
be repressed. Those who refuse to honor love are cruelly punished.
Sexual pleasure is not to be denied or postponed, nor is procreation
its aim. Jeanne Flore celebrates sexuality for and of itself; here
woman is ruled by desire, which is not presented as tragic or
reprehensible, except when denied or suppressed.

Admittedly, because of the bars of semi-seclusion and parental
arrangements of marriages, a maiden's love could not easily run a
romantic course in sixteenth-century French society. Consequently, it
is not only women who might imagine a relaxation of sexual mores,
but also men, and more especially young men. Mockery of marriage
was not new in the Renaissance; it was already traditional in Greek
and Roman comedy, not to mention its prevalence in medieval farce.
Not surprisingly, therefore, the *devisantes* are prepared to practice
what they preach, inviting young men for a visit and entreating them
to remain for the night, taking the initiative in what is an obvious
reversal of traditional gender roles, and just the kind of reversal
which a male author and audience would appreciate and applaud.

In the fourth story, which celebrates female sexuality and the
inability of old husbands to satisfy women's young desires, Madame
Minerve calls for wives to deceive their husbands:

Veu ce, nous n'avons doncques tort, amoureuses compaignes, si pour
mitiguer noz martyres venons à choisir qui puisse supplier aux faultes que
font noz maris impotens, lesquelz possible, quoy qu'ilz meslent le ciel et la

terre ensemble quand ilz nous surpreignent en noz larcins amoureux, sont
bien joyeulx de trouver oeuvre faite. (p. 168)

While not exactly reversing roles here, she gives the situation a new
twist when she portrays the wife as a martyr and justifies adultery as
a necessary means to self-satisfaction.

On the other hand, it is precisely because Jeanne Flore's heroines
live out their sexuality that they conform to the misogynistic stereo-
type of the wanton woman propounded by the antifeminist literature
of the *Querelle des femmes*. Renaissance medicine and medical authors,
uniformly male, informed primarily by the Galenic or Hippocratic
model, taught that women had a voracious sexual appetite and that
this was a purely physiological phenomenon. Satisfaction for them
was not associated with any pleasure other than simple relief of the
unbearable pressures emanating from the uterus. And whereas a
man was expected to be able to control his desires, it was believed to
be impossible for a woman and injurious to her health that she
should try. Thus in the third story a young girl, more enamored of
learning than of men, is afflicted by Venus with a fatal malady. The
doctor who examines her diagnoses her illness as sexual and
prescribes marriage as a remedy. Hoping to save her life, her parents
marry her off as quickly as possible to an old man who, unfortunately, is sexually dysfunctional. In despair, she finally stabs herself to
death, symbolically enough, on her marriage bed. Here we find the
counterpart of the hysterical woman who, in Hippocratic gyne-
cology, is unable to control her sexual appetite, and who, in the
antifeminist literature of the day, is an object of scorn and laughter.

There is something willfully paradoxical in Jeanne Flore's praise
of unrestricted sexual desire. Since the codes of conventional love
mandated chastity to the unmarried woman and fidelity to the
married, her appeal for absolute obedience to the dictates of Venus
is both provocative and polemical. Whereas a woman, traditionally,
is the pursued, here she becomes the pursuer, either bestowing or
withholding her love as she pleases; the man, at least in the second
story, dies helplessly of unrequited love, which is more in conformity
with the destiny of a woman in fiction as in life. Marriage, when it
appears, is a source of discord, and the heroine in the first story, who
is bound to an old, repulsive husband, is finally rescued by a young
and dynamic lover. Christian morality does not come into play; the
only rule of order is one of unhesitating allegiance to Venus, with
punishment reserved for those who fail to honor her properly. In this

sense, Jeanne Flore's representation of the nature of woman's love is liberating. Unfortunately, the argument works both ways, for in confirming the voraciousness of female sexuality, she confirms as well what popular and scientific tradition had said about it all along.

What finally are intended readers, presumably masculine as well as feminine, supposed to learn from the experience of the author's characters? If female, that they are justified in fulfilling their erotic expectations, legitimately, through marriage, or otherwise. If male, that women have equally strong sexual fantasies and desires. Hence there is a lesson for both, grounded simultaneously in past and present history. In cross-writing and displacing themes and stories from the past, Jeanne Flore imagines a strange, new, fictional reality. There is something utopian, even dream-like, in her world, and it is precisely this quality which awakens and stimulates the reader of her rewriting of the myth of Echo and Narcissus.

In Ovid's story there are several potential morals, and this is undoubtedly one of the reasons for its lasting appeal.[16] In the first place, it argues against the desire and pursuit of the unattainable. More specifically, it illustrates the destructive effect of self-love on others as well as on oneself. But the complexity and elaboration of his treatment are not directed solely to privileging any lesson which the story may imply, nor does the poet call attention to any of its moral implications. His interest is in combining the story of the punishment of Echo with the story of the punishment of Narcissus in a way which brings out the paradox, indeed the absurdity, of their interrelationship. Thus in its sequential development, Ovid's narrative alternates between the story of Echo and the story of Narcissus.[17]

Ovid first introduces a beautiful and proud Narcissus, then tells how the nymph Echo, condemned by Juno to repeating other people's words in abbreviated form, falls in love with him, only to be cruelly spurned. As a consequence of his rejection, her body wastes away, leaving only her synonymous voice. Narcissus is punished for his disdain when, chancing upon a forest pool, he falls in love with his reflected image. If for Echo the other was another, for Narcissus the other is himself, a reflected image which touch and desire are unable to reach. Realizing this in a monologue marked by rhetorical amplification and temporization, Narcissus dies at last from love of himself. In place of his body, his mourners find only an emblematic flower, white petals clustered round a cup of gold.

Ovid makes no moralizing generalizations on his characters or their fate. He simply tells a story which is at once intense and dramatic. Jeanne Flore, in her rewriting, underscores from the outset the lesson she reads into it. Thus she begins by admonishing women who are loved to love their lovers in return, reminding them of "Dido, Philis, Phedra, Adrianne, et Medée," who came to love reluctantly and who were abandoned subsequently by their lovers: "Et chascune de cestes cy . . . au premier eurent Amour et ses flambeaux à despris, jusques à ce que le printemps de leur aage se veit estre converty en pluyes ameres, et en esté tempestueux" (pp. 169–70). The example of their misfortune reminds her of Echo and Narcissus.

In retelling the story, the narrator begins with a brief reference to Narcissus' great beauty, followed by three pages of complaint on the part of the Nymphs who blame themselves for their inability to express adequately the consuming passion he inspires in them. Echo is introduced obliquely as one who, had she not been deprived of her "doulce loquence" (p. 173), might have found the words to do so. In keeping with her penchant for explanatory amplification, Jeanne Flore then recounts with copious detail the story of Echo's punishment by Juno for complicity in Jupiter's philandering, establishing thereby narrative causality between her loveless solitude and her subsequent rejection by Narcissus. When she finally encounters him in her lonely wanderings through the forest, she is unable to speak for herself, and can only express herself by repeating the final words he speaks, distorting their meaning to suit her own purposes.

Jeanne Flore's rendition of the scene of their meeting expands on the incidental comedy that Echo's linguistic disability entails. When Ovid's Narcissus says "Here let us meet," Echo, to follow up on her own words, comes forth from the woods and throws her arms around the neck she longs to clasp. Jeanne Flore's Echo reacts with considerably less dignity and restraint, as though she were being viewed though masculine eyes:

Prenant de là Echo esperance de jouir de ses amours, lascha la bride à ses ardens desirs, et donna telle hardiesse à son hatif vouloir comme de venir vers Narcissus, luy plorant et larmoiant par force d'amour dans le sein: et s'efforce luy monstrer à plain en profondement souspirer sa douleur surpassante toute aultre douleur. Et à l'heure quoy qu'elle doubta et trembla de paour, si est ce qu'elle baisa la bouche de l'amy fugitif. (p. 175)

And whereas Ovid's Narcissus says only "manus conplexibus aufer!" (390) ("Remove your hands from me!"), Jeanne Flore's apostrophizes her with a misogynistically coded epithet: "Je puisse, dist il, *lascive* Damoiselle, estre resolu en pouldre premier que je consente à tes vouloirs!" (p. 176). Moreover, while Ovid devotes more than twice as many lines to Narcissus as to Echo, Jeanne Flore gives more attention to Echo, evoking at length the almost hysterical intensity of her passion, implying that her loss of love is fully justified by past behavior. This may be a woman's interpretation of the fate of Ovid's Echo, but it is definitely not a feminist one.[18]

Finally, it is important to note that in Ovid, Narcissus' demise is induced by a young man who, upon being scorned, raised his hands and prayed that Narcissus himself might love and never win his love, whereas in Jeanne Flore it is Echo who asks that "cestuy, à qui nature a donné si excellente beaulté qu'il en a deschassé de soy toute doulceur humaine, soyt amoureux de soy mesmes et ne vive plus en paix, puisqu'il a en ce point desprisé tant de gentilles Damoiselles" (p. 176), making it perfectly clear that while their fates intersect, his is appropriate punishment for indifference towards the opposite sex. Additionally, and not insignificantly, while Ovid's Narcissus sees his own image reflected in the fatal pool, Flore's Narcissus wonders if he is not seeing a "Deesse" come down to earth, a logical Renaissance male rereading of the classical myth.[19]

Although Jeanne Flore retains the essential drama and general outline of Ovid's story, she omits the incident of the flower that bears Narcissus' name, presumably because, given the ideology which underlies all seven of the *Comptes amoureux*, anyone displaying contempt for love would not deserve the slightest hint of redemption. Her *translation* of Ovid's text is already *interpretation* in that she reads it differently, but not necessarily from a feminist standpoint. Her digressions, additions, and omissions tend to remotivate Ovid's myth, recontextualizing it into a story in which Narcissus becomes the brunt and the instrument of Echo's punishment for postponed love. Her version rereads an existing myth, and at one and the same time demands to be read as a myth itself.

It should be emphasized that Echo's death is portrayed as a function of feelings which she created within herself, making it appear as an inevitable consequence of the excesses of unsatisfied female desire. This reading is confirmed, moreover, by the closing moral instructing the *devisantes* not to neglect their lovers or delight in their martyrdom if they love heaven and themselves, for they will only regret their cruelty – a moral which has little to do with Narcissus. And while both Flore's and Ovid's Echo continue to echo even after death, her Narcissus simply dies, while Ovid's, received into the Underworld, continues, with final irony, to gaze upon himself in Stygian waters.

Ovid blames neither Echo nor Narcissus, but Flore clearly links his fate to her fault. Significantly, she omits Ovid's reference to the blind seer Tiresias whose prophecy that Narcissus will live to old age "if he himself shall not know" opens the story and is fulfilled by it. In both accounts, Narcissus is self-possessed and content before Echo intervenes. However, Flore frames her story differently, with a reference to Phoebus, "recteur du divin oeil eterne," who "par preuve sçait quel dommage reçoit celuy qui contre l'amour se veult rebeller" (p. 170), displacing Ovid's theme of self-love with that of women's unfulfilled love.[20] Far from being a submissive rewriting of a classical text, Jeanne Flore's story asserts its own meaning. Whereas a humanist would be intent upon finding and restoring the text's original meaning, she seems more inclined to reappropriate it, underscoring those features which translate most effectively her reading – which is, after all, what classical and Renaissance rhetoric understood by *invention*.

In this particular case, the narrator renews the story of Echo and Narcissus by representing it through feminine eyes. As described by her, both protagonists represent the torment and death resulting from unsatisfied desire. Her concluding address is an attempt to steer the readers and their fictional expectations in one direction, while the myth seems to go off in another. She instructs her *devisantes* to learn from Echo's example not to neglect their lovers nor rejoice in their martyrdom, but to love them with mutual affection.[21] Thus her lesson has the effect of turning Ovid's essentially undetermined myth of Echo and Narcissus into a problematic *exemplum* whose solution is unequally experienced by the two protagonists.

Although we have no proof that Jeanne Flore was or was not a woman, there is some indication that authorship of the *Comptes amoureux* was actually collective and partially, if not totally, masculine.[22] While her program for woman's sexual equality anticipates Marguerite de Navarre's in the *Heptaméron* or Louise Labé's in the *Débat de Folie et d'Amour*, it is focused, even distorted, by a shift from the contrived reality of the frame-setting to the fictive atmosphere, fanciful setting, and elaborate writing of the stories.

Moreover, since there is a marked discrepancy between the urgency of the feminist theme and the fantasy of its narrative setting in a dream world of dwarfs and giants, fabulous lions and snakes, magical clubs and ointments, enchanted castles and dragons, sorcerers and monsters, valorous knights and beautiful princesses, the reader, confronted with an admixture of seriousness and play, can only react with corresponding familiarity and detachment towards the author's display of discursive irony.

Finally, if this work is indeed an apology for women, it is strange that it has them willingly assuming many of the defects and weaknesses attributed to them by the misogynistic literature of the *Querelle des femmes*: lust, lasciviousness, infidelity, duplicity, aggressiveness. Moreover, when Jeanne Flore states in the concluding address to the reader that all she has written is "fiction de poësie," she acknowledges the fantasy of her feminism and the distance with which she has treated it. Irony of this sort is a polemical device, suggesting that the author holds other views, alerting us therefore to the possibility of other readings and other meanings.

What provokes and supports the assumption that Jeanne Flore's *Comptes* are to be read otherwise, with an eye to possible critical attitudes towards them, is, first of all, everything we know about the reading public in Renaissance France. A collection of stories dealing with the proposed liberalization and legitimization of female sexuality, especially one recovering and reversing easily recognized classical or Italian models, would have provided an essentially masculine public with the kind of referentiality needed to detect the distortions arising from ironic rewriting. Early modern readers would not have failed to appreciate the subtle humor inherent in the depiction of a group of women realizing their erotic fantasies through the medium of fiction. It is not certain, however, to what extent they would have realized that in locating their thematic ideology outside the laudatory or depreciative parameters of the *Querelle des femmes*, the *Comptes amoureux* effectively place the whole question of women's sexuality in a new and problematic context, one shared, moreover, by other women writers of the day.

READING AND WRITING IN THE TENTH STORY OF THE
HEPTAMERON

In privileging the concepts of *écriture* and *lecture*, twentieth-century theorists have diverted attention from the author as source and the work as object, focusing instead on writing as a version of speech and on reading as a subjective activity. When the meaning of a work is seen as the reader's distinctive experience of it, the authority of the author and work is subverted and assumed by the reader. Reading and writing are viewed in this perspective as correlative phenomena, the one participating in the fulfillment and determinacy of the other.

A similar complicity between reader and work seems to obtain in the *Heptaméron*. From the beginning, Marguerite de Navarre abdicates her status as author, first of all through explicit anonymity, inasmuch as the work was originally published without her name, then by displacement, in relinquishing the role of narrator and commentator to others. Not only do the *devisants* narrate the stories, they interpret them as well, reading them according to their own perceptions and prejudices.[23]

The immediate effect of Marguerite's absence from the text is to defer meaning in a play of differences. But this effect, contrary to twentieth-century expectations, contributes directly and indirectly to the process of ordering and constructing meaning. Directly, when we react, negatively or positively, to a particular reading by a particular *devisant*; indirectly when, confronted with a series of conflicting readings, we turn back to the story itself, reading it retroactively in an attempt to reconcile the contradictions arising from their inconclusive commentary. Thus while Parlamente *tells* the story of Floride and Amadour, Marguerite *writes* it, and it is her way of writing finally which circumscribes and directs the way in which it is to be read.

The narrator's professed objectivity makes it difficult for the reader to determine how to react to the characters and the intractable situations in which they come to be involved.[24] Is Floride or Amadour to blame for the tragedy which takes place? Or is it Love itself, which induces human beings to interact unseasonably and unreasonably? Is Marguerite's viewpoint gendered? If so, is her story not intended to condemn Amadour's violence and praise Floride's virtuous resistance? Is there moral resolution, and, if not, what lesson, if any, are we supposed to derive from their example? The answer to these and other questions is not clear from the way in which Floride and Amadour work out their respective fates, and the *devisants* tend to problematize the event even further. Moreover, narrative objectivity makes Marguerite's own viewpoint appear undecidable. Thus, lest the "beaulté de la rethoricque feit tort en quelque partye à la verité de l'histoire,"[25] she means for the story to tell its own truth, a truth inherent in the intricate and compromising relationship in which the protagonists allow themselves to fall.

Part of the difficulty in interpretation which readers of Marguerite have experienced has do with the confused way in which the work was transmitted. The *Heptaméron* is a collection of some seventy stories, the order and number of which varies considerably from manuscript to manuscript. The collection first appeared in print in 1558, edited by the humanist scholar Pierre Boaistuau. This edition was entitled *Histoires des Amans fortunez* and contained sixty-seven stories, arranged idiosyncratically. It omitted the discussions linking the stories as well as the name of the author, thereby deflecting any possible didactic or moralizing intent.

The following year, Pierre Gruget published a new and more comprehensive edition of the collection under the title by which it has been known ever since, claiming to have restored the tales to their proper order and naming Marguerite de Navarre as their author. To be sure, the seventy-two stories of this edition do not add up to the hundred projected in the prologue, making it fall short of the number completed by Boccaccio in the *Decameron*, Marguerite's acknowledged model. The organizing principle is quite regular and systematic: five men and five women alternately tell one story each day; a humorous tale follows a serious one; each day is bracketed by a prologue and an epilogue, and each tale is followed by a conversation among the participants, who proceed to disagree about the implications of the story just related. The stories are meant to divert and the commentary to instruct, but these functions are neither always completely separate nor distinct. Scholars have long attempted to establish the historical identity of Marguerite's ten narrators, and it is generally agreed that the names she ascribes them are partially or imperfectly anagrammatic, suggestive of the character or biography of the person in question. Thus Parlamente, the narrator of the tale which concerns us here, may or may not represent Marguerite herself.

A second source of difficulty arises from their originality. The most radical and seminal features of the *Heptaméron*, distinguishing it structurally and ideologically not only from the *Decameron* but also from other previous collections of stories, are first and foremost the dialogues of unequal, but increasing, length and complexity accompanying each of the stories, and secondly the absence throughout of professed auctorial intention or intervention. Once the anonymous narrator of the prologue (whom one may or may not be tempted to identify with Marguerite herself) has described the circumstances bringing the group together, recalled the history of an earlier project to produce a French *Decameron*, and prescribed the protocol to be followed at present, there is no longer any clearly identifiable directing voice, and therefore no fixed point of view.

Although the meaning of a given story may seem self-evident, the discussion it prompts among the various *devisants* tends to multiply and problematize it. Since no single interpretation is privileged and no consensus or conclusion is reached, one can infer, rightfully or not, that either Marguerite presumed that her meaning was sufficiently implicit from the way it is told, or that the book is unfinished, and that in its completed form it would have included an epilogue in which the various and conflicting points of view would have been reconciled, making both meaning and moral explicit. As this is not the case, a problem in reading arises: how are we to understand a book that advances a variety of interpretations without ever choosing among them? In a word, is it possible to cut through the competing commentaries and read Marguerite writing as Marguerite, situating and prejudging her characters, maneuvering and manipulating both *devisants* and readers for her own purposes?

In recounting the story of Floride and Amadour, Parlamente tells us something about the way the narrator views it; in writing it, Marguerite tells us something about the way the author conceives it, and their respective viewpoints may or may not coincide or be identical. In any event, there is room for play in the space between the writing and the telling, as evidenced first of all by the narrator's relative neutrality – that is, her lack of explicit moralizing, even when, as in the attempted rape scenes or the incident of self-mutilation, she has the obvious opportunity, even responsibility, to do so; secondly, by the writer's abstract and analytic style, which seems to be objective and nonjudgmental; finally, by the casting of the *devisants* not only as commentators of the tales which make up the collection, but also as characters in their own right, with conflicting personalities and moralities. And it is in this tenuous and indefinite space that Marguerite operates rhetorically, without interfering directly (that is, pedantically) in the didactic process, without informing us how to read and understand her story.

Preliminary to any proper appreciation of what Marguerite intends her stories to mean, a review of the consequences of the principal conventions governing their selection, as spelled out in the Prologue, is in order. First of all, their orality. Conceived and recorded as conversations among a group of *devisants*, and through them with us, these are stories that are to be heard rather than read, and which consequently require a different kind of reception from us than from them. Since the spoken word disappears, but writing remains, the reader has the advantage of a tangible and verifiable record, one that can be perused and analyzed. Unrestricted by the fiction of oral presentation, we are able to weigh words, to *see* how they interact and collaborate in the transmission of meaning.

The second prerequisite is that all of the *nouvelles* in the collection be true, either witnessed by the narrator or heard from somebody worthy of belief. Repeatedly the narrator assures the audience of the truth of the story. But what are we to understand by "true"? That the stories are historical, providing an exact transcription of actual events, or that they merely imitate or coincide with such events, thereby anticipating Balzac's "All is true"? In either case, the *devisants* are unable to agree on ultimate meanings because their concern is not with the facts of the story, its "truth" in that sense, but with consequences, with the way it turns out and the reasons it turns out that way. Each one rewrites the story in the light of his or her idea of the way it could or should have turned out if the protagonists had conducted themselves in the right way, that is in the ways they deduce retrospectively, leaving the reader with a plethora of interpretative options.

Finally, there is the stipulation that the stories are to be contemporary, as the word *nouvelle* implies, as well as entertaining, therefore not too long, enabling the *devisants* to pass the time pleasantly. Hence Oisille's two reasons for finding the Châtelaine de Vergy story, despite its credibility, unsuitable for inclusion in the present collection: "l'une pour sa grande longueur; l'autre, pour ce que ce n'est pas de nostre temps; et si a esté escripte par ung autheur qui est bien croyable, et nous avons juré de ne rien mectre icy qui ayt esté escript" (p. 400). Parlamente, on the other hand, argues for an exception on the grounds that it will be new to most of them: "Il est vray . . . mais, me doubtant du compte que c'est, il a esté escript en si viel langaige, que je croys que, hors mis nous deux, il n'y a icy homme ne femme qui en ayt ouy parler; parquoy sera tenu pour nouveau" (p. 400).

But to what extent are all of the stories oral, new, and true? Jourda has shown that some half-dozen are adaptations or near-translations (the Châtelaine de Vergy story is acknowledged as such), fourteen are historically verifiable, six probably so, and perhaps others could be. For the rest, more than half the total, Marguerite undoubtedly drew on personal experience, anecdotes, court gossip, oral tradition, and the like. It has been suggested, moreover, that she collected rather than composed the majority of her stories – that she first heard them from friends and acquaintances, editing them as she wrote them down. While we may choose not to believe, as Brantôme assures us, that she composed most of them while traveling in her litter, writing them as quickly and easily as if she were taking dictation, it remains true, nonetheless, that they are meant to reproduce the spoken rather than the written word.

In fact, despite the priority both editors and readers have afforded the stories, they contribute considerably less to the work's originality than the accompanying discussions. Mostly derivative – if not actual quotations of other stories, then at least quotations of stereotypical stories or situations – the *nouvelles* function essentially as a plot or a ploy to capture the reader's interest and attention (which helps to account for the prevalence of stories dealing with sex and sexuality), whereas the discussions provide convincingly impromptu performances of Marguerite's dialectical skill and invention.

Insofar as the *devisants* are both narrators and audience, they can be seen as models of authors and readers, figuratively incorporated into the text. Each narrator, in prefatory remarks, and each listener, in the subsequent discussions, provides a commentary on the activities of story-telling and critical interpretation. This recourse to self-referentiality could signal a desire to include the excluded, to overcome the distance separating author from reader, to point out that, over and beyond the hermeneutic manipulations of the individual *devisants*, the story has a meaning of its own, recoverable in its rhetorical structure.

Although Parlamente indulges herself as narrator, most noticeably in the plot-retarding monologues, she is also mindful of her audience's pleasure, voluntarily abridging the incidental aspects of

her story of Floride and Amadour, as she points out on several
occasions:

commencea la guerre grande et cruelle entre les deux Roys, laquelle ne suis
deliberé de racompter, ne aussy les beaulx faictz que feit Amadour, car
mon compte seroit assez long pour employer toute une journée (p. 67)
Je laisseray à dire les voiages, prieres, oraisons et jeunes, que faisoit
ordinairement Floride pour le salut de Amadour (p. 69)
Je vous laisseray à penser les propos que Floride et luy peurent avoir
ensemble (p. 70)
Je n'entreprendz poinct vous dire la douleur que sentoit Amadour
escoutant ces parolles. (p. 75)

And at the end of the story, despite its great length, she adds that it
could have been much longer: "Je sçay bien, mes dames, que ceste
longue nouvelle pourra estre à aucuns fascheuse; mais, si j'eusse
voulu satisfaire à celluy qui la m'a comptée, elle eut esté trop plus
que longue" (p. 83). While one can detect solicitude for the audience
in these disclaimers, one can also read them as rhetorical devices
which the narrator uses not only to confirm her sure direction in
spite of the shifting and somewhat rambling nature of the story, but
also, and even more important, to suggest, through its several
abridgments, the achievement and complexity of the whole in
relation to the essentials retained here.

If there is something peculiarly Renaissance in Marguerite,
however, is it not her renunciation of the traditional authority of the
author and the privileging of individual interpretation through the
interventions of the *devisants*? Dialogue, beginning with Plato, is a
means of criticism and debate, of contesting accepted values without
arriving at an unqualified conclusion; and such is the eventual effect,
if not its actual function, of the exchange that takes place at the end
of each story in the *Heptaméron*. Informed by opinion rather than
guided by rule, Marguerite's *devisants* are unable to come to common
agreement. While contemporaries would not have failed to appreciate this clash of conflicting interpretations and the splintered
morality it reflects, the modern reader, less spiritually minded, has
tended to be more concerned with the story itself and the inter-
personal and gender-related questions it raises.

The tenth *nouvelle* establishes at once a double moral perspective.
As Floride's tale, it is an example of victory over heart, body, love,
and lover;[26] as Amadour's, it is an example of the inadequacy of
"grande hardiesse," linguistic as well as physical.[27] Initially speech,

or its lack, is a substitute for action. Thus Amadour, at his first encounter with Floride, is reduced to silence: "là où il estoit estimé le mieux parlant qui fust en Espaigne, devient muet devant Floride" (p. 57). Young and inexperienced, Floride does not interpret correctly the meaning of his silence and confides in him without anticipating any future commitment on her part. Amadour then marries Avanturade in order to remain in touch with Floride. Unfortunately, his wife's sudden death deprives him of easy access to her company and forces him to abandon his strategy of patience and deferment. Speech having proved insufficient and faced with the prospect of permanent separation, Amadour resolves to chance a premature return on his investment in time and patience: "se delibera de jouer à quicte ou à double, pour du tout la perdre ou du tout la gaingner, et se payer en une heure du bien qu'il pensoit avoir merité" (p. 72). His thwarted or aborted rapes result in Floride's eventual disfigurement, and both of these crucial events require interpretation.

If feminist criticism has been relatively slow in investigating the *Heptaméron*, it is no doubt because of difficulty in reading Marguerite writing as a woman. One such attempt concludes that Floride's point of view dominates the tenth story and that this is indicated, for instance, in the fact that when she disfigures herself, the narrator does not describe the change in *her* face, but her reaction to *his* face when he sees what she has done: "Et . . . Floride veit son visaige et ses oeilz tant alterez, que le plus beau tainct du monde estoit rouge comme feu, et le plus doulx et plaisant regard si orrible et furieux qu'il sembloit que ung feu très ardant estincellast dans son cueur et son visaige" (p. 78).

Actually, this passage would seem to be less a description of Floride's "reaction" to Amadour's face at the sight of hers than of the changes which take place in his face, changes brought on by *his* angry reaction to *her* willful disfigurement:

S'il me fault mourir, je seray plustost quicte de mon torment; mais la difformité de vostre visaige, que je pense estre faicte de vostre volunté, ne m'empeschera poinct de faire la mienne, car quant je ne pourrois avoir de vous que les oz, si les vouldrois-je tenir auprès de moy. (p. 79)

Rather than proving "in a spectacular way how the heroine's point of view dominates the narrative," or that "what the reader sees is what Floride sees, not what Amadour sees,"[28] this passage seems to indicate that the narrator is particularly attentive to the play of facial expression (*contenance*) as a sure indicator of hidden emotion, regardless of the gender of the person. In a word, perceived incoherences in behavior may have less to do with a "woman writer's inability to make her heroine the subject of a plot structured by Amadour's desire to make her an object"[29] than with the dynamics of narration itself, which, in order to assure intensity and renewal, requires a series of entanglements and peripeteia.

It has been said that sex is not much fun in the *Heptaméron*, and this is certainly true of the tenth *nouvelle*. When love is limited to language, there is understanding and subtle pleasure, but when desire enters the picture, it tends to take a violent turn. Nevertheless, those critics who read the two rape scenes only as illustrations of Amadour's bestiality have missed the irony, even the comedy, inherent in their sudden reversal. In both instances, when Amadour's attempts are abruptly suspended by Floride's cries for help, the tragedy of the scene turns to farce. Thus at the denouement of his first unsuccessful attempt, Amadour, in utter despair, throws himself back on the bed with such great violence that the gentleman who comes at Floride's call thinks he has breathed his last. Infinitely more practical and composed than either of them, Floride asks the gentleman in question to go and fetch some fresh vinegar in order to revive her would-be seducer. At the second attempt, Floride cries out to her mother, and Amadour, not quite as ready to die as he has just declared, has enough time to gather himself together so that, when the Countess enters, he is already standing by the door, with Floride at a respectable distance.

Floride is justifiably angered by what occurs, but this is her anger and not the narrator's, who neither praises her virtue nor moralizes its effects. Placed on the defensive by Amadour's attempts to claim the *repos* he feels they have both earned, she decides simply to avoid her former confidant, thus procuring both his anguish and her own unhappiness. Unable to renounce what he feels is the just outcome of his long courtship and equally unable to obtain satisfaction through persuasion or force, he resolves finally to put an end to his torment through death: "vous esperez me tormenter plus en vivant que mille morts ne sçauroit faire. Mais combien que la mort me fuye, si la chercheray-je tant, que la trouveray; car en ce jour-là seullement, j'auray repos" (p. 81). Though his demise relieves her of any obligation to him, victory for her is hollow, and she retires to a convent, never to be heard from again. Thus the meaning of *repos*, the outcome both seek, is translated ironically into closure, promoting the end of their story and their lives.

Despite Parlamente's ambivalence, as narrator of the story, towards her protagonists, critics have tended to praise Floride and condemn Amadour, depicting her as innocent and virtuous and him as calculating and violent. To be sure, Parlamente uses a number of negatively charged words, seemingly portraying him as a kind of Julien Sorel in his relations with Floride. Thus when Amadour, upon first seeing Floride, "*se delibera* de l'aymer" (p. 56), the verb *se deliberer* has seemed reprehensibly "deliberate" to critics concerned more with ideology than philology.[30] While the usual meaning of "se délibérer à," from the thirteenth to the seventeenth centuries, is in fact "se déterminer à," etymology tells us that one who deliberates is one who weighs and ponders (*deliberare: de + libra* = "scale,"), and context tells us that here the word is meant to translate the fatal process by which Amadour succumbs to Floride's beauty.

Amadour's decision to marry Avanturade has seemed equally duplicitous, especially since the word *couverture* conveys the impression of stealth and dissimulation: "il espouza celle dont il estoit plus aymé qu'il n'y avoit d'affection, sinon d'autant que ce mariage luy estoit très heureuse *couverture* et moyen de hanter le lieu où son esperit demoroit incesamment" (p. 60). Ruthless calculation seems to determine his subsequent conduct as well: "Ayant gaingné ce poinct-là de ceste grande estime, se conduisoit si saigement et *froidement*, que mesme celle qu'il aimoit ne congnoissait poinct son affection" (p. 60). *Se delibera*, *couverture*, and *froidement* all suggest a devious seducer, bent upon satisfying his illegitimate desires.[31]

On the other hand, although these words have negative connotations, Marguerite does not always use them negatively, as reference to her other works shows. Moreover, Amadour's marriage *was* a fortunate cover, providing him with the means to frequent Floride, allowing him to conduct himself *froidement*, that is to say without displaying the physical effects of his passion.[32] Finally, and most important, all three words are clearly judgmental in that they describe the troubled beginnings of a dubious relationship, one requiring that both of the protagonists play an increasingly duplicitous and difficult role.

In the *Heptaméron*, Marguerite frequently depicts characters whose reason is wrong rather than right, who "deliberate" illogically, whose jealousy, concupiscence, cruelty, and anger lead to treachery, rape, and even murder. Yet, again and again, she makes it clear that right can spring from wrong.[33] Amadour is a victim of love, his life and conduct radically changed by his impossible passion for Floride. His love is not calculated nor calculating; rather he is deceived by love into thinking that his love will be returned, and it is upon this premise that he embarks on a troubled and fatal course resulting in eventual damnation and salvation for both.[34]

A summary of the plot of the tenth story has identified the sequence of events that compose it. These events are the reality, the "real" of the story, but we need still to examine another kind of reality, the real of the syntax linking the different events together. What plot there is – and it is reduced in this story to a number of events and their consequences – serves to provide order to the inception, progression, and subsequent destruction of an ambivalent and ambiguous relationship. This is another way of saying that incident is less important in the tenth story than intensification: that Marguerite, as we have seen, is less interested in recalling each and every circumstance appertaining to the story of Floride and Amadour than in selecting and developing only those elements of their story which directly affect and justify the meaning of its outcome. From the beginning, therefore, all of the connections she initiates between the characters are impossible, questionable, contested, denounced. The story of their increasingly tangled relationship is narrated and figured by the interlacing action of a series of irreconcilable strands. The text is comprised of conflicting perspectives and decisions, promoted and aggravated by a number of crises or reversals which are the primordial necessities of any narrative development.

First of all, there is no union which is not a source of discord. All of the characters are inextricably tied together, but there is no link, whether through blood, marriage, love, or desire, which is shared or which is in conformity with accepted moral or social norms. The Comtesse d'Arande is a widow who has brought up her daughter according to the strictest codes of virtue, honor, and obedience. Despite Floride's preference for the Infant Fortuné, her mother marries her with self-serving purpose to the Duc de Cardonne, because with him she will stay closer to home. This fatal decision initiates the first link in what is to become a chain of causes and effects: Floride loves the Infant Fortuné, but is married to the Duc de

Cardonne; Amadour loves Floride but marries Avanturade; Amadour embarks upon an affair with Poline, which she welcomes, but which he has no desire to pursue, making her suspicious and both Avanturade and Floride jealous. Actions and reactions arise from these unnatural unions, creating a series of inextricable circumstances which move the narration inexorably towards inevitable catastrophe.

Secondly, the relations between the characters, Floride and the Duc de Cardonne, Floride and her mother, Amadour and Avanturade, Amadour and Poline, Amadour and Floride, are further complicated and modified by deceit and dissimulation. References abound to masks, concealment, studied looks, and ruses. There is also the slow unfolding of Floride's love for Amadour, coupled with her unsuccessful efforts to hide its progress from herself, her mother, and him. Since all of the various characters seek to convey the impression of conformity of being with being seen, dissimulation is one of the prime sources of tension within and between them. Amadour hides his intentions behind words, whereas Floride struggles to maintain self-possession through absence or feigned indifference:

Mais, voyant sa mere pleurer très fort, laissa aller quelques larmes pour luy tenir compaignye, afin que, par trop faindre, sa faincte ne fust descouverte. (p. 68)
Mais, craignant que la joye qu'elle avoit de le veoir luy fist changer de visaige . . . se tint à une fenestre, pour le veoir venir de loing. Et, si tost qu'elle l'advisa, descendit par ung escallier tant obscur que nul ne pouvoit congnoistre si elle changeoit de couleur. (p. 70)

In the third place, dialogue has a similarly conflictual and disjunctive effect. Thus when Amadour finally breaks his silence and confides in Floride, hoping thereby to increase the degree of intimacy between them, his eloquence merely succeeds in arousing her suspicion: "J'ay si grand paour que, soubz vos honnestes propos, il y ayt quelque malice cachée pour decepvoir l'ignorance joincte à ma jeunesse, que je suis en grande perplexité de vous respondre" (p. 64).

In the fourth place, writing here is concerned with the strict presentation of situation. The picturesque and the particular are limited or eliminated. The fact that there is little or no physical description, either of people or places, is a clear indication of Marguerite's intention to emphasize relationships. Relative pronouns *qui, que, lequel,* and the conjunctives *et* and *que,* are the most significant grammatical features, especially prominent in the syntax of Floride's and Amadour's explanatory monologues. This is not an uncommon phenomenon in sixteenth-century prose, but it is especially relevant in a story where no relationship is straightforward or transparent.[35] In a word, the tenth *nouvelle* is "true" from the standpoint of its writing, in that the story it tells is both reflected in and consonant with the style in which it is told.

In the fifth place, there are a number of pivotal events, intended to promote the release and revelation of emotions, arousing joy or deception: Floride's marriage with the Duc de Cardonne; Amadour's decision to marry Avanturade, to court Poline, to bare his heart to Floride; his repeated departures for the battlefield and subsequent returns; his long imprisonment; Avanturade's death; the two rape scenes. These events introduce turning points in the development of the plot, dramatic and unexpected crises which orient the story in new and different directions.

The gradual qualification of degrees of love introduces a final determining element in the promotion and progress of the text. Thus the incipient desire which Floride feels for Amadour is depicted as "quelque chose plus qu'elle n'avoit acoustumé" (p. 65), that is, something slowly and inwardly experienced at first rather than outwardly manifested or expressed. Her growing attraction becomes more demanding once jealousy enters the picture: "Et commencea l'amour, poulcée de son contraire, à monstrer sa très grande force" (p. 66). All of these semantic unfoldings are textual unfoldings as well, bringing contrary strands together, informing and configuring a relationship which is both tangled and intolerable. And while the text itself, through its convoluted narrative structure, seems clear in its denunciation of this troubled relationship, the narrator's point of view, seemingly neutral, is actually equivocal.

In fact, Parlamente's voice introduces two distinct ideological strands, conveying different interpretations of the story according as one reads it from Amadour's or Floride's standpoint. Thus she has words of praise for both, while intimating that Floride's victory is also love's defeat. Further, without questioning the "truth" of Parlamente's story, the *devisants* are quick to take issue with her claim that Floride was tried to the limits of her endurance and put up a virtuous resistance in the face of it all. Their debate revolves around the meaning of "virtue" as it relates to a number of courtly concepts, *honneur, parfaict amour, debvoir, maistresse, serviteur,* all of which are defended according to the gender or particular moral code of the speaker.

Thus the word virtue, which, as etymology tells us, means virility, manly courage, is a quality in which Amadour is found lacking by the male *devisants*, for he failed in his conquest of Floride. For the female *devisants*, virtue means chastity, integrity, and self-respect, and Floride is steadfast in its defense. Although Amadour is as audacious in love as on the battlefield, his virtue, thwarted by Floride's virtue, results in conflict and catastrophe: "Et pour en venir à l'intention de mon compte, je vous diray que sa trop grande hardiesse fut esprouvée par la mort" (p. 82). For Parlamente, both Amadour and Floride remain "virtuous" in their separate ways, inducing her, in a worldly conclusion, to invite her female audience, "en prenant exemple de la vertu de Floride," to diminish "ung peu de sa cruauté, et ne croire poinct tant de bien aux hommes, qu'il ne faille, par la congnoissance du contraire, à eulx donner cruelle mort et à vous une triste vie" (p. 83).

If neither is to blame, what then is the lesson of the story? Since there is no general agreement among the *devisants*, are we to conclude that there is none, that Marguerite means to amuse but not to instruct? Or does she expect us to be better readers than they are and realize that the fault lies elsewhere, not in the respective virtues of her protagonists but rather in their fatal confrontation? Taken separately, their stories are related to one another, but asymptotically, in that both Floride and Amadour are victims, less of unreciprocated desire than of its impossible fulfillment. Their stories intersect nevertheless, and it is the consequences of their intersecting which are the real subject of the tenth *nouvelle*.

This rereading of the tenth *nouvelle* has focused on elements and structures of writing susceptible of revealing Marguerite's intentions, despite the conflicting interpretations of the *devisants*. When viewed as characters, the *devisants* are as "true" as the stories they tell. Conceived by Marguerite in the image of the readers of the day, they are self-centered, worldly, without a uniform moral code or transcendent expectations. Their inability to agree implies criticism of their ability to judge. Whereas they consider their idiosyncratic rewriting of the story to be an acceptable form of reading, for Marguerite it affords an example of wrong reading. Further, their commentary is similar to a gloss, and the revalorization of the text to the detriment of the gloss is one of the principal achievements of Renaissance writing. Right reading is reading according to the rules of the text, and the text writes right, as the story of Floride and Amadour shows, in crooked and tangled lines. Thus, while the *devisants* deconstruct the meaning of the text as each sees fit, we are expected to reconstruct it, returning to the text itself to reevaluate the significance of its foldings and unfoldings, an exercise in reading which the advent of the printed work rendered more feasible.

The tangle of the text is indeed a trap, designed to involve us in its problems and pleasures, drawing us effortlessly and resolutely into a web of converging, even opposing lines of development, resisting easy resolution rather than deferring it indefinitely. Authority, abrogated by the author and relegated to the *devisants*, is transferred peremptorily to the reader. Caught between objectivity and subjectivity, interpretation is informed finally by a reciprocal logic founded on the primacy of writing itself. The text, which relates the story, may write our reading; but it is the text of the text, that is, the particular form writing assumes in order to be true to its meaning, which shapes the story, revealing its right direction and ultimate intent. With no author to tell us how to read, it is reading itself which puts our judgment to the test.

While Marguerite remains resolutely in the margins of the *Heptaméron*, allowing her story to tell itself, rhetoric, which she dismisses in the Prologue, makes its way surreptitiously back into the text itself, guiding us slowly but surely through the thicket of possible misreadings. She depends upon her readers' perception of the moral and cultural disjunction between the world of Christian, courtly ideals and the amoral, frequently bestial world of her characters, regardless of gender, to set their sights aright. Her text opens up a space between these two worlds for cultural and political debate, in that it deals with the status of marriage, the place of men and women in society, and the troubled relationships between them. From her strategic position as detached observer, Marguerite quietly contests both the precepts and techniques of misogynist history, rewriting the *Querelle des femmes* with her own rules on the wiles of fiction.

Two different stories or collections of stories, one certainly by a women, the other probably so, have provided us with two different, even contrasting, reactions to Renaissance feminism. Whereas Marguerite de Navarre exchanges the polemics of misogyny for the rhetoric of fiction, Jeanne Flore imagines a world in which women are more or less everything misogynists claim them to be. In their separate ways, both tend to problematize the question of women's place and sexuality in the world. Floride's comportment, for instance, remains ambiguous throughout the tenth story, initially because of naïveté or lack of experience, but eventually, once love has taken over, through silence, indecision, and ambivalence. The reader is left, along with the *devisants*, with the difficult task of finding the answer to the fundamental question which the narration raises but never answers, that is, who is to be blamed for the inevitable outcome of their story, Floride or Amadour? Are not both to be pitied, although for different reasons? Are they to be held accountable for their actions, or are we supposed to see them as hapless victims of their own natures as well as of a tragic set of circumstances?

On the other hand, Jeanne Flore's women exist in a world which appears much more ludic than tragic, in that they realize many of the very same traits which misogynistic literature attributes to them, making it difficult to decide whether we are to admire them as living examples of sexual freedom or to be amused by the coincidence of their sensual appetites and actions with masculine prejudices and expectations. Yet both authors presuppose and depend upon the participation of their audience for the right reading of their texts. Placed within the social context generated and conditioned by the publication of countless polemical works concerning women, both the *Heptaméron* and the *Comptes amoureux* acquire sharper focus and greater cultural pertinence, making them more pronounced in their moral judgment and statement. These are tales that are meant to be *read*, that is, whose meaning must be worked out through the complex cultural and rhetorical layerings which compose the early modern text. It is in this sense and for this reason that these two works can be said to fictionalize the questions raised by the *Querelle des femmes*. Rather than taking sides, they make readers decide which side is right or wrong, assigning them thereby an area of literary activity and moral responsibility all their own.

CHAPTER 3

Anonymity and the poetics of regendering

It is already sufficiently difficult, as we have just seen, to distinguish between writer and rhetoric in self-consciously objective texts; it is almost impossible when the writer remains of necessity on the periphery of the written word, marginalized by ideological design, social status, civil or religious pressures. The fusion, even confusion, of writer and writing is a salient characteristic of early modern literature, prioritizing performance over person and rhetoric over self, especially in the transitional period between manuscript and print cultures as writers measure their professional responsibilities towards patrons and audience alike.

The advent of printing, and the possibility of increased circulation it afforded writers and their writing, tended to make recognition of authorship a priority in a system which depended almost exclusively upon patronage for its viability. Proprietary interest is reflected in the various efforts of Renaissance authors to spell out their own names and to create a place and a presence for themselves in their texts.[1] This intention is evidenced first of all by the prominence afforded such paratextual matter as title page, *privilège*, author's portrait, and prologue; it is marked also, but more discreetly at first, by instances of self-promotion within the confines of the text itself, becoming much more blatant in Ronsard and the other Pléiade poets.

This chapter will be concerned first of all with the self-referential *je* in early Renaissance poetry written by men. As commissioned poets, the Rhétoriqueurs were obliged to write on set topics at set times, according to the protocol of the particular court to which they were attached. Their official duties were to speak for others and not for themselves, which means that their works, both in prose and poetry, remain strictly impersonal. Conversely, beginning with Marot, the first-person singular is ubiquitous, but it stands most

frequently as a rhetorical substitute for the more properly autobiographical self. In fact, "I" is almost always anonymous in early
modern literature, compounding the problem of the relation
between author and actor. The more intrusive it becomes, the less
reliable it tends to be. In this sense, early modern writing is both
liberation, a way of displaying the author, and at the same time
restriction, self-expression being governed both by the formal principles of structure and the changing conditions of production and
audience.

The second part of this chapter will address the way in which
women writers reposition and regender the literary "I," endowing it
with reactive authority and mediated presence. The voices which
emerge for these writers remain partially derivative insofar as they
take shape in relation to male models and mentors, expressing
themselves through the self-conscious regendering of traditional
rhetorical conventions. This emphasis on the techniques of referentiality requires a close reading of the texts under consideration, but
always in view of the larger question of the way in which marginality
is perceived and structured by writers in the cultural context of the
day. Thus these pages on Pernette du Guillet and Louise Labé are
not intended to provide yet another feminist reading of their poetry,
but rather a reading of the way in which a feminist reading, in
overlooking Renaissance rhetorical tactics and strategies, can deflect,
even distort, their meaning.

THE "I" AS ANOTHER

In a letter to Georges Izambard dated May 15, 1871, Rimbaud wrote
two arresting and seminal paragraphs on poetry and poets, which he
repeated and expanded somewhat in another letter, dated May 17,
1871, this time to Paul Demeny. In these two letters, Rimbaud
contends that the true poet must be a seer, capable of looking
beyond the real world. "Je veux être poète et je travaille à me rendre
voyant," he wrote in the first letter, and in the second, "Je dis qu'il
faut être *voyant*, se faire *voyant*." The poet becomes *voyant*, he explains
in the May 15 letter, through "le dérèglement de tous les sens," a
statement he developed in the second letter with the addition of
three preliminary adjectives: "par un long, immense et raisonné
dérèglement de tous les sens."[2] According to this proposition, the
"I," as the transmitter of unsolicited and spontaneous visions, is not

personally involved in the poetic process. "Car JE est un autre", he concludes in both letters, appending, in the second, an extended musical analogy designed to describe the source and quality of inspiration: "Si le cuivre s'éveille clairon, il n'y a rien de sa faute. Cela m'est évident." The poet is merely a receptive witness, an instrument played upon by autonomous forces: "j'assiste à l'éclosion de ma pensée: je la regarde, je l'écoute." While the poet provides the initial impulse, afterwards the poem pursues its own peculiarly independent course: "je lance un coup d'archet: la symphonie fait son remuement dans les profondeurs, ou vient d'un bond sur la scène."[3]

The dramatic conclusion that "I" is another signifies a troubling disjunction between the poet and his poem. Had Rimbaud written "Car JE *suis* un autre," his formula would have provided little to puzzle over. In objectifying the "I," however, his remarks effectively eliminate its referential character and, consequently, the poet's active participation and presence in the operation of the poem. The "I" who is "other" assures the autonomy and indeterminacy of writing, untrammeled henceforth by the exigencies or contingencies of self.

Rimbaud's declaration seemed new and revolutionary at the time. As such, it had an enormous impact on the subsequent development of French poetry, although it is little more than a recasting of traditional doctrine on inspiration. The idea of the poet as *mage* or *voyant* came to Rimbaud through Romanticism; it originated, however, in Renaissance recastings of the classical myth of the poet as *vates*. Anticipating Rimbaud's "Je est un autre" is Ovid's *est Deus in nobis*, equating inspiration with possession and enthusiasm.[4] In Platonic and Renaissance theory, it is indeed the voice of divine fury that speaks through the poet. This is the "other" whose presence manifests itself, spiritually and physically, in the *forcènement, transe, délire, folie, vaticination, ravissement* marking the conversion of the person into a poet.[5]

For the most part, classical and Renaissance theoreticians would agree that poetry is formed, mediated, and modulated by remembered patterns of thought and language, that the speaking "I" is at once individual and universal. The modern conception of the literary voice is marked by the primacy accorded self-expression since Rousseau and Romanticism. Invention in this context no longer implies finding and refining what is already known, but creating something "new" and "original" out of inner resources. Conversely, in the sixteenth century, invention and imitation are not seen as contrary, contradictory, or antagonistic, in part because of the classical and Christian tradition of the centrality of humanity. The individual is perceived as open, on the one hand, to society, that is to say, the collectivity of court or community, and, on the other, to the presence of that part of humanity which makes us similar to others. A person is formed by giving shape and coherence to a relationship with the exterior world – civil, social, religious – all the while remaining an example of the human experience in one of its individually different configurations. Nothing then is ever completely old or new, and the "I" is never fully devoid of its more public connotations.

Significantly, *I* as *ego* in the modern sense of the word was unknown in sixteenth-century thought, and writers had no reason consequently to experience anxiety over its expression or repression. The *moi* was already "haïssable," reserved for the confessional, and there was little or no public interest in its specificity. "Je est un autre" is therefore a perfectly appropriate designation for French Renaissance authors. If the private self intrudes into sixteenth-century texts, it is almost always conditioned by rhetorical training as well as contemporary cultural constraints. Thus Marot, despite the autobiographic penchant of much of his epistolary poetry, recounts his own trials and tribulations within a prototypal context, which includes, among others, intertexual echoes of Villon's "Je ris en pleurs et attens sans espoir," and Ovid's *Tristia*.[6]

The writers arbitrarily designated as Rhétoriqueurs[7] constitute the first distinctive generation of Renaissance authors to appear in print. Because of their situation as *indiciaires* or *secrétaires* at noble courts, they were not autonomous in their choice of themes. Constrained by the demands of their official position to write on the events and circumstances – births, marriages, deaths – which marked the lives of the noble family in whose service they were employed, they themselves are never directly the subject or object of their texts. Whenever, therefore, their official duties committed them to compose a celebratory or deploratory work, they were confronted with the problem of initiating and sustaining interest in a topic in which their participation was strictly professional. Relegated to anonymity by the circumstances of their birth and conditions of their office as well as by the inherited principles and conventions of medieval poetics, the Rhétoriqueurs were reduced to manifesting their individuality indirectly and marginally, through a masterful display of verbal acrobatics and prosodic complications.

The Rhétoriqueurs had a noble, even aristocratic conception of poetry, more so in fact than much of their practice would immediately suggest. While they believed in inspiration, their insistence on art and erudition tends to make their works appear perfunctory and impersonal. Above all, they demonstrated ingenuity in latinate lexicon and syntax, acquired prestige in their ability to locate and enumerate rich and rare rhyme schemes (*rimes équivoquées, fratrisées, concatenées, couronnées, rétrogrades, senées, bilingues*), and in their manipulation of complicated strophic patterns (*chant royal, ballade, rondeau, épître*). Contrived harmony of sounds, either by alliteration or assonance, was systematically but meaningfully pursued, since, as Jean Lemaire de Belges declared, "Rhetorique et Musique sont une mesme chose."

The fact remains that these poets, convinced as they were of the importance of form, were less immediately concerned with content. For them, a competent display of technical virtuosity was sufficiently substantive in itself. Rather than *poeta vates*, the Rhétoriqueur is *poeta faber*, a forger of rhyme and rhythm, correlating originality with contrived ingenuity in versification and word-play. Thus Cretin, in his *Chant royal*, conflates God the creator, "L'altitonant supreme plasmateur, / Monarque et chef en l'art d'architecture," with the poet, artisan and architect of a verbal universe. Similarly, a pattern of acrostic alliteration sustains the rigid strophic structure of Molinet's *Oroison sur Maria*, repeating both horizontally and vertically the separate letters of the Virgin's name, gradually composing a calligrammatical paradigm designed to represent, musically as well as graphically, the geometry of perfection itself:

> Marie, mere merveilleuse,
> Marguerite mundifie,
> Mere misericordieuse,
> Mansion moult magnifie,
> Ma maistresse mirifie,
> Mon mesfait maculeux me matte,
> M'ame mordant mortifie;
> Mercy m'envoye m'advocate![8]

With the advent of printing, auctorial self-promotion is more intrusive. Thus while Cretin, Molinet, and Jean Lemaire de Belges continue to assure recognition of their authorship through verbal manipulation, punning signatures, or emblematic devices,[9] they begin nevertheless to intervene more directly in the conduct and reception of their works, asserting their presence in paratext and text. Paratextual involvement is usually personal, in that the author speaks in his or her own name, preparing and presenting the text to patron and public. It is the place of the exordium to put the reader in a favorable state of mind towards the speaker, and Molinet accomplishes this through traditional rhetorical formulas of self-disparagement, with specific reference to inadequacy, rude speech, and intellectual inferiority. Comparing his *moy simplet* with the *noble oiselet* of his *Ad laudem irundinis*, he enters obliquely, but fraudulently, into the text itself. A veritable dialogue ensues between poet and poem, making the writing process itself a medium of personal experience:

> Tant gente es tu de corps, de becq et d'elle
> Que a bien loer ta digne corpulence
> Fallent mes sens, qui riens n'ont d'excellence.[10]

Compared with the excellence and nobility of the *hirondelle*, or the eloquence and learning of previous praisers of its virtues, the poet considers himself initially to be of little talent, unworthy therefore of the difficult task he has set for himself:

> Tant d'orateurs, plains de philosophie,
> Ont tant prisié ta vertu salutaire
> Que moy simplet, qui peu te glorifie,
> N'ay rien d'exquis, dont soyes assouffie,
> Si voeul tout clore et si ne me puis taire . . .   (p. 597)

Denigration of himself leads to denigration of his art, equally primitive, he feels, in comparison with the swallow's great and novel ingenuity:

> Mes dictiers sont du temps du roy Clotaire
> Emprés ton hault et nouvel artifice . . .   (p. 597)

Nevertheless, in realizing the uniqueness of the swallow's nature and the mighty gifts it contains, his "rough mind" is encouraged to raise its unworthy voice in dissonant song and praise. With emphatic enumeration of the swallow's superior qualities and, in comparison, his own failings, Molinet initiates a paradox which is not fully resolved, in true dramatic fashion, until the very end of the poem. In the interval, the *hirondelle* is slowly transformed from a humble bird into an object of great beauty and value:

> Et sy vault bien sa pesanteur d'argent
> Cent mille fois et cent fois bien cent mille;
> Tu n'as plume qui ne vaille une ville
> Toute d'azur et d'or une cité,
> Car tu n'es riens que preciosité.   (p. 598)

Philosophers of old, the poet maintains, *Isidore, Ambroise, Aristote, Macrobe*, have celebrated the swallow's curative powers, declaring it to be a greater physician than *Apollon, Mercure, Hippocrate* or *Esculape*. In applying epideictic topics of circumstances, physical attributes, qualities of character to a bird, Molinet is intentionally disconcerting; but this is his strategy for setting up a problem in interpretation which only recourse to etymology can resolve successfully. For who, except the learned reader, would know that the Greek word for swallow is *khelidôn*, from which derives *khelidonia* – celandine, a plant which grows commonly in rubble or debris; or that the swallow is reputed to use the juice of this plant to restore sight to its offspring; or that celadonite, a kind of agate or semi-precious stone, is fabled to be found in its belly? Through an exchange of properties, the simple swallow suddenly becomes much more complex and worthy of praise than originally anticipated, justifying retrospectively the poet's opening expression of inadequacy and hyperbolic description of his subject:

> Sy convient mettre avant la celidone,
> Qui en toy naist et prend son origine;
> Si grand vertus le haultain ciel luy donne
> Que l'oeul crevé, que tout mire abandonne,
> Il resuscite et tout vif l'enlumine . . .   (p. 600)

Molinet's swallow is never really a swallow seen or described from nature, but rather the sign of something else, and his text is meant to inscribe a trajectory from bird to symbol. In listing physical characteristics and hidden properties, the poem is first of all a kind of *blason*. As such, it partakes of the didactic tradition of bestiaries and lapidaries, involving at once practical, moral, and religious readings of the dissimulated virtues inherent in animals, plants, and precious or semi-precious stones. On the other hand, it falls into the encomiastic tradition of paradoxical literature in its celebration of a small and insignificant object. Ultimately, it is allegorical, in that the *hirondelle*, although unworthy on the surface of such extravagant praise, actually comes to merit it once its deeper significance is understood. Thus, after distributing the swallow's traits and attributes according to the letter of pagan lore and literature, Molinet recapitulates them figuratively, deciphering them within a Christian framework of Incarnation and Redemption, so that transition from bird to crucified Christ informs the rhetorical dynamics of this curiously complex text:

> Sainct oiselet, ce n'est point sans mistere
> Que Dieu transmet en toy faveur celeste:
> Il y gist sens de moralle matere,
> Non pas pour cerf, pour linx ne pour panthere,
> Ne pour corps nulz aërin ne terrestre,
> Mais pour splendeur ou tout homme s'arreste,
> Le createur, qui son sang espandit,
> Quand en la croix lumiere nous rendit.   (p. 600)

Molinet's initial self-denigration is remotivated finally by his strategic repositioning of poet and subject, for in praising the swallow, he praises himself as the subtle decipherer of its hidden meaning. Humbled before the *noble oiselet*, the *moy simplet* is exalted at last as the successful author of a delicately heuristic undertaking:

> La blance fleur de ton purain fourment
> M'a donné soing de maulre ma farine,
> A pouvre vent, mais soubtil quelquement.   (pp. 601–2)

Molinet is at once the self-conscious architect and the interpreter of his poem, structuring its subject in such a way as to enable the reader to decipher its deeper meaning. To this end, the text is made to explicate itself, leaving nothing to chance or ambiguity. As the "inventor" of his allegory, Molinet inscribes its right reading within the logic of the text, assuring his authority over the triviality of wayward language and arbitrary interpretation. Seemingly undecided in its preliminary proliferation, meaning is ever more sharply focused as the poem progresses. Narrative and authorial voices coincide finally, defining and legitimizing the poet's own presence in an artful poem in praise of a swallow.

Despite the self-effacing requirement of Rhétoriqueur poetics, Jean Lemaire de Belges's elegy for a dead parrot similarly introduces the person of the author into the body of the text. Written to console Marguerite d'Autriche, duchesse de Savoie, his first *Epistre de l'Amant vert* is a mock and self-mocking *déploration*. Following the sudden and dramatic death of her young husband Philibert le Beau, Marguerite had returned to "Germany" to visit her father, leaving Lemaire behind. During her absence, a dog killed her pet parrot, providing her *indiciaire* with both a pretext for an unsolicited poem and a reminder of his past service and present need for continuing patronage.

Ironically, Jean Lemaire's poetic career was marked, even marred, by a series of unexpected and untimely deaths. Almost immediately after he entered into a noble household, his patron would become fatally ill. This unfortunate pattern repeated itself on more than one occasion, requiring each time the writing of a eulogy, which, since the patron's death meant the poet's dismissal, Jean Lemaire was careful to dedicate to a prospective replacement. Thus upon the death in 1503 of his first patron, Pierre de Bourbon, he wrote a *déploration* entitled *Le Temple d'Honneur et de Vertu*, presenting it to Louis de Luxembourg, comte de Ligny. Impressed with Jean Lemaire's talents, the count decided to take him under his protection, and inevitably, a few days later, fell sick and died. Obliged once again to compose an elegy, Jean Lemaire wrote the *Plainte du Desiré*, dedicating it to Anne de Bretagne.[11] Fortunately for her, perhaps, she failed to extend the anticipated support, and Lemaire then turned to Marguerite d'Autriche, who retained him as "indiciaire et historiographe" in June 1504. In September, her husband Philibert le Beau died, at the young age of twenty-four, from drinking water at a cold fountain after the heat of a hunt, and Lemaire set to writing the *Couronne margaritique*, a vast and laborious project in prose and poetry. After a few opening pages on the events leading up to the duke's death – the fatal hunt, the heat of September, the ensuing thirst, the ice-cold fountain – and expressions of grief, the remainder of the work is devoted to praise and consolation for the widow.[12] Justifiably concerned for his future upon her departure to Germany and weary perhaps of official *déplorations*, Lemaire wrote his first *Epistre de l'Amant vert*, hoping to attract attention to his plight, while diverting both himself and the recipient from more serious matters.

Jean Lemaire presented his epistle to Marguerite in 1505, upon her return to Savoy. Afterwards, it was circulated in manuscript form and acclaimed by courtly readers. During the autumn of 1505, he composed a *Seconde épistre de l'Amant vert*, in which the dead parrot writes to his lady and mistress from beyond the grave, describing his passage through the animal underworld and entrance into the paradise of beasts, where he is reunited with the *Esprit Vermeil*, Marie de Bourgogne's parrot, victim of an equally tragic death. The original edition of both *épistres* was printed in 1511, together with a dedicatory letter addressed to Jean Perréal, asking him to recommend them to the benevolent attention of Anne de Bretagne.[13] For this purpose, Jean Lemaire modified the text of the second *épistre* so as to associate praise of Anne with that of Marguerite, undoubtedly hoping finally to enter into her service at the Court of France.

Inasmuch as the *povre corps tremblant* of the *Epistre de l'Amant vert* is both poet and parrot, Lemaire's text is self-consciously playful from the very start. The ambiguity of the narrative "I" is a pretext for banter, even bold familiarity. The "amant vert" of the title is at once bird and courtly lover, privy to the intimate life of the ducal household (scenes of which he will have occasion to recall) and required, as a domestic of a kind, to please his mistress. This accounts for his ironic despair at her departure, which he presents here as the final, fatal separation of a lover from his beloved:

> Las! seuffre ung peu ta haultesse et prestance
> Ses beaux yeulx clers (pour ung hault benefice)
> Prester lecture à ce derrain office.
> Derrain diz je, quant à moy qui t'escripz,
> Car, mettant fin à mes chantz et mes criz,
> Je delibere et sans faincte propose
> A mes briefz jours mettre certaine pose.   (p. 5)

In its initial positioning of author and subject, the *mediocritas mea* topos focuses on the dual fate of the parrot/poet. Whereas Molinet's swallow is more and more abstract, until volatilized at last into a symbol, Lemaire's parrot becomes increasingly more concrete and human, assuming the role finally of the "mal aimé" in a mock-heroic drama of abandonment and suicide. Thus Lemaire's parrot "parrots" him, introducing the poet into his poem and allowing him to play out the fate he anticipates for himself if Marguerite, who has gone off and left him, fails to answer his plea for compassion and support:

> Helas! Que y je meffaict?
> T'ay je despleu, o chief d'euvre parfaict?
> Ai je noncé chose qui face à taire?
> A riens meffait son humble secretaire . . .   (p. 6)

The reader, initially unaware of the union of poet and parrot, assumes that the narrator is an unhappy courtly lover. In deferring the true identity of the *amant vert*, Lemaire is able to exploit the parrot's voice with playful audacity to accuse Marguerite of cruel indifference to his plight. Throughout, the text oscillates between voices: at times it is the poet's alone we hear, recalling in his capacity as *secretaire* the dramatic events of Marguerite's life; at other times, the poet/parrot, speaking about a past of devoted and constant service; finally the "pucelle aux passants," recapitulating the parallel careers of poet and parrot: foreign birth, removal to a cold and windy clime through love and renown of a lady, loss of native language and acquisition of a learned one:

> Laissa Eygpte et le fleuve du Nil
> Espris d'amours en ung cueur juvenil . . .
>   Sa langue malheureuse
> Laboura tant à son futur dommaige
> Qu'elle oublia son langaige ramaige
> Pour sçavoir faire ou sermon ou harengue,
> Tant en françois comme en langue flamengue,
> En castillan et en latin aussi,
> Dont à l'aprendre il souffrit maint soucy.   (pp. 12–13)

Distance enables Lemaire to speak frankly of himself and the precariousness of his situation with elegance and wit, without ever completely relinquishing the respect and anonymity his position requires. When, however, he allows himself the license of alluding to the beauty of Marguerite's nakedness or of referring to himself as a silent and envious witness to her sexual pleasure, we have a foretaste not only of Marot's elegant, courtly *badinage*, but also of the erotic fascination which characterizes much Renaissance prose and poetry:

> Quel autre amant, quel autre serviteur
> Surpassa oncq ce hault bien et cest heur?
> Quel autre aussi eut oncq en fantasie
> Plus grand raison d'entrer en jalousie,
> Quand maintes fois, pour mon cueur affoler,
> Tes deux mariz je t'ay veu accoller?   (pp. 8–9)

Finally, Molinet's eulogy and Lemaire's two *épistres*, together with some fifty by Marot, are important documents in the history of the transition between manuscript and print cultures. Whereas these *épistres* were conceived and written originally for the eyes of the person addressed, they acquired a different and much more public function once they appeared in printed form. No longer destined solely to fulfil a professional obligation or assure a future livelihood, they were now intended to amuse and impress a wider circle of readers, providing the private author with a public forum. To a greater extent than has been thought, early modern texts drew readers from very different social and economic levels, creating an undetermined and unexploited marketplace for the distribution of new forms of reading and writing. With publication, written works were subject to the rules of the trade and the whims of the anonymous reader, making it necessary to devise specific prefatory practices and rhetorical strategies to encourage yet delimit entrance into the text.

The printed image was often a proposal or a protocol for reading, suggesting a correct understanding and a proper meaning for a work.[14] This is equally true of the personal image, the self-portrait the writer draws for the reader, providing a textual intermediary between the two. But in the transition from Molinet's swallow and Lemaire's parrot to Marot's "pauvre Clément," autobiography gradually displaces anonymity. At the outset of his career, however, Marot stands firmly in the impersonal Rhétoriqueur tradition, partly because he came to it through his father Jean, partly because, like those writers, he is a court poet, working under similar social conditions. It is not until his imprisonment in 1526 that he converts to a first-person narrative. In his *épistres*, we find a Marot who is naïve, mistreated, and misunderstood. Despite his repeated misfortunes, his tone remains light, his rhythm rapid, his style direct and colloquial. But this display of linguistic charm is expected to fulfill a very precise function, for underneath its playfulness lurks the muted urgency of a suppliant intent upon contriving a favorable image and conveying a convincing message, even if this means conflating his voice with that of another.

As editor and rejuvenator of Villon's works (1533), Marot was familiar with expressions of self-pity, similar instances of which appear at some time or other in his own works. There is much which is suspect in their shared, self-serving "sincerity." Both want to proclaim their injured innocence, and poetry for them serves as a kind of alibi. Marot could have learned from Villon how to exploit misfortune to advantage, the tone and tactic to adopt in order to interest and amuse the reader. Clearly, his self-portrait is informed less by autobiographical imperatives than by circumstantial events, making it indispensable for him to satisfy the expectations of his recipient in order to be successful in his request. Enforced distance from his intended audience makes textual presence all the more compelling, and Marot was aware both of the techniques and necessity of achieving proximity.[15]

Much of Marot's individuality comes from preempting a central place in his poetry, yet situating himself precariously on the periphery of the contemporary social, political, and religious norm. In the first place, like Lemaire and his parrot, his origins and native language were foreign:

> A brief parler, c'est Cahors en Quercy,
> Que je laissay pour venir querre icy
> Mille malheurs: ausquelz ma destinée
> M'avoit submis. Car une matinée
> N'ayant dix ans, en France fuz mené
> Là, où depuis me suis tant pourmené
> Que j'oubliay ma langue maternelle,
> Et grossement apprins la paternelle
> Langue Françoyse es grands Courts estimée.[16]

Secondly, the Court, he claims, was his "maîtresse d'école," leaving him with little time for humanist books and learning. Spokesman of the first generation of Renaissance poets, his acknowledged readings remain disconcertingly medieval:

> J'ay leu des Sainctz la Legende dorée,
> J'ay leu Alain le tresnoble Orateur,
> Et Lancelot le tresplaisant menteur,
> J'ay leu aussi le Romant de la Rose,
> Maistre en amours . . .[17]

Despite dependency on the Court for patronage and, consequently, the necessity for self-effacement, Marot seeks untiringly to promote a certain image of himself, self-consciously bridging the traditional interval between life and letters. Unlike Lemaire, who writes for Marguerite, Marot has one eye on the King and the other on the public. He aims at pleasing both audiences by telling them what they want to hear in an off-handed way, rather than recounting his innermost thoughts or feelings. The Marot we come to know is the Marot he wants us to know: provocative, unpredictable, ingenuous, yet involved, partially in spite of himself, in all of the ideological controversies of the day.

On the more practical side, his "élégant badinage" serves to overcome two interrelated problems, one physical and the other rhetorical. Exiled from Court, it allows him to impose a presence, to please the King and interest him in his request. Maintaining a

delicate balance between absent writer and present reader, he
dialogues with the King, promoting a sense of complicity between
theme. Thus in his *Epistre au Roy, du temps de son exil à Ferrare*, he
accuses the Sorbonne of ignorance because of its opposition to the
lecteurs royaux, but also because it was instrumental in having his
books and papers confiscated. Admittedly, some were prohibited;
but, as a poet, he had the license, even the right, to read and retain
them:

> Et juge sacrilege,
> Qui t'a donné ne loy ne privilege
> D'aller toucher, & faire tes massacres
> Au cabinet des sainctes Muses sacres?
> Bien est il vray, que livres de deffence
> On y trouva: mais cela n'est offence
> A ung Poëte, à qui on doibt lascher
> La bride longue, & rien ne luy cacher. . .[18]

Although Marot left France for Ferrara after the *Affaire des
Placards*, it was not out of guilt, but because he was being unjustly
persecuted. Moreover, in repairing to the court of Renée de France,
Louis XII's daughter, he never really left royal service. In any
event, it is the "Sorboniqueurs" who are the guilty party, and the
King should punish them for obscuring the light of his proposed
reforms. In accusing the King's enemies, Marot excuses himself;
manipulating his argument, he places himself on the side of the law.
While the *épistre* is personal in its message to the King, it also
affords a place of public representation for Marot. Thus his
"pauvre Clément," like Molinet's "moy simplet" or Lemaire's
"povre corps tremblant," is a dramatized narrator, a character in
his own right, pleading his case before his King and the world: a
private, but decidedly public figure.

Cretin, Molinet, Lemaire, and Marot represent different phases
and different stages in the gradual entrance of the author into the
text. In manuscript culture, the author is frequently depicted in the
act of presenting his or her work to a protector, thus instituting a
kind of interpretative pact between the two. In print culture,
however, public circulation provided writers with common but
detached readers. Effectively distanced, writers found it increasingly
expedient to adopt a public voice, much like the Prologue of the
classical stage, in order to program their argument and offset the
impersonality of the printed page. While the formulation of the

poetic "I" was accomplished with elegant ease by Marot and even greater assurance by Ronsard and the poets of the Pléiade, it was with some difficulty and self-conscious reluctance that Pernette du Guillet and Louise Labé entered into the public area of the text, partially because of traditional constraints on women's speech, but mostly because of the tactical problem of expressing themselves in a masculine world of thematic and rhetorical conventions.

Although there are numerous ways of locating oneself in the physical world, the textual equivalent usually involves comparison with antecedent example. With the accumulated experience of over two thousand years behind him, Renaissance man was able to identify easily and comfortably with traditional literary models and discourses. Whether evoking the exploits of war or the effects of passion, there was ample precedent to follow. For women writers, however, with almost no such history, the process was more problematic. Whom were they to imitate, how and what were they to write? Beginning with Sappho, women have almost always preferred to adopt existing discursive norms, recasting them from a self-consciously other point of view, at times with ironic or parodic overtones. Thus during the Renaissance, when the number of women writing and publishing increased dramatically, especially in Lyons where cultural and social factors proved favorable to their social and literary emancipation,[19] gendered reappropriation became the order of the day.

Invariably, it was the image and panoply of the feminine other which inspired and shaped the erotic deliberations of Renaissance writers. Exceptionally, however, as in the case first of Pernette du Guillet and then of Louise Labé, it was the male figure who is the object of desire, requiring a shift in focus as well as in language. Now the dialectic of courtly and Petrarchan love was routinely masculine, and neither had at her ready disposal an equivalent vehicle for the expression of female erotic fantasies. Initially, therefore, they had to overcome a series of seemingly intractable problems, at once psychological, cultural, and literary, the most outstanding of which was the formulation of a feminine, even "feminist," language of love, adequate to, yet distinct from, the prevailing Neoplatonic, Petrarchan discourse which, in giving voice to men alone, continued to emphasize the passive status and situation of women in love and society.

PERNETTE DU GUILLET'S PLATONISM

Whereas Louise Labé edited and published her own works during her lifetime, Pernette du Guillet's remained in manuscript form at her death in July 1545, at the age of twenty-five, possibly a victim of the plague.[20] At her husband's request, the poet humanist Antoine du Moulin examined her "brouillars" and, as he explains in his prefatory epistle, unable to classify them satisfactorily, published them as he found them, as much to satisfy those who had heard her recite them privately as to serve as an example for other women of Lyons to emulate.[21] Thus several poems in the *Rymes de gentile et vertueuse dame D. Pernette du Guillet, Lyonnoise* may be rough drafts, and some are obviously unfinished; but the collection as a whole reflects her relationship, whether real or imagined, with another poet, presumably Maurice Scève.[22]

Louise Labé's name has been associated especially with Petrarchism and Pernette's with Platonism, and it is certain that at the time both were writing, it would have been difficult to escape the influence of either.[23] However, rather than debating the reliability of a particular dialectics of love like Labé, neither fully accepting nor rejecting its tenets, Pernette seems content to retain its conventions, working and writing easily and convincingly within its confines. On the other hand, although she aspires to become another, she tends to become more herself, increasingly sure of her own wit and verbal skill.

Metamorphosis for Pernette, as for Narcissus, would seem to be essentially self-referential and self-contained, signifying a desire to coincide with an image of herself as she perceives it through the eyes of another. As such, amelioration inspires her in her relation with Scève, inducing her to seek perfection in love and letters through his example and approbation. Imitation for her is therefore a means to self-knowledge rather than a sign of subservience. She presents her texts as responses to his influence, effectively usurping his reputation to further her own self-representation. Further, she appropriates his conceits, imagery, even rhymes, as in the *dizain* in which she assays the breadth and depth of her will to succeed. Juxtaposed to a relevant theme by Scève, her own performance appears at once more diffuse and less inclined to metaphoric or syllogistic resolution:

> Ma voulenté plus grande que l'effect,
> Si elle estoit justement mesurée,
> Rendre ne peult mon desir si parfaict,
> Qu'elle ne soit en luy demesurée.[24]

If, as it has been frequently proposed, Pernette considered Scève her mentor, then it follows that she expected her poetry to reflect his instruction and obtain his approval. One can only surmise the extent of their relationship, even wonder if Pernette, upon reading Scève's *Délie*, was not simply reacting to the seductions of his verse and reputation, hoping that her *Rymes* would admit her into correspondence with an admired model.[25] A poetic exchange, in any event, would seem to be confirmed by her hesitant and playful interpretation of the cryptic *R* with which a reader, presumably Scève, marked the copy of a *dizain*:

> R, au dizain toute seule soubmise
> M'a, à bon droict, en grand doubtance mise
> De mal, ou bien, que par R on peult prendre.
> Car, pour errer, R se peult comprendre,
> Signifiant que le loz qu'on me preste,
> Soit une erreur, ou que R est riens, ou reste
> Mais si par R on veult responce avoir,
> Je dy, combien que n'aye le sçavoir,
> Ne les vertus que ton R m'advoue,
> Qu'errer je fais tout homme, qui me loue.   (pp. 14–15)

As earlier commentators have pointed out,[26] Pernette adopts here a familiar technique of Rhétoriqueur poetry, influenced perhaps by a passage in Jean Lemaire de Belges's *Le Regretz de la Dame Infortunee, sur le trespas de son tres-cher frere unique*, although Marot and others provide a number of equally obvious antecedents. However, the source of this technique is certainly less important than her particular application of it. Whereas Jean Lemaire's *M* has mortuary connotations, Pernette's *R* is more ambivalent, allowing her to interrogate its implications, much as a pupil might a pedagogue's, but in playful or parodic fashion.

Though Pernette's writing responds structurally and thematically in a number of poems to Scève's *Délie*, she avoids his tendency towards sustained intensity in thought and expression. Where she achieves a striking measure of originality is, first of all, in the relative simplicity of her language, as though her attention and efforts were concentrated on processing ambiguity, hoping thereby to assure perfect coincidence between words and meaning; secondly, in the self-conscious playfulness with which she explores Scève's conceits, reducing their characteristic seriousness to word-play; finally, in refusing to imitate or attempting to rival Scève's linguistic and formal hermetism, electing rather to react obliquely, through fable, myth, enigma, or parody.[27]

In the main, the language of Pernette's poetry is reductive, in that it tends to express complex relations in an elementary and uncomplicated manner. At times, she relies on verbal reduplication to carry and develop her idea:

> Le corps *ravy*, l'Ame s'en esmerveille,
> Du grand plaisir, qui me vient entamer,
> Me *ravisssant* d'Amour, qui tout esveille. (p. 20)

So much so, in fact, that in another example, tautology, which serves to suggest profundity in Scève, adding nuance to an increasingly obsessive and ingenious analysis of the meaning and pertinence of various abstractions, remains literal in her hands, almost to the point of parody:

> Le *bien du bien*, que la raison ordonne. (p. 24)

While her handling of rhetorical and syntactical devices owes much to Scève and the Rhétoriqueurs, she is not always equally successful in achieving density of thought through paradigmatic interrogation of similar words or sounds. Here, for instance, repetition seems to take the place of argument:

> Pour *contenter* celuy qui me *tourmente*,
> Chercher ne veulx remede à mon *tourment*. (p. 23)

Word-play of this kind is characteristic of epigrammatic poetry, but Pernette tends to simplify the pattern in her responses to poems in which Marot or Scève raise similar problems of amorous doctrine.[28] Thus in her "L'heur de mon mal, enflammant le desir, / Feit distiller deux cueurs en un debvoir" (p. 21) is clearly inscribed Scève's "L'heur de nostre heur enflambant le desir / Vnit double ame en vn mesme povoir";[29] but her resolution, contrary to the oxymoronic resignation of his "Fais que puissions aussi long sentir / Si doulx mourir en vie respirable," calls unassumingly for lasting and mutual satisfaction: "Fais donc aussi, que nous puissions avoir / En noz espritz contentement durable!" (p. 21). In the two texts which follow, she takes up the problem of "doulx mourir" once again, attempting to reconcile it with "contentement," proposing first of all that "Le grand desir du plaisir admirable / Se doit nourrir par un contentement," leading her to conclude first of all: "On veult mourir, s'on ne l'a promptement: / Mais ce mourir engendre une autre vie" (p. 22) and, finally, less problematically: "Car, en mon mal voyant qu'il se contente, / Contente suis de son contentement" (p. 23).

There are a number of other texts which rely on word-play, as in this parodic rendition of Marot's celebrated *Petite Epistre au roy*:

> Tu te plains, que plus ne rimasse,
> Bien qu'un temps fut que plus aymasse
> A estendre vers rimassez,
> Que d'avoir biens sans rime assez:
> Mais je voy, que qui trop rimoye,
> Sus ses vieux jours en fin larmoye . . .[30]   (*Epître II*, p. 119)

Pernette ends up blaming "rime" as well as the "rimasseur" for claiming that writing is its own reward, adding an unexpected "grimace" to Marot's witty and more allusive text:

> Et tu verras qu'à ta rimasse
> Comme moy feras la grimace,
> Maudisant et blasmant la rime,
> Et le rimasseur, qui la rime,
> Et le premier, qui rimona,
> Pour le grand bien, qu'en rime on ha.

Or in this playful clash between a series of prioritizing deliberations in -*ique* and her lighthearted and commonsensical rejoinder:

> Aucuns ont dict la Theorique
> Estre devant que la Practique:
> Ce que bien nyer on pouvoit.
>   Car, qui feit l'art, jà la sçavoit,
> Qui est un poinct qu'un Sophistique
> Concederoit tout en dormant:
> Quant à moy, je dy, pour replique
> Qu'Amour fut premier, que l'Amant.   (p. 72)

In another example, she uses rhyming homonyms in the manner of Jean Lemaire de Belges, signaling her presence and participation in the playful working out of an otherwise traditional theme:

> Mais si au ranc des desolez
> Il me fault par ce point venir,
> Je vous supply vous souvenir

De regarder plus *amplement,*
Que tel en son dire *ample ment,*
Comme contre moy remply *d'ire,*
Et qu'il ne dict rien simplement,
Que je n'entende qu'il veult *dire.*

(p. 48)

Elsewhere, characteristic wit is manifested in possible puns on French *sévère* and the Latin version of Scève's name, *saevus* – "severity" being a common concept in the Renaissance language of love, usually applied, however, to women:

D'un qui est haultement en ses escriptz divins,
  Comme de mon, *severe.*

(p. 54)[31]

Puis que, de nom et de faict trop *severe.*

(p. 55)

In another example, Cupid's farewell is rendered in Greek:

Et au partir luy dit: callimera.

(p. 66)

And in the following epigram, the Greek word *Imera* is used to refer to her *Jour*:

Mesmes qu'il est mon Imera

(p. 67)

Additionally, one of her longest poems is a *Coq à l'asne* (pp. 93–5). Here, as in Marot's or Rabelais's inaugural experiments with this particular genre, there are a number of ambiguous and satirical allusions:

Seroit ce pas grand deshonneur
De la laisser ainsi pucelle? (p. 93)

Mais c'est chose par trop notoire,
Que l'on ne peult bien faire croire,
Qu'une robe faicte à l'antique
Ne montre le corps si ethique,
Bien qu'il soit un petit trop juste
Pour courtisaner à la buste.

(p. 94)

Lastly, there is her playfully sensual rewriting of the Actaeon myth, in which she imagines herself bathing naked in a "clere fontaine," and, contrary to Diana, not only aware of her lover's approach but enticing him, Siren-like, with her song, yet prepared to ward him off with her splashing if he attempts to touch her. Her wish is that the water might have the power to change him into Actaeon not, however, so that he be transformed into a *cerf* and devoured by his dogs, but, as she puts it in a redeeming pun, so that he become her *serf* and *serviteur* (p. 59). Pernette revises the Ovidian and

Petrarchan versions of the story, recounting it from her perspective rather than Actaeon's, luring the lover on and keeping him off at the same time, moderating his sexuality as well as her own. Bringing her fantasizing to an end, she prefers finally that he remain in the service of the Muses, anticipating that mutual happiness will be theirs eventually through poetry:

> Lequel un jour par ses escriptz s'attend
> D'estre avec moy et heureux, et content.   (p. 60)

Placing her inspiration within the confines of traditional Renaissance conceits, it is the malady of love, she writes in her opening *dizain*, which summons her "[à] regraver [s]a dure impression / D'amour cruelle et doulce passion" (p. 8). It would seem that she does not conceive of her poetry as secondary, nor herself as consigned to repeating masculine literary models. To be sure, she remains strictly within the canonical limits of genre and versification established by the Rhétoriqueurs, Marot, or Scève, but she does not experience her own writing within this tradition as a constraint to self-expression, a poetic prison from which she needs to free herself. Her quest would seem to be directed elsewhere, beyond the already tired rhetoric of the *Querelle des femmes*, less towards self-identification or self-justification than to the pursuit of knowledge through commerce, personal or literary, with another.

"Je fuiray loing d'ignorance le vice" (p. 12), Pernette writes in another of the opening *dizains*, but what does she mean by ignorance? Since she associates it with vice, its corresponding virtue must be knowledge. But knowledge of what? Of books, learning as the humanists of the day understood it, or that knowledge which, according to the Platonic contention, is the only good, the mother of all virtue? And what does she mean when she writes in the same *dizain*: "Puis qu'il t'a pleu de me faire congnoistre, / Et par ta main, le VICE A SE MUER, / Je tascheray faire en moy ce bien croistre, / Qui seul en toy me pourra transmuer" (p. 12)? If Scève (whose anagram, occurring at the beginning and end, frames this *dizain*) is to be the agent of transformation, then is the virtue to which she aspires moral or poetic or both? Is she anxious to learn to know vice for what it is, and thereby to follow virtue, or to write as Scève writes, avoiding divergence or error in this sense? The syntactic parallelism between *en moy* and *en toy* suggests a union that limits ideally the male

Petrarchist's solipsism, whereas *ta main* could refer metonymically to writing, both his and hers, as the agent and result of change.[32]

Her original ignorance she translates metaphorically as darkness:

> La nuict estoit pour moy si tresobscure
> Que Terre et Ciel elle m'obscurissoit,
> Tant qu'à Midy de discerner figure
> N'avois pouvoir, qui fort me marissoit.　　　(p. 9)

The dawn which comes out of the darkness, already a Renaissance commonplace, refers to the reemergence, after Gothic obscurantism, of the wisdom of Antiquity, and it is illumination of this kind, moral as well as intellectual, which Pernette associates with the light of day. Less self-assured than Labé, she relies on Scève's tutelage, hoping through him to avoid error. Does this mean that, contrary to Labé, Pernette sees herself as a passive figure in the masculine world of letters? Initially, this may be so, but almost immediately upon awakening under Scève's influence, she is prepared to raise her voice in confident praise:

> Mais quand je vis que l'aulbe apparoissoit
> En couleurs mille et diverse et seraine,
> Je me trouvay de liesse si pleine
> (Voyant desjà la clarté à la ronde)
> Que commençay louer à voix haultaine
> Celuy qui feit pour moi ce Jour au Monde.　　　(p. 9)

To propose that the *Rymes* recapitulate the personal story of Pernette's development from initial passion to eventual virtue may appear logically consistent with the narrative intentions of the text as we know it. It is important to remember, however, that this particular reading is founded on Antoine du Moulin's posthumous ordering of Pernette's manuscripts, and that his ordering does not necessarily reproduce hers. Thus our understanding of the story they seem to relate is predicated on his, and it is not inconceivable that a different arrangement would produce an entirely different story. This being said, his decision to prioritize "Le hault pouvoir des Astres" (p. 8), while arbitrary, affords an appropriate chronological entrance into the *Rymes* in that it serves to announce Pernette's birth into the world of poetry.

At once we recognize the play of a unique and distinctly female voice within the masculine discourse she adopts, which introduces a subjective reversal of its conventionalized themes and images. Significantly, in this liminary *dizain*, the autobiographical intrusion

("Quand je nasquis") directs the reader's attention away from "celle divinité" (designating, presumably, Scève) towards her: "Qui me cause l'imagination / A contempler si haulte qualité" (p. 8). In "imagination" resides the faculty of capturing and reflecting the image of the "high quality" of the other, an achievement which accrues to her intellectual credit.

The sequence in which the episodes follow is another matter altogether, especially since Du Moulin's edition depends also, at least partially, on a division into separate categories. Consistent with contemporary practice as exemplified by Marot, he proceeded to group Pernette's manuscripts by genre, according to the economy described in his preface ("Epygrammes, Chansons, et autres diverses matieres de divers lieux," p. 3), making it problematic to read the *Rymes*, despite a number of interesting attempts, as a *journal intime*. What we do find, however, in a significant number of these texts, is clear evidence of the way in which Pernette tends to "contempler si haulte qualité," imprinting her own distinct rhetoric on the subject and conventionalized style of love. Finally, the originality of her "rhyming" with Scève's "reasoning" lies less perhaps in her variations on his images and themes than in her intense maneuvering of their respective poetic voices.

Clearly, some of the poems in the *Rymes* and the *Délie* answer one another. The question which arises in this respect is to what extent and in what manner Pernette manages to retain a degree of autonomy in her intense exchange with a person whom she considers her intellectual and poetic superior. Unremitting in acknowledging her gratitude for all she has learned from him, is she able nevertheless to maintain the authority of her own voice in their continuing dialogue? Does her poetry not call into question the role postulated for her in his, inasmuch as she idealizes him even more that he idealizes her? Since he seems to her to be attracted to her sexually, she feels constrained to ask him to restrict his interest to sharing with her in the intellectual stimulation which he has successfully awakened in her:

> Non que je vueille à dextre, et à senestre
> Le gouverner, et faire à mon plaisir:
> Mais je vouldrois, pour noz deux cueurs repaistre,
> Que son vouloir fust joinct à mon desir.   (p. 77)

Her idea of love as perfect and disinterested is based on a code of behavior which opposes the light of reason to the folly of passion. As such, it is radically different from Scève's more openly sensual focus. Thus the role Pernette imagines for herself in her poetry is not identical with the one Scève assigns her in his. Whereas he conceives of her as his distant and lunar other, she sees in him the immediate source of her own fulfillment. It is somewhat misleading therefore to speak of a dialogue between Scève and Pernette du Guillet. Both may speak the same language, but each understands it differently. Her Neoplatonism is less erotic than his, more concerned with the immediacy of exchange and stability than with the paradoxes and problematics of love. Since both assert their inferiority to the ideal other, neither can fully satisfy the other's expectations:

> Si je ne suis telle que soulois estre,
> Prenez vous en au temps, qui m'a appris
> Qu'en me traictant rudement, comme maistre,
> Jamais sur moy ne gaignerez le prys. (p. 39)

Typically, in a number of *dizains*, Pernette recalls a controversial topic from traditional debates on the doctrine of love and resolves it cleverly and expeditiously. Wondering whether a lover is indebted more to Love than to his Lady, she concludes with what she calls "un tres grand poinct": "C'est que sans Dame Amour ne seroit point" (p. 32). Or, in another instance, asking whether one can have two Loves, she answers with a similar conceit: "Peult Dame avoir à la Vertu si grande / Que de l'Amant la qualité demande / Double merite, ou double passion" (p. 33). Rhetorical questions are answered rhetorically, with elegance and wit; or better, as Saulnier remarks in another context, "chez Pernette, la rhétorique se moque volontiers de la rhétorique."[33]

Not only in these several examples, but throughout the *Rymes*, Pernette's self-portrait of a young, relatively uncomplicated individual, direct in both thought and language, acquires shape and focus through sustained comparison to her intellectual superior. Thus her references to the "grand renom de [s]on meslé sçavoir" (p. 10), "[s]on eloquent sçavoir" (p. 13), "[s]on esprit, qui esbahit le Monde" (p. 38), "sa philosophie" (p. 58), and her ignorance (pp. 31, 52) and lack of grace and merit (p. 60), are reinforced metaphorically by frequent contrasts between sun and moon, light and dark, day and night. Antithesis, then, structures her stance, depicting her as marginal or, at least, secondary in relation to him. But is this a true reflection of a relationship, presumably with Scève, or merely a poetic or thematic strategy consistent with the dialectics of Platonic love and the dynamics of the epigrammatic form? Is this, in a word, autobiography or discourse? Is Pernette recounting an episode in her life or reworking and regendering the rhetoric and literary conventions governing the language of love, reversing the traditional humility of the male lover towards the person he loves? Are we to identify her, in a word, with her projection of the speaking subject? Is she not, rather, the author of herself as much as Scève or Ronsard, and, as such, the manipulator of her own identity?[34]

In any event, the image of Pernette which emerges from her poetry is that of an individual intent upon a relationship (which she terms *amitié*) with a person she admires and wishes to emulate, but who finds both herself and her writing unworthy or unequal to the task. Moreover, compared to Scève's, her poetry is relatively unproblematic in conception and execution, depending more on linearity than on structural or thematic complexity for its effect. Attuned especially to the contents of her poems, most readers have been content to qualify her intellectual reticence as a kind of *degré zéro de l'écriture*. Saulnier, for instance, locates her originality in what one might call a rhetoric of sacrifice: "peu de figures de style, peu d'ornements ajoutés; il est rare – et c'est tant mieux – qu'elle s'essaye à des combinaisons très savantes."[35] According to this perspective, lack of technical or linguistic sophistication, even an occasional awkwardness, are intentional effects, strategically designed to promote a certain idea of the poet and her desired relation with the object of her inspiration. What is clear finally is that in reading Scève's poetry as though it had been written for her, Pernette preserves the difference between them as her own literary domain. Their relation may be fiction, but fiction recounted from her perspective and fulfilled through her poetry. In a very real sense, Pernette is her own author, both reader and critic of a work which remains on the margins of another, thereby proclaiming its own presence and autonomy.

LOUISE LABÉ'S PETRARCHISM

In articulating the specificity of the relatively unexplored world of feminine desire, Labé similarly relies inevitably on the insights of the predominant literary code, reversing its point of view and regendering its language as required. Consequently, the various themes, syntactical patterns, and metaphors which speak to the authenticity of her passion are fundamentally derivative, informed by the antithetical play of the Latin elegiac poets, the *basia* of Johannes Secundus, the conceits of Petrarchan sonnets, all of which translate originally a specifically masculine point of view. Is then her originality to be restricted to the artful remaneuvering of conventions and commonplaces with which, at first reading, she manages to induce a conviction of sincerity, or should we look beyond the immediacy of remembered rhetoric to interventions, both explicit and implicit, which question and even invalidate its pertinence where women are concerned? In a word, does her writing signify only *within* the imposed parameters of the predominant discursive system which, inevitably, continues to permeate her works, or does it operate *against* it as well, allowing a marginal perspective to determine her own poetics of love's deceits and deceptions?[36] Finally, to what extent is her regendering poetically rather than politically motivated?

Since the primary intention of rhetoric is to impose a textual order which restructures reality and affirms discursive autonomy, the fact that Labé's love may have existed in her imagination only is, rhetorically speaking, completely irrelevant. The language in which she describes its effects is derived from the literature of men, which is for her the language of unrealized promises and fantasized expectations. Rather than reading this language uncritically, she questions its integrity, exposing its ambiguities and duplicities. Thus her poetry deals more with rhetorical seduction than with life and love, with literature rather than autobiography; it reorganizes and reevaluates experience, filtering it through the very language which, with its persuasive authority, is the origin of her deception. Her particular angle of recuperation creates a sense of semantic drift or loss, which is prerequisite to a displaced rereading, with ironic possibilities, of the gendered language of poetry.

Labé's works are dialogically structured, inscribing alternate texts, one representing the code of male seduction, and the other her reaction to and reinterpretation of this code. She exploits the difference between meaning and meaningfulness, playing one against the other, making her self-conscious reprise of the language of Platonism and Petrarchism readable only in relation to the way in which its original context is modified and repossessed, frequently with ironic intent.

Irony is a form of implicit commentary, which occurs whenever a text seems to assume an attitude towards its own subject matter. Thus while Labé reiterates the phenomena and paraphernalia of the traditional code of love, she reacts to its various pretensions as they relate retroactively to her own expectations. *Having* loved rather than *being* loved is the theme of these texts, love past invoked by one who is no longer fully under its spell, and it is this particular bias which accounts for much of their originality. Spent passion affords the opportunity as well as the lucidity to analyze its cause and effects, to unwrite the language in which it was first written. While, on the one hand, her poetry supports the contention that love is learned, formed, and formulated through literature, it tends to confirm at the same time the crucial difference between life and literature, undermining thereby the very dialectic it so successfully recovers.

The world of Labé's love is the world of poetry, and when we enter this world, we experience a sense of familiarity with its themes and techniques, most of which are conditioned by a series of seminal texts. Ficino's commentary on Plato's *Symposium* and Petrarch's *Rime sparse* codified the language dealing with the inception of love, its concomitant torments, conduct, and progress, and it is through individual imitation and interpretation of this language that Renaissance writers create and impose their own recognizable imprint.[37] When, however, Labé writes of love, she means to represent its course from her own standpoint, but without the attendant convenience of a previously regendered code. Thus she had either to improvise a new language or rework the old, moving within its confines in such a way as to make it doubly decipherable, recognizable as a reflection of male discourse, but scrutinized from a female point of view. In order for this difference to obtain, her writing operates ironically, analyzing, even subverting, the legitimacy of the Neoplatonic and, more especially, the Petrarchan tradition it pretends to perpetuate.

It is her right to write which Labé first defends in the dedicatory epistle addressed "A M.C.D.B.L.," an acronym for *A Mademoiselle Clémence de Bourges, Lyonnaise,*[38] in maintaining that the moment is opportune for women to demonstrate their ability to acquire and propagate letters and science:

Estant le tems venu, Madamoiselle, que les severes loix des hommes

n'empeschent plus les femmes de s'apliquer aus sciences et disciplines: il me
semble que celle qui ont la commodité, doivent employer cette honneste
liberté que notre sexe ha autre fois tant desiree, à icelles aprendre: et
montrer aus hommes le tort qu'ils nous faisoient en nous privant du bien et
de l'honneur qui nous en pouvoit venir. (p. 41)[39]

Next, she moves from blaming men for preventing women from
taking advantage of the benefit and honor learning imparts to
encouraging them to put their own ideas into writing and to accept
ensuing public recognition: "Et si quelcune parvient en tel degré,
que de pouvoir mettre ses concepcions par escrit, le faire songneuse-
ment et non dédaigner la gloire" (p. 41). But she fails to specify the
particular form their participation is to assume. Does she mean that
women are to write as men, imitating and equaling them in their
literary practice, or are they to distinguish, within and in opposition
to that practice, a rhetoric of their own?[40]

From beginning to end, in prose and in poetry, Labé's works
revolve around this problematic as it relates to the theme of love –
which, given its pervasiveness in the literature of the day, especially
perhaps in Lyons, is not an unexpected focus. It is initially significant, however, that she treats the subject of unreciprocated love,
whether in prose or in poetry, in dialogue form, with its separate
voices structured along clearly gendered lines, since it is from this
confrontation of opposing points of view that much of her originality
derives. This particular slant accounts for a number of textual and
intertextual examples of gendered prejudice and grammatical
anomalies.[41] In a word, her writings participate in the continuing
Querelle des femmes, but with opposing sides reassembled in a common
forum.

First published in 1555 by the celebrated Lyonnais printer Jean de
Tournes, Labé's *Evvres* include a prose *Débat de Folie et d'Amour*, three
Elégies and twenty-four sonnets. In many respects, the *Débat de Folie et
d'Amour* is more radical and personal than the sonnets, yet both
display similar themes and ideologies. In the *Débat*, we find love,
which writers of the day treat invariably as a serious and noble
subject, presented in a detached fashion, somewhat in the tradition
of the Lucian and Erasmian paradoxical encomium – as, for
example, when Mercury parodies Petrarchan oxymorons: "Avoir le
coeur separé de soymesme, estre meintenant en paix, ores en guerre,
ores en treves: couvrir et cacher sa douleur, changer visage mile fois
le jour: sentir le sang qui lui rougit la face, y montant: puis soudein

s'enfuit, la laissant palle . . . bruler de loin, geler de pres . . ." (p. 98).
Labé addresses her sonnets to an anonymous fellow poet, whom she
treats as a literary equal rather than as a model to emulate, and
whose language her own calls into question. In both prose and
poetry, therefore, traditional literary discourse is similarly under-
mined, with words and meaning conjoined in dialectical confrontation.

Already in the *Débat*, Labé dissociates and animates the traditional
expression *fol amour*, playing one term against the other. Exploiting
the mythical origin of the image of blinded and blindfolded Cupid,
she proceeds to dramatize the unexpected yet predestined encounter
and conflict of *Amour* and *Folie*. The ensuing trial exposes the
idiosyncrasies and inadequacies of the two competing ideologies
informing Renaissance discourses of love.[42] Cupid, with his eyes
open, organizer and defender of the order and harmony of the
world, can be taken to represent Love as conceived in the Neoplatonic tradition. Such, in any event, is the meaning his figure acquired
in early modern depictions, painted or sculpted.[43] This love is not
blind, since it is through its eyes that celestial beauty is perceived.
Blind love, on the other hand, produces disorder and chaos, desire
without transformation or transcendence, the folly which is sensual
or sexual passion.

If Apollo is chosen to defend Cupid, is it not because he is the god
of the arts and therefore of universal peace and harmony? Conversely, Mercury, god of medicine and philosophy, but also of
eloquence, cunning, and deceit, is aptly chosen to defend Folly.[44]
According to Apollo's opening deposition, Folly's blinding of Love is
a willful and spiteful act, designed to bring about disarray: "Injurier
cet Amour, l'oultrager, qu'est ce, sinon vouloir troubler et ruïner
toutes choses?" (p. 67). And since blinded Cupid will no longer be
able to act autonomously, Folly will have the opportunity to introduce discord into what was heretofore an ordered and orderly
world:

Car ou Amour voudra faire cette harmonie entre les hautes et basses
personnes, Folie se trouvera pres, qui l'empeschera: et encore es lieux ou il
se sera attaché. Quelque bon et innocent qu'il soit, Folie lui meslera de son
naturel: tellement que ceus qui aymeront, feront tousjours quelque tour de
fil. Et plus les amitiez seront estroites, plus s'y trouvera il de desordre
quand Folie s'y mettra. (pp. 77–8)

In his rebuttal, Mercury defends the union of Love and Folly as a kind of *discordia concors*, the successful conjoining of complementary opposites. To be sure, Love promotes order, but Folly is a purveyor of desire, and one without the other is both unnatural and incomplete:

Je croy avoir satisfait à ce qu'avois promis montrer: que jusque ici Amour n'avoit esté sans Folie. Il faut passer outre, et montrer qu'impossible est d'estre autrement. Et pour y entrer: Apolon, tu me confesseras qu'Amour n'est autre chose qu'un desir de jouir, avec une conjonccion, et assemblement de la chose aymee. (98–9)

Mercury's defense consists in agreeing with Apollo's accusations, while giving them a positive twist. Consequently, without denying that Folly is synonymous with desire and a source of disorder, he argues that the advent of the one fully compensates for the loss of the other:

Amour donq ne fut jamais sans la compagnie de Folie: et ne le sauroit jamais estre. Et quand il pourroit ce faire, si ne le devroit il pas souhaiter: pource que lon ne tiendroit conte de lui à la fin. Car quel pouvoir auroit il, ou quel lustre, s'il estoit pres de sagesse? (p. 101)

In his reassessment of traditional categories, Love, he concludes, should not end in Wisdom, as the Neoplatonists would have it. On the contrary, without Folly, Love is powerless to act or to attain fulfillment.[45]

In the *Débat*, Apollo and Mercury argue their cases forcefully, and their deliberations, when one is weighed against the other, may seem to result in a draw, especially since Jupiter's judgment refuses to decide between them once and for all. Undecidability allows Labé to present, with seemingly equal eloquence and authority, both sides of the argument, playing one against the other in keeping with the rules of rhetorical disputation. But the disproportion between Apollo's opening testimony in Cupid's favor (sixteen pages) and Mercury's retort in defense of Folly (twenty-two pages), which gives the latter a decided textual advantage, is particularly crucial to Labé's understanding of the respective priorities of Cupid's idealism and Folly's realism. Cupid may be male and insist upon maintaining his dignity and hegemony, but Folly, as female, is fully aware of her rights and prerogatives as well as her ability to impose them.

In the *Débat*, the protagonists are mythological, and their story is recounted as fiction, but fiction with a purpose. Thus Folly, for Labé, is fundamentally Erasmian. But whereas Erasmus develops his idea of her Silenus-like nature as a figure of authentic Evangelical wisdom, Labé pits male Cupid against female Folly in a clearly gendered variant of the medieval *conflictus*, weighing their respective qualities and deficiencies, casting them and the cause of their disagreement in a playful and somewhat disrespectful light. Mythology here is humanized, only to be ridiculed – or at least pictured – as all too human. And while the *Débat* removes the opposing ideologies of the *Querelle des femmes* to the distant spheres of an almost Rabelaisian Olympus, the poetry grounds them in the anguished exchange of male and female perceptions of the ritual and consequences of love.[46]

This is not quite the same as saying that Labé should be read as a feminist document (a sometimes facile exercise, not always successfully resisted by commentators). In fact, it would seem more accurate and obviously less anachronistic, given the complementary roles assigned to *Folie* and *Amour*, to consider her work as an argument in favor of understanding and harmony between men and women in love.[47] In this way, her *Evvres* can be seen to revise a subject which the literature of the day presented more or less unilaterally, generally through masculine eyes, including almost all of those Renaissance "feminist" apologies which, in countering medieval misogynistic diatribes, continued to inject an element of "quarrel" into the *Querelle des femmes*. While it is true that Labé urges her female readers (are they intended to be her sole readers?) to abandon gendered occupations and ornaments,[48] it is equally true that her advice is considerably less radical or revolutionary than it has been made out to be in recent years.

However, Labé's participation in this debate is "modern," if by modern we mean that she is involved in reading contemporary literary and social norms from a personal and particular viewpoint. But where she remains one with her century is in her identification of the irrationality induced by love with *mania* – first in herself, then, by reflection, in women in general – rather than with *furor*, which, in its Pléiade, especially Ronsardian trappings, is a noble, essentially masculine conceit.[49] Thus, whereas Renaissance poetics advances the myth of divine inspiration, *inflatus* and *furor poeticus* are viewed by Labé as purveyors of rhetorical duplicity, inciters of destructive passion in the lives of women.

In short, the Petrarchan and Pléiade imagination is essentially masculine, focusing and concentrating the voice and vision of the lover, while fragmenting and dispersing the beloved in a series of metonymic or metaphoric figurations, an eye, a flower, a precious jewel, a statue, or a goddess. It is not Cassandre, Méline, or Olive who is the focus of the poem, but the poet himself, who, in amplifying his own point of view, deflects the reader's attention from the object of his love.

Labé, however, projects herself as a woman into this exclusionary paradigm, not as the prevailing rhetorical code imagines her, virtuous, distant, cruel, but burning with unrequited desire, a tormented victim of male deceit and indifference. It is not only because she dared to express her need of physical love which, until then, was a domain reserved to men, that she scandalized her contemporaries, or, at least, her male counterparts, but also because, in displaying female ardor, she tended to contest the view of traditional physiology and psychology that women were essentially cold, reserved, and silent. Here, for the first time in the Renaissance dialogue of love, the insistent voice of a woman is heard, translating the point of view of the unsatisfied other who, having responded to the language of love, has found herself betrayed by its promises. If, then, the *Débat* can be said to argue for the harmonious conjoining of the separate voices of Love and Folly, it is the loss or lack of this desired union which the poetry of the *Sonnets* similarly regrets:

> Voilà du Ciel la puissante harmonie,
> Qui les esprits divins ensemble lie:
> Mais s'ils avoient ce qu'ils ayment lointein,
> Leur harmonie et ordre irrevocable
> Se tourneroit en erreur variable,
> Et comme moy travailleroient en vain. (xxii)

Although the narrative element in Renaissance love cycles is always somewhat tenuous, it provides, nevertheless, a sense of chronology and coherence to what otherwise would prove to be little more than a random collection of disparate texts. In Labé's sequence, development is abbreviated to a succession of salient moments, grouped and organized thematically to evoke, first of all, in the liminary sonnet in Italian, the incidence of love and its unexpected aftermath; then, the conditions and reactions of the lover, both positive and negative, followed by the troubling and disruptive effects of erotic fantasies, myths, and mythology, concluding with an appeal for understanding from love's other victims.

Superficially, then, Labé's sonnets provide stylized transcriptions of Petrarchan themes and topoi, but without any of the onomastic word-play characteristic of the genre. What, for instance, is her lover's name? What is he like physically? What are the events or occasions which mark their common adventure? There are no answers to these and the many other questions, both biographical and autobiographical, which her *canzoniere* raises, and the reader must be satisfied finally with a stenographic abstract of the mechanics of the genre. If, in this language, the eye or the breath, a lute or a glove, are metonymies of love, it is because they reify various aspects of an unsettling psychological and sentimental experience. Thus passion is represented through a conventionalized semiology, adjusted and renewed in proportion as the poet is successful in competing with the exigencies of rhyme or rhythm. Labé, however, steps outside this restrictive circle and views it, so to speak, from the margins. While it is through the perspective of a conventionalized rhetoric that she defines her amatory expectations, it is in derogation of its regulatory norms that she succeeds in achieving presence and originality.

It is especially in her elegies that Labé assumes an overtly feminist rhetoric. The first and the third present a woman's apology for writing about love and the second a passionate lament for the absent lover. In the first elegy, she adopts a personal stance, describing her futile resistance to love's pervasive and irresistible force, then asking for understanding from her women readers, warning them finally that they could suffer a similar fate. The third elegy repeats and amplifies the themes of the first, developing further the idea that time has not yet rid her of her suffering. In between appeals for sympathy, the second elegy recapitulates the story of her love, her lover's departure for Italy and her yearning for his return.

Despite a number of details of an autobiographical nature, these elegies, together with the accompanying sonnets, read at times like a parody or even a pastiche of Petrarchan conventions. To be sure, parody need not be confused with or lapse into pastiche, if it captures and valorizes the spirit of the language and style it imitates. What might be called parody in Labé is, as etymology implies, a language rivaling with but distinct from the one it means to approximate. This helps to explain why, if, as critics keep insisting, hers is a sincerely passionate love, and, in this sense, different in experience and expression from the perfunctory or merely rhetorical exercises of the many sonnet sequences of contemporary Petrarchan poets, it is recalled in a language whose readability affords a number of definite ironic possibilities.

Whereas pastiche and parody involve explicit linguistic manipulation, irony results whenever one suspects that the author is implying a judgment on the subject matter. As term and rhetorical figure, irony is ubiquitous from classical Antiquity through the Renaissance, and is usually defined as saying the contrary of the intended meaning. This being the case, its occurrence postpones or defers ultimate meaning and requires reader involvement in its decipherment. Thus while poetry affords a way of constructing a world other than the real world, irony is a way of pointing out that it never fully coincides with reality. In this sense, irony impinges upon three central themes in Labé's elegies: war, memory, time. All three are common to poets of the day, but she configures them in a convincingly individual way.

Both the frequency and the meaning of Labé's military lexicon have been diversely interpreted, but most usually in a literal sense, as biographical reference. She has been pictured as armed, waging war, participating in jousts, and certain lines, it is true, seem to confirm this reading:

> Qui m'eut vù lors en armes fiere aller,
> Porter la lance et bois faire voler,
> Le devoir faire en l'estour furieus,
> Piquer, volter le cheval glorius,
> Pour Bradamante, ou la haute Marphise,
> Seul de Roger, il m'ust, possible, prise.   (p. 116)

On the other hand, since poetry is both a physical and a spiritual experience, writing itself induces her to represent her vocation in military terms. Furthermore, love is frequently viewed as a combat between a man and a woman, a struggle for conquest and possession, and Labé's metaphors seem to come under that category. Moreover, when she opposes a distant, heroic past to a more recent time of suffering and submission, it is Love itself which is the enemy, the foe against which she has fought heroically, but in vain:

> Il m'est avis que je sen les alarmes,
> Que premiers j'ù d'Amour, je voy les armes,
> Dont il s'arma en venant m'assaillir.   (p. 108)

Another difference voiced in this first elegy is between time without poetry, when love subsumed memory, and a time of poetry, once memory enters into play. To write, she explains in her dedicatory letter, is to renew past pleasures, assuring them of an indelible record. Memory functions as a kind of intertext, providing the material which writing serves to transmit and perpetuate, making literature more pleasurable than life. For whatever we imprint in our memory is merely a shadow of the thing remembered, whereas writing, she submits in the *épître dédicatoire*, is a second memory, more accurate and durable than the first, allowing us to relive the past more clearly and with greater pleasure:

Mais quand il avient que mettons par escrit nos concepcions, combien que puis apres notre cerveau coure par une infinité d'afaires et incessamment remue, si est ce que long tems apres, reprenans nos escrits, nous revenons au mesme point, et à la mesme disposicion ou nous estions. Lors nous redouble nostre aise: car nous retrouvons le plaisir passé qu'avons ú ou en la matiere dont escrivions, ou en l'intelligence des sciences ou lors estions adonnez. (p. 42–3)

There are, then, two kinds of memory, one natural, and the other artificial, the product of art. Natural memory is imbedded in our minds and subject to the fantasies and fluctuations of the imagination; artificial memory, fixed on paper, is lucid and unchanging. The self-consuming fires of *furor eroticus* have given way, with time, to song, inspired by Apollo, protector of poets, allowing her finally the privilege and freedom of retrospective complaint:

> Au temps qu'Amour, d'hommes et Dieus vainqueur,
> Faisoit bruler de sa flamme mon coeur,
> Encore lors je n'avois la puissance
> De lamenter ma peine et ma souffrance.
> Encor Phebus, ami des Lauriers vers,
> N'avoit permis que je fisse des vers:
> Mais meintenant que sa fureur divine
> Remplit d'ardeur ma hardie poitrine,
> Chanter me fait . . .   (p. 107)

For Labé, love and poetry are not simultaneous occurrences. It is only after the fact, once her pain is past, that memory enters into play. Through poetry, then, the present is superior in pleasure to the past: "Et outre ce, le jugement que font nos secondes concepcions des premieres, nous rend un singulier contentement" (p. 43). But remembrance of things past puts words and deeds in a different light, initiating a crucial space in which imagination has room to maneuver and play. In the *Débat*, it obtains in the familiarity with which Labé treats classical mythology; in the elegies and sonnets, in her reevaluation of the conventional dialectics of love.

The originality of the elegies lies less in their form or versification, both of which owe much to Marot, than in their political and rhetorical stance. In addressing her apology to women readers and asking for their understanding, she means to alert them to the tyranny masculine rhetoric exercises on their perception of love and life. In the sonnets, however, she recalls the lure of the language of love which, in her experience, has failed to live up to its promise or her expectations. In her rendition of Petrarchism, antithesis is more than thematic play; it reflects rather the lucidity with which she compares past and present time and memory. Thus she recapitulates the causes and effects of seduction in the second sonnet (the first in French), structuring it as though it were a typical *blason*, addressed by a lover to his love:

> O beaus yeus bruns, ô regars destournez,
> O chaus soupirs, ô larmes espandues,
> O noires nuits vainement atendues

Yet these opening lines are deliberately misleading, in that it is not immediately clear who is actually speaking.[50] An unidentified voice is heard, but whose standpoint does it represent? Whose eyes, looks, sighs, and tears are these? Who has been waiting nights and days? Is this the language of the beloved, recalling the means and moments of seduction, or the language of the lover, invoking the beloved's seductive charms? The paratactic structure, the shifts from looks to sufferings to the cruelty of fate, convey a sense of troubled obsession; but it is not possible to distribute these random apostrophes syntactically, assigning them definitively to one or the other lover. In fact, they would seem to belong indiscriminately to both, as if to reproduce and conjoin alternate voices in the dialogue of love.[51] Nevertheless, the source and speaker of the separate remarks remain uncertain and this, in itself, would seem to suggest the disembodied voice of an individual in process, undefined and uncertain as to its authentic place in relation to the other.

Despite their initial ambiguity, these disparate signs are collected and identified as "tant de flambeaus pour ardre une femmelle!", that is to say, as representations of the reactions of a woman in love. As such, they recuperate and regender the Petrarchan topos of the inception of love which, traditionally, translates a masculine viewpoint, reflecting his reactions rather than hers. While Petrarch and his proponents remain generally content with a unilateral display of love's delirium, Labé, on the contrary, requires mutual recognition of its effects. For Ronsard, the verb *aimer* is resolutely intransitive. "Mon Dieu que j'ayme," he writes (*Cassandre*, XXI), and only rarely does his sensibility extend beyond the magic circle prescribed by the ravages of love on him. But since for Labé love is reciprocal, she can never fulfill its prerequisites by herself. Thus, after enumerating the various traits which, for her, signify fatal passion, she faults the other for remaining indifferent to their effects. Her exclamations translate surprise and consternation at the fact that the language of love, which she has learned from his lips, does not mean the same for him as for her:

> De toy me plein, que tant de feus portant,
> En tant d'endrois d'iceux mon coeur tatant,
> N'en est sur toy volé quelque estincelle.   (II, p. 122)

In wondering why he fails to reciprocate a positive response to her charms, Labé initiates a reversal in the roles of observer and observed that underlie men's poetry in praise of women.

Although we may feel justifiably that sonnet VIII, "Je vis, je meurs: je me brusle et me noye" (p. 125), is an empty rhetorical exercise, and that IV, "Depuis qu'Amour cruel empoisonna" (p. 123), or XI, "O dous regars, o yeus pleins de beauté" (p. 127) add little to the already highly documented thematics of love, there may be something more to be said about the obvious, even emphatic triteness of Labé's language and the seemingly unself-critical way in which she exploits literary conventions. In short, it may not be enough to limit her successes to those few instances in which technique and language are made to subserve the poetic personality, especially if we consider, as Valéry would have us, not only what a poem *says*, but also what it *does*, for what Labé's sonnet does is usually quite different from what it says. In fact, most of what Labé says had been said, and even better said, before, which leads us to question the reason for her reliance on and relation to so many undisguised, almost verbatim borrowings of texts and techniques.

It seems clear that she was not expecting her borrowings to go undetected, but that, on the contrary, she was counting on the reader's familiarity with the commonplaces of Petrarchism to recognize them as such. In fact, rather than rewriting them as an exercise in reappropriation and concealment, she tends to retain them as they are, incorporating them however into a different context. Her intertexts serve therefore as signatures of the writing her own writing discredits, objectifying its conventions in a meaningful way. Her originality, then, lies less in the skill with which she manipulates the dialectics of the day (the wounds of love, the icy fires, the remedy sought in the disease itself, the appeal to cruel fate), or in subtle deviations from its expected course (usually determined by a variation on a word or theme) than in the irony with which her writing questions its continued appropriateness where her own experience is concerned.

In successive sonnets, Labé recognizes in herself the various signs and stages promoted by Petrarchism, only to discover, in each instance, that its rhetoric is perceived and realized differently by men and by women. Thus sonnet III evokes a physiological phenomenon with a conventional conceit:

> O longs desirs, ô esperances vaines,
>   Tristes soupris et larmes coutumieres
>   A engendrer de moy maintes rivieres,
>   Dont mes deux yeus sont sources et fontaines.   (p. 122)

which, when viewed in the retrospective light of its hyperbolic consequences, appears ludic in pretension and language:

> Car je suis tant navree en toutes pars,
>   Que plus en moy une nouvelle plaie,
>   Pour m'empirer ne pourroit trouver place.   (p. 123)

While Labé's sonnets have long attracted attention for their supposedly transparent expression of unrequited love, uncritical admiration has tended to obscure the ironic and parodic counterpoint underlying her discursive practices. The sharp contrast in sonnet XXI between the generalizing speculations of the quatrains:

> Quelle grandeur rend l'homme venerable?
>   Quelle grosseur? quel poil? quelle couleur?
>   Qui est des yeus le plus emmieleur?
>   Qui fait plus tot une playe incurable?
> Quel chant est plus à l'homme convenable?
>   Qui plus penetre en chantant sa douleur?
>   Qui un dous lut fait encore meilleur?
>   Quel naturel est le plus amiable?

and the highly selective intervention of the tercets:

> Je ne voudrois le dire assurément,
>   Ayant Amour forcé mon jugement:
>   Mais je say bien et de tant je m'assure.
> Que tout le beau que lon pourroit choisir,
>   Et que tout l'art qui ayde la Nature,
>   Ne me sauroient acroitre mon desir.   (pp. 132–33)

provide an example of two moments, two opposing times, two different voices involved in a disabused evaluation of the magic and logic of love.[52]

If, in this sonnet, the rhetorical reattribution of conventional female attributes to the male beloved requires a dramatic, even theatrical reading, as opposed to the deliberate and more sustained expression of the tercets, then quite clearly, the quatrains are intended to reflect Petrarchan discourse, whereas the tercets, more circumspect and restrictive, represent the voice of critical reaction. The enchanted person may have come under the spell of a lover's charms, but the disenchanted poet doubts that she can be objective in the matter. Her initial questions appear in a different, more ironic light, consequently, in view of her later uncertainty: "Je ne voudrois le dire assurément."[53] Thus, while she writes within the confines of Petrarchist rhetoric, Labé's counter-rhetoric serves to question its continuing credibility and authority.

In sonnet XXIII she reproaches her lover for his long absence, criticizing his use of hyperbolic praise devoid of proof of devotion. Mocking his vow to die before the demise of his love for her, she parodies the language of his empty compliments. Viewed from the disabusing distance of present reality, his Petrarchan metaphors and promises seem all the more ironic:

> Las! que me sert, que si parfaitement
>   Louas jadis et ma tresse doree,
>   Et de mes yeus la beauté comparee
>   A deus Soleils, dont Amour finement
> Tira les trets causez de ton tourment?
>   Ou estes vous, pleurs de peu de duree?
>   Et mort par qui devoit estre honoree
>   Ta ferme amour et iteré serment?   (p. 134)

Critics have long commented on the supposed sincerity of these sonnets, claiming perfect coincidence between context and content. Yet since her language of love is mostly derivative, sincerity would seem to lie elsewhere, more especially in her appraisal of its inherent inadequacies. Petrarchism is for Labé the language of literature, not of life. Thus her sonnets exhibit its conceits, only to have personal experience deflate them. She inaugurates thereby a dialogue between the competing languages of illusion and delusion, with her "sincerity" countering and correcting his "insincerity."

The continuing presence of the poet-critic is signaled in the way the text turns back upon itself, reviewing and assessing its proposals and progress. Labé is never fully immersed in the language of passion, transported or absorbed by its intensity; rather, through ironic distance, she invokes another and different reading of its rhetoric. For instance, while the quatrains and the first two lines of the opening tercet in sonnet XVII translate the "errors" induced by repeated attempts to conquer love, first in flight from the presence of the object of desire, then through worldly diversions, and finally in solitude, the concluding lines propose an hypothetical, yet impossible, correction for diverse efforts of evasion:

> Mais j'aperçoy, ayant erré maint tour,
> Que si je veux de toy estre delivre,
> Il me convient hors de moymesme vivre,
> Ou fais encor que loin sois en sejour. (p. 130–1)

In situating the story of her "errors" in the past, Labé introduces the principle of a temporal, and consequently structural, difference, encouraging memory and judgment to evolve side by side, actuating thereby a seminal exchange between experience and writing.[54] Where she realizes herself most clearly therefore is in her reevaluation of a language which is not her own and which she views from the vantage point of one who is outside its semantic realm. Originally she thought she shared the language of love with another, only to discover eventually that each spoke and understood it differently. Whereas for him, she now knows, words were instruments of persuasion and seduction, for her they are truth, the unmediated language of the heart and mind. It is in this clash and conjunction of opposing dialectics that Labé emerges as a poetic entity, conscious of the deviousness of conventional rhetoric and independent finally of its influence.

For example, in the initial quatrain of sonnet XVIII, she modifies Catullus' hyperbolic arithmetic ("Da mi basia mille, deinde centum, / Dein mille altera, dein secunda centum, / deinde usque altera mille, deinde centum, 5.7–9), reducing the number of mutual kisses from hundreds and thousands to a more realistic nine:[55]

> Baise m'encor, rebaise moy et baise:
>   Donne m'en un de tes plus savoureus,
>   Donne m'en un de tes plus amoureux:
>   Je t'en rendray quatre plus chaus que braise.

Then, in the second quatrain, she encourages her love to delight in their shared kisses and implicit promise of eventual union:

> Las, te pleins tu? ça que ce mal j'apaise,
>   En t'en donnant dix autres doucereus.
>   Ainsi meslans nos baisers tant heureus
>   Jouissons nous l'un de l'autre à notre aise.   (p. 131)

But whereas Catullus, mindful of the inevitable night of eternal sleep, equates loving with living here and now ("Vivamus, mea Lesbia, atque amemus"), Labé is more inclined, in Neoplatonic fashion, to consider that through mutual love, each "dies" as an individual, only to be reborn in spiritual union one with the other:

> Lors double vie à chacun en suivra.
> Chacun en soy et son ami vivra.   (ibid.)

Finally, in a literal reconsideration of the theme, she concludes that happiness for her requires escaping from herself:

> Permets m'Amour penser quelque folie:
> Tousjours suis mal, vivant discrettement,
>   Et ne me puis donner contentement,
>   Si hors de moy ne fay quelque saillie.   (ibid.)

But since "discrettement" implies both "separately" and "prudently," does she not mean that, living apart, therefore prudently, from her lover, she is unrealized, and that this situation could only be remedied if and when she were able to make a sally outside of herself – which thought, of course, as she puts it, is madness – presumably in order to unite herself with him?

Here as elsewhere in her sonnets, Labé confronts masculine rhetoric with feminine logic, discrediting the former's pleas and promises. Thus her particular contribution to a renewal of the *basia* motif and *animae dimidium meae* topos depends less on the purported authenticity of her sensuality than on the self-consciously playful manner in which she describes its fantasized fulfillment. Rather than carrying the theme through to a closing conceit, developing it as a whole and in a continuous manner, she reviews it from the perspective of the tercets, giving it a sudden, ludic twist. Her poetry, once again, retraces and, in a sense, retracts the language it borrows, making it mean more and otherwise than intended, certainly more than the contemporary reader, familiar with its original context, could possibly have anticipated.

In perhaps an even greater number of texts, however, Labé focuses on her own reactions to the pleasures and torments of love. Thus, in sonnet XVII, which in many ways is one of her most successfully dramatic poems, a set of hypotheses and aspirations are aptly conjoined and worked out tentatively in a single, sustained, and complex sentence. Structurally, with its *si* punctuating a series of conditional alternatives, this sonnet is similar in its opening dynamics to Du Bellay's "Si nostre vie est moins qu'une journée," one of the final sonnets in the cycle he devoted to Olive. Both translate Platonic themes of transcendence and immortality, Du Bellay's through the scale of beauty, Labé's through the kiss of life. Poetically, however, each accomplishes a different trajectory, Du Bellay's ascending mimetically to "l'Idée," Labé's remaining resolutely earth-bound, ending, after insistent and progressive elimination of various obstacles, in the triumph of love over death:

> Lors que souef plus il me baiseroit,
> Et mon esprit sur ses levres fuiroit,
> Bien je mourrois, plus que vivante, heureuse.   (p. 128)

And in her final sonnet, a farewell to her female readers, she recalls the innumerable sufferings to which love has subjected her, concluding that, in order to avoid greater unhappiness, they should profit from her experience, reacting even more cautiously and ironically to the wiles of masculine rhetoric:

> En ayant moins que moy d'ocasion
> Et plus d'estrange et forte passion,
> Et gardez vous d'estre plus malheureuses.   (p. 135)

The debate between love and folly, the theme of Labé's dialogue in prose, resounds throughout these twenty-four sonnets. Neither one nor the other is ever fully dominant, and the play between them is constant. What one senses in Labé, and misses, say, in Ronsard, is on the one hand, a questioning of convention, and on the other, a propensity for its appropriation, but in a reduced and more concentrated form. Her work remains circumscribed by the folly of love and the love of folly, a troubling paradox whose resolution, with speculative consequences, is deferred indefinitely in her poetry and prose. "Pour la dificulté et importance de vos diferens," Jupiter decrees at the end of the *Débat de Folie et d'Amour*, "nous avons remis votre afaire d'ici à trois fois, sept fois, neuf siecles. Et ce pendant vous commandons vivre amiablement ensemble, sans vous outrager l'un l'autre. Et guidera Folie l'aveugle Amour, et le conduira par tout ou bon lui semblera." (p. 103) Her strength, despite a certain narrowness of scope, lies finally in the unfamiliarity of her self-consciously feminine attitude towards conventions within which her male counterparts, in ever-increasing numbers, continued to work and write. One suspects that it was, in part, unconventionality of this kind which fomented charges by a number of her masculine readers of an equally unconventional lifestyle.

When, in fact, a woman decided to go public, whether through publication or otherwise, Renaissance cultural convention considered her to be sexually permissive. We need only to remember Boccaccio's rendering of the story of Semiramis who, during her son's minority, ruled the Assyrians in his stead. First he praises her for her military and political skill, concluding that it heightened her glorious majesty as much as it gave rise to admiration in those who looked upon her.[56] Then he condemns her fall into sexual, even incestuous, promiscuity, reporting that she gave herself to many men, even to the very son whose power she had managed to maintain.

Although Christine de Pisan prefers to ignore Boccaccio's pre-occupation with Semiramis' sexuality, depicting her rather as a builder of cities, Louise Labé evokes the example of the Queen's transformation from active ruler to victim of love in order to account for the dramatic change in her own life:

> Ainsi Amour de toy t'a estrangee,
> Qu'on te diroit en une autre changee.
> Donques celui lequel d'amour esprise
> Pleindre me voit, que point il ne mesprise
> Mon triste deuil: Amour, peut estre, en brief
> En son endroit n'aparoitra moins grief.   (*Elégie I*, p. 109)

Ultimately unsuccessful in her resistance to Cupid's repeated assaults, she feels justified in asking for understanding from those readers who have similarly succumbed, claiming an exemplary role for a woman who has gone public. Equally apprehensive, Antoine du Moulin defended his decision to make Pernette du Guillet's poetry available to the public, explaining that he resolved to do so only after her death and with her husband's full knowledge and consent. In this way, he hoped to avoid compromising her reputation as an honorable and virtuous woman.

The changing conditions of contemporary culture are reflected in Labé's paratextual expressions of concern over the proper reception of works by women. The Renaissance was not only for men, as Rabelais, through Gargantua's letter to his son, is careful to point out. By divine goodness, he writes, light and dignity have been brought back to letters. Now all the branches of science have been reestablished and languages have been restored, Greek, Hebrew, Chaldean, and Latin. Printing, so elegant and exact an art, has been invented. The world is full of learned men, erudite teachers, and vast libraries, and even "femmes et filles ont aspiré à ceste louange et manne celeste de bonne doctrine."[57]

The invention of printing made books more readily and widely available, as Rabelais remarked, and also altered the fundamental composition of the reading public once and for all. No longer almost exclusively clerical and masculine, it began to include more and more women from various social and economic classes, in proportion as educational opportunities were opened to them, eventually making it possible to identify them as a distinct and separate group. Pernette du Guillet and Louise Labé address their works to the women of Lyons, slanting their rhetorical strategy in such a way as to solicit and facilitate comprehension and acceptance of their passage to public recognition. This does not mean necessarily that they designed and destined their works for a female audience exclusively. It does imply, however, that they and their editors were not unaware of the potential of writing for a wider, even virtually untapped, market of readers, or that this new writing, to be successful, would need to take a stand against the prevailing rhetorical code. It is in this sense that the women writers of Lyons reshape, even redefine, the *Querelle des femmes*, a quarrel which printers, in furtherance of their own interests, continued to foment and promote.

Where women writers are concerned, print culture refers to the production of writing in a newly gendered form, addressed to a broader and less homogenous public. No longer satisfied with being the silent object of man's desire, they proclaim their right to public audience, only to be reviled for aggressiveness. Shattering publishing and cultural stereotypes, women become the focus of another chapter in the *Querelle des femmes*, one pitting writer against writer over matters of literary propriety. Refusing anonymity, they begin to occupy a place in the margins of literature, despite continuing attacks on their morals or learning. Old misogynistic arguments and old rhetorical strategies are recalled in a concerted attempt to silence pens which were rapidly becoming, it was realized belatedly, much sharper and more effective protagonists.

CHAPTER 4

The women in Montaigne's life

While early modern poetic language, from Marot to D'Aubigné, is
frequently subjective, it is not always clear in what degree it is
autobiographical, designed to translate personal rather than universal experiences. The same can be said of prose writers such as
Rabelais or even Montaigne who, in presenting themselves in public,
remain spectators of their own performance. Writing, they see
themselves writing, and their "I" is partially another, designed to
fascinate or exemplify. No longer excluded from scrutiny by professional or paratextual protocol, the self-conscious author is clearly
a product of the age of printing, constrained to solicit the benevo-
lence of publisher, patron, and reader alike. However, both as a term
and a concept, the *moi* is not part of the language or psychology of
identity in sixteenth-century France. The Renaissance "I" signifies
the writer's presence, but without any real sense of equivalency with
a distinctly inner reality.

The French word *identité* derives from the Late Latin *identitas*, from
identidem, "repeatedly," a word which is probably a contraction of
the expression *idem et idem*: "same and same," that is, the repetition
of essential or generic character in different examples or instances.
Identity therefore remains constant in relation to change; it is the
solid but impenetrable center located in the periphery of self, the
"forme maistresse, qui luicte contre l'institution, et contre la tem-
peste des passions qui luy sont contraires."[1] Thus the *moy-mesme*
which is the professed matter of Montaigne's book measures the
difference and inscribes the redundancy between *je* and *me* in
expressions such as *je me vois, je me taste, je me roulle en moy mesme*, but its
autonomy remains strictly relational, circumscribed by comparison
with others, even another oneself.

The ambivalence of Montaigne's "I" is common to most if not all
first-person narrations in Renaissance literature. Whenever auto-

107

biographical references occur, they are designed either to impress the reader or to offer self-justification. Personal facts and events may support an argument, but they rarely stand on their own, as unmediated or unmotivated records. This is as true of Benvenuto Cellini's *Vita*, Gerolamo Cardano's *De vita propria sua* or Marguerite de Valois's *Mémoires*, in which purpose and apology figure prominently. Thus, Cellini may boast of his sexual conquests to further the image of his adventurous nature, and Cardano may regret the "Sardanapalian life" he led while rector at Padua or the unfortunate marriage which, through the sins of his son, was the cause of all of the calamities which befell him for the rest of his life, while Marguerite de Valois is concerned with the politics of marriage and the compelling reasons for not divorcing her husband, Henri de Navarre, as her mother insisted.[2]

In the case of Montaigne's own family, biographical and autobiographical information concurs imperfectly, mostly because of the way in which he displaces facts in the interest of more general considerations, making true appreciation of his account problematic. The place that Marie de Gournay comes to occupy in his life and book is similarly unclear, partially because of the uncertainty surrounding the authenticity of the passage in the posthumous edition of the *Essais* in praise of their friendship, but also because of her readiness to convert his appreciation of her into a vehicle for self-promotion. She makes Montaigne and his book hers in the story of her life, recasting them in her own image both through her successive editions of the *Essais* and her own numerous publications. But does she exploit friendship for Montaigne professionally, that is as a means to escape from the marginality to which both gender and literary norms consigned her? Whatever the reason, in joining her name to his, she was successful in gaining entrance into the privileged world of criticism and critical editions, areas previously reserved for humanist scholars. Vigorously resented, her encroachment occasioned a new version of the *Querelle des femmes*, in which Marie de Gournay, in defending Montaigne, defended herself and her right to Montaigne.

MONTAIGNE'S WOMEN

Whereas much has been written, especially somewhat recently, about Montaigne and Marie de Gournay, little attention has been given to the other women in his life, namely his mother, wife, and six daughters, only one of whom, Léonor, lived through and beyond childhood.[3] This neglect, moreover, applies to Montaigne himself, who has little to say in his writings about the women with whom he lived and shared many years of his life. On the other hand, he shows considerable interest in them as readers, addressing them publicly and individually in the several chapters he dedicates to them, as well as collectively in "Sur des vers de Virgile," a chapter in which he deals more specifically with sex and sexuality, subjects, he feels, which will entitle him to their more private attention: "Je m'ennuie que mes essais servent les dames de meuble commun seulement, et de meuble de sale. Ce chapitre me fera du cabinet." (III, v, 847 B)[4]

Montaigne's biography poses fewer problems and has occasioned fewer polemics than his autobiography. While we find nothing in the various accounts of his life similar to the disputes over the philosophy, religion, or politics of the *Essais*, there have been questions about the quality of his family life, even a lively debate whether or not his wife, purportedly disappointed with her new husband's attitude towards sex and marriage, had an affair with his younger brother.[5] While reports of his marital misfortunes are seemingly exaggerated and mainly conjectural, his domestic situation was somewhat exceptional and may have had something to do with his decisions both to retire to his tower and, subsequently, to set off on a long, prolonged, and potentially hazardous journey to Rome.

Fictionalization renders Rabelais's writings on women and marriage unreliable as social documents, but Montaigne's self-revelatory remarks seem relatively transparent. Nevertheless, when read against the context of his domestic situation, they acquire a somewhat different connotation. While the *Essais* contain little actual information about Montaigne's family life, we know from other sources that there was friction between him and his wife, even hostility at times, and this may be one of the reasons he decided to repair to the tranquillity of his tower. While he has little to say in the *Essais* about his own wife and marriage, much of what he has to say about women and marriage in general is negative. Conversely, he is generous in his admiration of a number of women, both from Antiquity and his own time, comparing them favorably to men in more than one instance. Perhaps we have not always read this discrepancy correctly, in part because we have forgotten how to decipher the workings of Renaissance rhetoric, but also because of a common critical fallacy, especially prevalent since the advent of Romanticism, which confuses the lives of writers with their writing.

Inevitably, critics have tended to conflate and confuse the *Essais* with biography, using one to explain and confirm the other. More and more, however, we have come to realize that the self-portrait Montaigne promised us in his remarks "Au lecteur" is not, as Villey and others had thought, essentially autobiographical. On the one hand, although he speaks of himself throughout his book, his presence, resolutely peripheral, is essentially that of a writer positioning and situating himself in relation to the question, quotation, or theme of the day. On the other hand, he states that the *Essais* afford him pleasure in allowing him to discharge his bile in generalities, implying that specific antagonisms lie sometimes not too far beneath the calm surface of the text. In "Sur des vers de Virgile," for instance, where his self-portrait acquires its most intimate, almost confessional dimension, personal references are modified and deflected by philosophical comments on life and literature. And while some judgments on sex and marriage may be dictated by personal attitudes or experiences, they are folded into the larger context of an inquiry into the differences and similarities between men and women.

In fact, virtually all of the occasions Montaigne finds for talking or writing about himself involve a relationship with another.[6] He presents his *Essais* as a substitute for a lost friend, one with whom he was able to communicate as with himself, and his reactions to his family prompt him to write some of his most intimate passages. In "De l'affection des peres aux enfans" (II, viii), he explores a number of limitations on that sentiment, including his physical abilities and psychological make-up in comparison with his father's, the position and authority of women as wives and mothers, his views and those of his wife on the raising of children. In arguing against fathers who measure the love and attention which nature intended them to show towards their children, who use wills and testaments to control their families and prolong their authority into the future, he could readily have included himself – despite his claims to have acted differently – as a son who respected but challenged parental authority, a husband who honored his wife but resorted to legal means to assure his own authority over her and his household, and a father who would have nothing to do with his daughter's education.

Montaigne draws an interesting portrait of his father in "De la praesumption" (II, 17), a chapter in which he describes at length some of the factors contributing to his own psychological make-up. His remarks about his father's athletic prowess and ongoing concern for the consolidation of the estate and preservation of the buildings of the château are explained, in part, by his admiration for qualities he himself did not possess. They serve as well to point out traits which, while seemingly appropriate to his father's extroverted nature, appear unimportant, even incomprehensible, to an introspective writer of essays.

It was Montaigne's fate to live exclusively among women, at least following his trip to Italy and the departure of his youngest brother, raised until then at the family château. While he never speaks of his own wife, he alludes to wives and marriage in a way which suggests that their union was one of habit and resignation rather than of passion or even happiness.[7] In fact, much of what he has to say about women in the *Essais* is general in character, and references to his domestic life are disconcertingly brief as well as few and far between.[8] Is it not strange that a man who writes "je suis moy-mesmes la matiere de mon livre" ("Au Lecteur", A) should devote so little time and space to himself as husband and father? The question to be addressed here is whether this reticence has more to do with personal inclination than the gendered prejudices of Renaissance writing.

First, let us examine the place of Montaigne's wife, daughter, and mother in his life and possible reasons for their marginalization in his book. Next, his tendency to generalize personal relations and attitudes and the rhetorical practices which, far from excluding them from the *Essais*, actually give them more prominent, if displaced, attention. The remaining, interrelated question, of the influence of printing on the way in which Montaigne structures his writing in general and on women in particular, will be taken up last. Suffice it to say here that, in the opening section of the *Apologie de Raimond Sebond*, Montaigne suggests a crucial difference between readers of another, less sophisticated age and his own – between, that is, different ways of reading and different degrees of respect and authority accorded learning and books. Over time, he realized, the culture generated by the advent of print had been considerably modified by the success of print itself. With profusion, books were read more quickly and cursorily, and Montaigne's own style of writing was designed to counter the easy reading habits of his generation. Anti-rhetorical in prejudice, it is rhetoric of another sort, geared specifically to the problem of capturing the attention of a new kind of public, at once more diffident and more apt at anticipating the snares and conclusions of traditional arguments.

It has been said that we know almost nothing about Montaigne's wife. This is true if we rely on the *Essais*. However, we do have twenty-three letters she wrote to her spiritual director, Dom Marc-Antoine de Saint-Bernard, some seventeen years after her husband's death, and they show her to be a complaining and meticulous old lady, without much imagination or personality.[9] If these traits prevailed during Montaigne's lifetime, it is safe to assume they would have had an impact on the conduct of their years together, a supposition reinforced by the opening paragraphs of "De trois bonnes femmes" on criteria for judging a good marriage. When he writes that there are few good women, especially where the duties of marriage are concerned, "car c'est un marché plein de tant d'espineuses circonstances qu'il est malaisé que la volonté d'une femme s'y maintienne entiere long temps" (II, XXXV, 744 A), or that "Nous dispenserons volontiers qu'on rie apres, pourveu qu'on nous rie pendant la vie" (ibid., B), and, in a 1595 addition, "Est ce pas de quoy resusciter de despit, qui m'aura craché au nez pendant que j'estoy, me vienne frotter les pieds quand je commence à n'estre plus" (ibid., C), his "generalities" would seem suddenly to take on a decidedly personal turn.[10]

On the other hand, we know that his wife was a practical and efficient person, who took excellent care of his household and properties, a duty for which he maintains he himself had no capacity and which, in the *Essais*, is translated into universal rules of conduct: "Le plus utile et honnorable science et occupation à une femme, c'est la science du mesnage"; "Si le mary fournit de matière, nature mesme veut qu'elles fournissent de forme" (III, ix, 975 B). We know moreover that she brought him a substantial dowry and provided him with family connections which proved useful to him in the early years of his parliamentary career.[11] One suspects, however, that there may not always have been agreement on matters of money or on the manner of their daughter's education. In any event, few if any of these intimate matters actually enter into Montaigne's narrative of himself, and we are left to read them back into the text whenever he talks about domestic relationships in general.

Montaigne says next to nothing of his daughter, but his few words would seem to indicate that she was not particularly alert or wide-awake.[12] The most negative indication she gave of this was when, after Montaigne's death and shortly before her own, she disposed of his library, entrusting it to Gaudefroy de Rochefort, grand vicaire d'Auch, whence it was gradually dispersed and all but lost.[13] Could it be that this was out of spite, that Léonor acted that day in the name of all the women of Montaigne, those whom he had so often abandoned for the silent companions of his tower?[14] In any event, her gesture was too late, for posterity had already taken over.

Even more problematic is Montaigne's mother, that descendant of the presumably Jewish Lopez who, following her husband's death, remained with her son until and beyond his own death, almost never leaving the grounds of the family château. If, then, Montaigne remembered his father in the *Essais*, why does he exclude his mother? Is his silence due to the fact that she was still alive at the time and therefore not yet entitled to the honor of a *memento mori*, or is it more meaningful, signifying perhaps an underlying antagonism between them, a tension which personality and Protestant leanings would have greatly aggravated? Obviously, a difference of confession in a person under the same roof and at that period of religious wars would not have contributed to the harmony or even the security of the household. Whatever the reason, when Montaigne left the image of his wife and daughter as an ex-voto at the shrine at Loretto in Italy, his mother was not included in his pious homage.[15]

In fact, before 1875, no one else paid any particular attention to Montaigne's mother. In that year, however, Théophile Malvezin published a book establishing the peninsular origin of the Lopez or Louppes family, hesitating between Spain and Portugal.[16] His main interest lay elsewhere, however, namely in proving their Semitic origin. He was convinced that Antoinette de Louppes was descended from a family of *conversos* that had emigrated to France at the end of the fifteenth century, together with a significant number of other converted Jews, to escape religious persecution in their homeland. Settling in the Bordeaux region, they became progressively wealthy through various successful commercial enterprises and were gradually assimilated, mostly through intermarriage, into the local Christian society.

The fact that Malvezin was the first to raise the question of Montaigne's Jewish ancestry is intriguing. Neither Montaigne himself nor any of his contemporaries ever alluded to the possibility, and had it been known or even suspected at the time, there were any number of detractors who would not have failed to point it out, among them the very noble Scaliger who, since he took it upon himself to remind his recently ennobled neighbor that his father had been a seller of salted herring, would have been just as pleased to be able to report his Jewish origins.[17] Equally troubling is the fact that Malvezin's thesis, although grounded on the flimsiest of evidence, was immediately adopted by Lanson, Stapfer, Strowski, Villey, Armaingaud, and Plattard, that is to say by a whole generation of literary historians who suddenly began to detect certain social, psychological, even stylistic traits in the *Essais* which they attributed unhesitatingly to Montaigne's Jewishness.

For instance, Paul Bonnefon's portrait of Montaigne is informed by a number of racial stereotypes:

> Il importe davantage à la psychologie du fils de savoir que la mère avait du sang étranger dans les veines, et du sang d'étranger d'origine juive. Peut-être est-il permis de voir là l'explication de la tolérance de Montaigne, le secret de sa nature si souple, s'accommodant si volontiers aux circonstances. C'est d'eux [de ses ancêtres] encore qu'il tenait sa faculté d'assimilation, un certain cosmopolitisme de goût qui le poussait aux voyages et le faisait se trouver bien à l'étranger.[18]

For his part, and somewhat less tendentiously, Albert Thibaudet remarked that a drop of Jewish blood may account for Montaigne's "mobilism."[19]

Whatever the reason, it has become a commonplace of Montaigne criticism to mention his Jewish ancestry – as distinct from his Jewish background, since no one seems to feel that he was brought up in the Jewish religion or culture – even though most of the supporting evidence remains conjectural and circumstantial. Moreover, as Roger Trinquet has pointed out in his careful and thorough review of the whole question, it should be remembered that had there been any Jewish blood in Montaigne's veins, it would have been considerably diluted over the years:

> En fait, la conversion de ces Lopez – à supposer qu'ils eussent été juifs à l'origine – remontait sans doute au début du xvᵉ siècle . . . En l'espace de trois ou quatre générations, plusieurs mariages avec des filles d'anciens-chrétiens se produisirent vraisemblablement . . . réduisant d'autant la part de l'ascendance proprement sémitique de Montaigne.[20]

With some scholars wanting him to be Jewish (and social historians could probably tell us something about the possible connection between the Dreyfus affair and the sudden proliferation of such claims at the close of the nineteenth century), and others wanting him to be English,[21] Thibaudet's insightful portrait of his essential Frenchness affords a salutary, perhaps even necessary, readjustment of a number of critical distortions.[22]

Aside from the obvious fact that mothers do not, much before Proust, usually figure as subjects in French literature,[23] might there not be some explanation other than racial or religious for Montaigne's silence where his own is concerned? There is evidence, both documentary and deductive, to show that she was authoritarian and that differences of temperament and conflicts of interest marked their troubling and troubled relations. There exists, for instance, the act of agreement which Montaigne, upon his father's death, entered into with his mother, because of doubts which had already arisen between them or which might arise in the future over the conditions of her late husband's will: it stipulates that while she had a legal right to remain at Montaigne until her death, she would no longer have any "superintendence and mastery" over the household "other than honorary and maternal." While it was agreed that she would be "lodged and nourished with all filial respect and enjoy the service of two maids and a manservant," her son was to enjoy henceforth "the full command and mastery of the said château of Montaigne, its accessories, entrances, and exits."[24]

The very fact that Montaigne seemed to have felt it necessary to have a legal act drawn up to define and delimit his mother's rights and privileges suggests a history of incompatibility between the two, and a struggle for control over a household which had been hers for forty years and was now his. In anticipating that mother and son might not be able to live and get along congenially together in the same house, and in spelling out the conditions of such an eventuality, their formal agreement tends to confirm the reality of mutual mistrust and misunderstanding. When at last Montaigne entered into his inheritance and finally achieved financial and domestic independence from his mother, he was already thirty-five and had been married for three years. It is not unlikely, therefore, that these difficulties had an influence on his decision to take refuge in his tower as well as in shaping, even sharpening, those "espines domestiques" to which he refers in "De la vanité" (III, ix, 950 B), or on his remarks, especially in "De l'affection des pères aux enfans" (II, viii), on troublesome relations between sons and mothers, husbands and wives, and elsewhere, between men and women in general.[25]

Have historians read misogyny into Montaigne in much the same way as they read Jewishness? Robert Cottrell has studied the gender polarity marking the *Essais*, pointing out that in the Stoically colored world of late Renaissance humanists it was traditional for women, lumped together with children and the common people, to be categorized as soft and weak, whereas men are viewed as strong and resilient.[26] Traditional rhetorical commonplaces were still much in vogue, and these in turn continued to influence the shaping and structuring of ideas, even of thought. When therefore Montaigne, prompted by quotations from Virgil and Lucretius, examines marriage and female sexuality in "Sur des vers de Virgile," he is led quite naturally to retrieve any number of topoi on the subject from the storehouse of popular and literary memory and to reconsider their status in relation to his own experience.

In his long commentary on the passage in which Virgil depicts a moment of marital passion between Venus and Vulcan, Montaigne distinguishes clearly between sexuality and marriage. In considering arguments for and against marriage, he concurs, in conformity with Roman and medieval Christian prejudices, that it is a reasoned arrangement for procreative purposes, but that sexual passion is better left to extramarital relations:

L'amour hait qu'on se tienne par ailleurs que par luy, et se mesle lâchement aux accointances qui sont dressées et entretenues soubs autre titre, comme est le mariage: l'aliance, les moyens, y poisent par raison, autant ou plus que les graces et la beauté. On ne se marie pas pour soy, quoi qu'on die; on se marie autant ou plus pour sa posterité, pour sa famille. (III, 5, 849–50 B)

Intent upon maintaining a sense of self outside the bonds and boundaries of the family, he concludes ironically that, for his part, he would have avoided marrying Wisdom herself, even if she had wanted him.

Montaigne's principal source in this crucial essay for examples of female sexuality is Juvenal's Sixth Satire (which runs to the extraordinary length of nearly 700 lines, taking up therefore all of one book), a poem designed to provide a notorious adulterer called Postumus with a series of misogynistic arguments against marriage. Since, as we have seen, rhetoricians were accustomed to debating the pros and cons of this and any other question, a good deal of the material in this satire was probably already derivative, selected from the vast repertory of themes and examples they had collected for pedagogical purposes. From Juvenal's extensive catalog of female excesses, many dealing with their boundless lust and insatiability, Montaigne recalls the anecdote of the Empress Messalina's nocturnal exploits in a brothel, from which, at dawn, she returned still unsatisfied (III, v, 854 B).[27] A quotation from Martial, in which a wife reproaches her husband Bassus for his inability to satisfy her sexual wants (III, v, 855 B), confirms this example, followed by a reference to Catullus' Clodia and her hundreds of lovers (III, v, 857 B). Examples of female depravity are counterbalanced, however, with examples of masculine excess, justifying the conclusion that men and women are comparable, at least from a sexual standpoint.

Of course, sexual equality is not the same thing as gender equality, and here the record is somewhat less clear. On the other hand, while there are numerous passages in the *Essais* where Montaigne speaks of women positively, the sum of his remarks does not add up necessarily to his "idea" of women. In fact, he almost always refers to them in relation to and in comparison with men. Once again, in his most definitive statement on the matter, he finds men and women fundamentally similar. Both are cast in the same mold, and whatever differences exist between them are primarily social and cultural: "je dis que les masles et femelles sont jettez en mesme moule: sauf l'institution et l'usage, la difference n'y est pas grande" (III, v, 897 B).

Montaigne's commentary on sex outside of marriage is prompted by a quotation from Lucretius on the illicit loves of Mars and Venus. In the long digression on the art of writing which follows, he refers to language in gendered terms. If French is "feminine" and Latin is "masculine," according to his bilingual prejudice, is this because French, being derived from Latin, has suffered a loss of vigor and meaning in his eyes and is, consequently, of a lesser nature?[28] Notwithstanding, he describes French as "gratieus, delicat et abondant," especially in comparison with a particular Gascon dialect which he admires as "singulierement beau, sec, bref, signifiant, et à la verité . . . masle et militaire plus qu'autre que j'entende" (II, xvii, 639 A). Although French is not inferior to Latin lexically, he finds it inadequate in expressing concepts: "Je le trouve suffisamment abondant, [c] mais non pas maniant et vigoureux suffisamment. Il succombe ordinairement à une puissante conception" (III, v, 874 A).

Not only is Montaigne's appreciation of language gendered, but his classification of various styles as well. Thus he admires the strength and energy of Sallust, Caesar, and Tacitus, but finds Cicero and Pliny the Younger lacking in vigor.[29] To the "mignardises et delices" (I, xl, 250 A) of Terence, he prefers the natural virility and manliness of Virgil and Lucretius:

> leur langage est tout plein et gros d'une vigueur naturelle et constante; ils sont tout epigramme, non la queuë seulement, mais la teste, l'estomac et les pieds. Il n'y a rien d'efforcé, rien de treinant, tout y marche d'une pareille teneur. [c] *Contextus totus virilis est; non sunt circa flosculos occupati.* [b] Ce n'est pas une eloquence molle et seulement sans offence: elle est nerveuse et solide, qui ne plaict pas tant comme elle remplit et ravit, et ravit le plus les plus forts espris.[30] (III, v, 873 B)

In order to compensate for the perceived weakness of French in lexicon and style, he comes to rely progressively on disruption and allusiveness, "à ne dire qu'à demy, à dire confusément, à dire discordamment" (III, ix, 996 c). If, therefore, *distingo*, as he claims, is the most universal component of his logic (II, i, 335 B), it is not only because he privileges exception and promotes digression, but also because his text advances "à sauts et à gambades" (III, ix, 994 B), separating and "distinguishing" individual words. Classical rhetoric, from Aristotle through Quintilian, warns against the disruptive nature of digression, the *egressio* or *excessus* which leads the orator astray, distracting him and his audience from the point of his argument. Now Montaigne is all digression, but purposefully so: "Je m'esgare, mais plutost par licence que par mesgarde" (III, ix, 994 B). Whereas the orderly arrangement and linear presentation of material (*narratio*) is a necessary art for an orator whose public is immediate and whose words are heard but once, a different kind of rhetorical practice is required of the writer who, because his public is anonymous, remote in both space and time, can no longer depend upon the persuasive tactics of voice and gesture. Since *verba volent*, but *scripta manent*, it is not enough for the written word, as it is for the spoken word, to express force and conviction. It must also present sufficient interpretative difficulties to retain attention, for the written word, unlike the spoken word, is a fixed thing which, to become vital, requires the reader's cooperation and participation: "Si prendre des livres estoit les apprendre, et si les veoir estoit les regarder, et les parcourir les saisir, j'aurois tort de me faire du tout si ignorant que je dy" (III, ix, 995 c).

How does a writer manage to induce the reader to give meaning and direction to his words? Traditionally, by recourse to the art of rhetorical devices designed to facilitate transitions and underscore salient words and passages. But Montaigne expects the matter of his book to make its own divisions, to show where it changes, concludes, begins, resumes, without introducing links and seams for the benefit of weak or heedless ears.[31] If he cannot arrest the reader's attention by the weight of his material, he is prepared to do so by his idiosyncratic presentation: "Puisque je ne puis arrester l'attention du lecteur par le pois, '*manco male*' s'il advient que je l'arreste par mon embrouilleure" (ibid., B). In substituting *embrouilleure* for the orderly arrangement of classical *dispositio*, Montaigne is perhaps the very first post-Gutenberg writer to realize the importance of adapting oratorical priorities to the changing requirements of a reading public.

Disorder and digression, in this perspective, acquire a positive connotation, since the reader, unlike the listener, is required to become actively involved in the unraveling and deciphering of the text and its meaning. Whereas the linearity of *prorsa oratio* is intended to coincide with the logical progression of an argument and thereby to facilitate the listener's apprehension of its inevitable conclusion, the *embrouilleure* of Montaigne's writing, like the *versus* or "turning back" on itself of poetic structure, constrains the reader to interpret the meaning of words according to their *contexture*,[32] considering them in conjunction with their contrived interrelationship (*callida iunctura*) with other words. What is essential to the successful functioning of *embrouilleure* is the instant of variance, the sharp swerve away from predictability, the discursive *clinamen* generating unanticipated shapes and deviations, which produces a kind of writing involving the reader necessarily in the realization of meaning.

Thus the idea of *embrouilleure*, which Montaigne mentions almost casually, implies a crucial and radical departure from ordinary practices of arrangement and reception. How to conduct a reader most effectively to a preconceived conclusion is no longer the question; but, rather, how to assure correlation between the formal exigencies of writing and the subtle intricacies of thought. Montaigne is intent upon achieving a text which reflects and reproduces the digressive complexities of the mind in search of order and meaning and which, consequently, resists easy and immediate comprehension, in opposition to one which, in progressing evenly and uneventfully towards a preconceived conclusion, tends to sacrifice differences and variables. He is not concerned with the reader's convenience, as he informs us in his remarks "Au Lecteur," merely his attention and good will in the working out of a question or idea. "Mon stile et mon esprit vont vagabondant de mesmes" (III, ix, 994 c), he maintains, and he leaves it to us to adapt our reading habits and rhetorical expectations to the complexities of a prose whose order and movement are meant to conform to the vagaries of a personal logic and the peculiarities of a private, and therefore strictly marginal, rhetoric.

For this reason, misogyny as a subject is much too unilateral for Montaigne's world or vision. Based upon old arguments and over-simplified conclusions, it acquires life and validity through the conjuncture of opposing points of view: "Nous sommes, quasi en tout, iniques juges de leurs actions, comme elles sont des nostres" (III, v, 885 B). When he writes of women, Montaigne goes far beyond the restrictive confines of the pedagogical *exercitatio*. Instead of adopting an extreme position on either side of the question, he prefers to explore the relatively untouched middle ground, focusing on what men and women have in common. Thus, there is neither a feminist Montaigne nor an antifeminist Montaigne, even though the *Essais* have much to say on either side of the question; only a Montaigne who brings them both together, who situates himself in relation to the way in which the question is posed. In examining women from the perspective of the way men view them and *vice versa*, he amalgamates and neutralizes the extremes of misogynistic litera-ture. When therefore he attributes unfailing sexual appetites to women, he emphasizes the contrast between the chastity men and masculine norms impose upon them and the reality of their common sexuality. Men, by assuming the right to make the rules of the game, have driven women to ruse and deception: "Les femmes n'ont pas tort du tout quand elles refusent les reigles de vie qui sont introduites au monde, d'autant que ce sont les hommes qui les ont faictes sans elles" (III, v, 854 B). Neither one nor the other is right, he proposes, but both.

Lastly and most important, Montaigne concludes that the distance between men and women is not as great as the tradition of misogynistic literature would have us believe. "Il est bien plus aisé d'accuser l'un sexe, que d'excuser l'autre" (III, v, 897 B), he writes at the end of his long and subtle commentary on sex and sexuality, ridiculing those who, unable or unwilling to look at both sides of the question, praise or blame one or the other.[33] Montaigne's funda-mental contribution to the subject of the place of women in life and literature is far from negligible, inasmuch as he abandons the rhetorical prejudice which shaped the antithetical arguments of the *Querelle des femmes* and considers them in their own right, in the light both of his own experience and what others have had to say about them.

However, what was originally a scholastic exercise, alternatively praising or demeaning women, retains some of its fundamentally ludic propensities in "Sur des vers de Virgile." Mindful of the complexity of a problem compounded by centuries of discussion and debate, Montaigne appears more concerned with asking questions than providing answers. While he points out inevitable differences between men and women, most of which appear to be cultural, he remains convinced nonetheless of their natural equality. It is "l'institution et l'usage" which interest him especially, for in the subtle process of exception lies not only the real substance and essential matter of the *Essais* but also the fundamental principle of *embrouilleure*.

Can rhetoric assist us finally in assessing Montaigne's writing on women? What we know about his domestic life would seem to indicate that he had sufficient cause for some of his negative comments. When, however, he moves from the personal (where he undoubtedly had problems) to the general (where he is more circumspect), he transcends the prejudices of unilateral evaluation through the weighing and balancing procedures of the *Essais*. Rather than looking at only one side of the question, he compares one with the other, according to a strategy which is much more critical, prompted less by the art of persuasion than by experience with difference. Since his book, as he says, wrote him as he wrote it, it is as much a register of progress as of his past.[34] On the other hand, since writing allows him to express himself in generalities, it was possible for him to be more or even less tolerant towards women and marriage in the *Essais* than in the routine of his daily life. In this sense, the personal is both subsumed and displaced by the universal, giving it a decidedly rhetorical twist.

MARIE DE GOURNAY'S MONTAIGNE

Self-conscious autobiography became especially prevalent among women writers. Imperatively, they began to rewrite the prevailing Platonic-Petrarchan dialectic from within, parodying its conventions and inverting its hierarchy in order to arrange a place for the inscription of their own voice and viewpoint. Thus while Louise Labé and Pernette du Guillet were instrumental in obtaining the right for women to speak for themselves *in* literature, Marie de Gournay, as editor of the *Essais*, established their right to speak for themselves, with demonstrated knowledge and authority, *about* literature. Thinking and writing like Montaigne, she becomes his authentic interpreter, speaking for him and like him:

> Et parce que mon ame n'a de sa part autre maniement que celuy de juger et raisonner de ceste sorte, la nature m'ayant faict tant d'honneur que, sauf le plus ou le moings, j'étois semblable à mon Pere, je ne puis faire un pas, soit escrivant ou parlant, que je ne me trouve sur ses traces; et croy qu'on cuide souvent que je l'usurpe.[35]

In this capacity, she is the only woman in Montaigne's life whose voice we still hear, usurped or not.

In some respects, Marie de Gournay's literary career is decidedly marginal, formed and informed by her relation with Montaigne, part fact, part fiction. We will probably never know for sure who is the real author of the passage in hyperbolic praise of her future role on his behalf, but we do know that it first appeared in the 1595 edition of the *Essais*, therefore following Montaigne's death, and that it is marked by exceptional recourse to rhetorical overstatement ("certes aymée de moy beaucoup plus que paternellement," "l'une des meilleures parties de mon propre estre," "Je ne regarde plus qu'elle au monde," etc.) and syndetic number ("et . . . et . . . et"). While it is true that a certain lyrical effusiveness is characteristic of many of Montaigne's "alongeails,"[36] the one in praise of Marie de Gournay is disconcerting in its rewriting and regendering of his prior profession of friendship for La Boétie:

> J'ay pris plaisir à publier en plusieurs lieux l'esperance que j'ay de Marie de Gournay le Jars, ma fille d'alliance: et certes aymée de moy beaucoup plus que paternellement, et enveloppée en ma retraitte et solitude, comme l'une des meilleures parties de mon propre estre. Je ne regarde plus qu'elle au monde. Si l'adolescence peut donner presage, cette ame sera quelque jour capable des plus belles choses, et entre autres de la perfection de cette tres-saincte amitié où nous ne lisons point que son sexe ait peu monter encores: la sincerité et la solidité de ses moeurs y sont desjà bastantes, son affection vers moy plus que sur-abondante, et telle en somme qu'il n'y a rien à souhaiter, sinon que l'apprehension qu'elle a de ma fin, par les cinquante et cinq ans ausquels elle m'a rencontré, la travaillast moins cruellement. Le jugement qu'elle fit des premiers Essays, et femme, et en ce siecle, et si

jeune, et seule en son quartier, et la vehemence fameuse dont elle m'ayma et me desira long temps sur la seule estime qu'elle en print de moy, avant m'avoir veu, c'est un accident de tres-digne consideration.[37]

Is this a text by Montaigne or a pastiche of a text by Montaigne? In style and syntax, it reads like Montaigne, but its authenticity has been seriously challenged for a number of compelling reasons. First of all, it occurs neither in the original version of "De la praesump-tion" nor in any subsequent version published during Montaigne's lifetime. Nor does it appear in the extant manuscript additions of the *Exemplaire de Bordeaux*, even though there was sufficient marginal space on the page in question for Montaigne to have inserted it there.[38] Nor is there any concrete trace elsewhere of the "esperance" he is reported to have placed in Marie de Gournay and published "en divers lieux," except, of course, as she herself was to fulfill its promise in editing the *Essais*, an eventuality which only she was in a position to predict. Finally, although a variant reading of this passage appeared in her 1625 and 1635 editions, it seems highly unlikely that Montaigne himself would have written two separate versions of the same text, the original 1595 manuscript "alongeail" and a truncated revision, or that the original of both would have been lost.[39] Conversely, since we know that Marie de Gournay was the editor of the editions in which text and variant first surfaced, it seems likely that even if she had nothing to do with the original, she had something to do with its sequel. In any event, perhaps because she had already exploited much of the same material in praise of herself elsewhere, notably in the successive prefaces of her editions of the *Essais*, this second version is much more restrained and abbreviated:

I'ay pris plaisir à publier en plusieurs lieux, l'esperance que i'ay de Marie de Gournay le Iars ma fille d'alliance: & certes aymee de moy paternelle-ment. Si l'adolescence peut donner presage, cette ame sera quelque iour capable des plus belles choses. Le iugement qu'elle fit des premiers Essays, & femme, & en ce siecle, & si ieune, & seule en son quartier, & la bienueillance qu'elle me voüa, sur la seule estime qu'elle en print de moy, long-temps auant qu'elle m'eust veu, sont des accidents de tres-digne consideration.[40]

In addition to arguments already advanced against the authenti-city of these passages, some material and some circumstantial, there is the undeniable fact that Marie de Gournay was not above resorting to literary deception.[41] Thus, in 1624, under the title of

Remerciement au roy, she published a revised text of Ronsard's *La Harangue du Duc de Guise aux Soldats de Metz,* stating in her dedicatory "letter" to Louis XIII that she had taken it from a manuscript containing some twenty poems corrected by the author, whereas, in fact, it was she herself who had "corrected," that is modernized, his language according to seventeenth-century reformist prejudices, a subterfuge to which she later admitted and which Guillaume Colletet denounced as follows in his *Vie de Ronsard*:

A ce propos il faut que je dise que je n'ay jamais approuvé le bizarre dessein de Marie Le Jars de Gournay, qui avoit entrepris de corriger les plus nobles poésies de Ronsard, pour les adoucir, disoit-elle, et les accommoder à notre style. Et de faict elle eut la hardiesse de mettre les mains sur celles-cy et de les publier mesme, avec quelques autres oeuvres, précédées d'un advertissement par lequel elle donnoit advis au lecteur qu'elle avoit heureusement trouvé un exemplaire de toutes les oeuvres de Ronsard, revues et corrigées par l'autheur et de sa main propre; ce qui estoit absolument faux, comme elle me l'advoua elle-mesme, en me donnant cet eschantillon d'oeuvres corrigées.[42]

Marie de Gournay's defense of Ronsard's poetry and of Montaigne's prose seems to be dictated by a common, yet somewhat contradictory, editorial strategy. Thus in an attempt to defuse adverse criticism leveled by modernist theoreticians of Malherbe's generation, she resolved, on the one hand, to rejuvenate Ronsard's language, even envisaging the rewriting of the entire corpus of his works and, on the other, to print the *Essais* as they were written, arguing against altering or modernizing Montaigne's language in any way whatsoever. If then she was not above rewriting Ronsard's poem and passing her version off as his own, it is also possible that she could have drafted Montaigne's retrospective praise of her adolescent promise ("Si l'adolescence peut donner presage, cette ame sera quelque jour capable des plus belles choses"), providing thereby, with unexpected irony in a chapter dealing with various kinds of anticipation, one final example of presumption (*praesumere*: to anticipate).

Marie de Gournay's authorship of this addition seems all the more plausible when we remember that the *Essais* afford at least one other example of her penchant for editorial tinkering. In "Que le goust des biens et des maux depend en bonne partie de l'opinion que nous en avons" (I, xiv), Montaigne's manuscript reference to an encounter with an anonymous girl ("Mais, outre ce que je sçay en

avoir esté imité en France par aucuns, j'ay veu une fille . . .")
suddenly becomes self-referential in her 1595 edition ("Quand je
vins de ces fameux Estats de Blois, j'avois veu peu auparavant une
fille en Picardie"),[43] making it likely that she herself penned in this
reference to Montaigne's first visit. It is quite true that Montaigne,
despite an exceedingly full schedule of activities during the nine
months or so he spent in Paris, where he was occupied by a political
mission and a new printing of the *Essais*, found time to receive Marie
de Gournay with whom, upon her initiative, he had lately been in
correspondence, and that subsequently, when she returned with her
mother to Picardy, he visited them there, probably on more than one
occasion, remaining in all some three months.[44] Thus chronological
and geographical details concur to identify Marie de Gournay as the
"fille de Picardie" and commemorate her first meeting with Montaigne. But since it is equally true that this is another passage of
which there is no trace in the *Exemplaire de Bordeaux*, we are led to
suspect that it was added by the editor herself. Obviously, as *fille
d'alliance*, she must have felt she had the right and the obligation to
clarify Montaigne's text posthumously, and to appropriate a place
for herself in the margins of a book over which she was beginning to
exercise a veritable proprietary interest.[45]

Whether or not the addition is hers is not necessarily the point.
What is, however, is that whoever its author, this passage situates
Marie de Gournay in relation to Montaigne, conferring on her a
title which "presumes" and legitimatizes her as his worthy inheritor.
Thus the passage in "De la praesumption" assumes and answers the
principal questions addressed in her important and controversial
"Préface" to the 1595 edition of the *Essais*, in that it assures her and
her readers of Montaigne's express confidence in her ability to
interpret his works.[46] Moreover, in this preface, which contains an
exhaustive examination of the various criticisms leveled against the
Essais together with a preliminary treatment of many of the subjects
she was to develop in subsequent works, she proceeds to defend
Montaigne as a writer and herself as editor, anticipating and
precluding attacks on her qualifications as a woman for the critical
task she had undertaken:

Bien heureux es tu, Lecteur, si tu n'ez pas d'un sexe qu'on ait interdit de
tous les biens, l'interdisant de la liberté, et encores interdit de toutes les
vertus, luy soubstrayant le pouvoir en la moderation de l'usage duquel elles
se forment: affin de luy constituer pour vertu seulle et beatitude, ignorer et

souffrir. Bien heureux, qui peuz estre sage sans crime, le sexe te concedant toute action et parolle juste, et le credit d'en estre creu, ou pour le moins escouté. De moy, veux-je mettre mes gens à cet examen où il y a des cordes que les doigts feminins ne doivent, dit-on, toucher, ou bien, eussé-je les argumens de Carneades, il n'y a si chetif qui ne me r'embarre, avec solenne approbation de la compagnie assistante, par un soubsris, un hochet ou quelque plaisanterie, quand il aura dit: "C'est une femme qui parle."[47]

Marie de Gournay was certainly the first and probably the only professional woman writer in Renaissance France. As such, her literary activity was both varied and voluminous. First of all, she was a remarkably erudite and meticulous editor of the *Essais*, deciphering and transcribing thousands of manuscript corrections and additions in preparation for her monumental 1595 edition; appending a running subject repertory and a life of Montaigne in the 1608 edition; identifying the authors of Greek, Latin, and Italian quotations and compiling a comprehensive index of subjects and authors in the 1611 edition; locating the sources and translating into French the quotations in the 1617 edition and preparing a final, carefully revised edition in 1635, in which, upon the printer's request that she expand the 1625 incipient modernization of the text, she reluctantly added a significant number of controversial modifications and corrections, including perhaps the amended passage in praise of herself.

Her own works, collected in *L'Ombre de la Damoiselle de Gournay* (Paris: Jean Libert, 1626), expanded and retitled *Les Advis ou Les Presens* (Paris: Toussainct Du-Bray, 1634), comprise some forty different publications in various genres, including fiction, poetry, autobiography, critical prefaces, and erudite treatises on a variety of subjects, ranging from rhyme and diminutives to metaphors and grimaces, translations from Tacitus, Sallust, Ovid, Cicero, and Virgil, letters, and philological and feminist works, constituting a sustained publishing record as well as an impressively varied intellectual and literary career.

What is of immediate interest in the present context is her long relationship, both personal and professional, with Montaigne, whose name she contrived to associate with her own in the title of her first published work, *Le Proumenoir de Monsieur de Montaigne par sa fille d'alliance* (1594), a "psychological" novel written while she prepared the 1595 edition of the *Essais* and the long preface that introduced it, the plot of which has nothing to do with Montaigne at all.[48] If she named her book after him, it was in memory of their long walks during his stay at Gournay-sur-Aronde, and of a particular conversation between them in which he encouraged her to write down her version of a story she had read and recounted to him. In the dedicatory letter which accompanied the manuscript she sent to Montaigne three days after his departure, she reminds him of their "proumenoir" and asks him for corrections and reactions. The manuscript, unmarked and possibly unread, was found and returned to her after Montaigne's death in 1592, and what, if anything, he thought of it remains unknown.[49] Despite his apparent lack of interest or encouragement, she had it published at once with his name as part of the title, along with a letter in which she ascribes its origin to his influence.

As a young and unknown provincial autodidact recently entrusted with preparing the posthumous edition of the *Essais*, Marie de Gournay was certainly not oblivious of the promotional advantage of advertising her privileged relationship with Montaigne.[50] This perspective comes through most clearly in the *Proumenoir* and in those parts of the 1595 preface in which she relates the story of her discovery of the *Essais* and subsequent friendship with their author.[51] When, however, she proceeds to react to and assess the negative criticism afforded his work, she begins to establish her own authority as reader and editor, outlining a theory of literary reception and linguistic evolution which she articulates more fully in a series of later works, and with which her detractors continue to identify her.

The 1595 preface begins with an attempt to attribute the "froid recueil, que nos hommes ont fait aux *Essais*"[52] to the fact that it takes a great mind to recognize greatness and that great minds are few. The inadequacy lies not in the writer but in the reader, and Montaigne, to her mind, has not yet been well served, except initially by Justus Lipsius and now, implicitly, by herself.[53] In her systematic and spirited defense of Montaigne's style, she argues against those real and imagined "censeurs" who condemn his latinisms and neologisms, his Gasconisms and archaisms, his obscenities and obscurities, his metaphors and examples, and who would prune or otherwise "purify" his language. In this respect, she speaks for herself as editor, but also for Montaigne as an author who was convinced that words were only a means, however defective and insufficient, of representing things, and who reacted preemptively against anyone who would attempt to reduce his meaning to the immediacy of their expression:

Je sçay bien, quand j'oy quelqu'un qui s'arreste au langage des Essais, que j'aimeroye mieux qu'il s'en teust. Ce n'est pas tant eslever les mots, comme c'est deprimer le sens, d'autant plus picquamment que plus obliquement. Si suis je trompé, si guere d'autres donnent plus à prendre en la matiere, et, comment que ce soit, mal ou bien, si nul escrivain l'a semée ny guere plus materielle ny au moins plus drue en son papier.[54]

For her, consequently, exceptional words convey exceptional meanings, and their full and integral retention, despite lexical reduction, whether artificially or naturally induced, is both desirable and indispensable: "On ne peut representer que les conceptions communes par les mots communs. Quiconque en a d'extraordinaires doit chercher des termes à s'exprimer. C'est, au reste, l'impropre innovation qu'il faut blasmer et non l'innovation aux choses qu'on peut rendre meilleures."[55] While inspired by Montaigne, Marie de Gournay's linguistic philosophy is largely her own, prompted in great part by animosity towards the reformist tendencies of a new generation of writers and courtiers:

Or, à mesure que jardiner à propos une langue est un plus bel œuvre, à mesure est-il permettable à moins de gens, comme dict mon Pere. C'est à quelques jeunes courtisans, sans parler de tant d'escrivains, qu'il faudroit donner de l'argent pour ne s'en mesler plus, lesquels ne cherchent pas d'innover pour amender, mais d'empirer pour innover.[56]

Another objection raised by early critics which she addresses concerned Montaigne's self-portrait: "Or revenons, pour dire que la plus generalle censure qu'on face de nostre livre, c'est que, d'une entreprise particuliere à luy, son autheur s'y depeint."[57] It is hardly surprising that a century in which the *moi* was termed *haïssable* would find Montaigne's project reprehensible, but Marie de Gournay's reaction is partially a pretext for her own self-indulgence. Thus, for example, Montaigne's marginal note: "Ce n'est non plus selon Platon que selon moy, puis que luy et moi l'entendons et voyons de mesme"[58] becomes the principle by which she measures her own intellectual autonomy: "Et le seul contentement que j'euz oncques de moy-mesmes, c'est d'avoir rencontré plusieurs choses parmy les dernieres additions que tu verras en ce volume, lesquelles j'avois imaginées toutes pareilles, avant que les avoir veues."[59] Few writers of the day were more provocatively self-assertive, making her the brunt throughout her life of numerous satires and caricatural sketches; but it is precisely through her continuing defense of Montaigne and opposition to his detractors that she situates herself as an author, with a rhetoric and a purpose of her own.

It is undeniable that Montaigne had a great impact on Marie de Gournay's intellectual development, especially her conception of herself and her perceived role as an editor and future author. She herself attached the title of *fille d'alliance* to her first publication, but it is not entirely clear finally whether it was given by Montaigne or adopted by her in an attempt to further her own literary ambitions. What is obvious, however, is that in referring to him as father, she means to recognize her coming into print through his auspices.[60] But in praising him and his work while deprecating herself and her own, she effects a strategically critical difference between them:

Les Dieux et les Deesses donnerent leur langue à ce livre ou desormais ils ont pris la sienne[61]

Ce livre est en fin le throsne judicial de la raison ou, plus proprement, son ame; l'helebore de la folie humaine; le hors de page des esprits; la resurrection de la verité; le parfaict en soy-mesme et la perfection des autres[62]

Lecteur, n'accuse pas de temerité le favorable jugement qu'il a faict de moy, quand tu considereras, en cet escrit icy, combien je suis loing de le meriter.[63]

It is because of this play of distances that the *Essais*, it has been proposed, "serve her less as an inspiration than as an authorization to seek and gain her own voice."[64] Thus the story she narrates in her "Préface" has as its essential subject *her* discovery of the *Essais*, *her* realization of their profound originality and worth, *her* friendship with their author, and *her* authority as witness to his life and interpreter of his works. She alone had perfect knowledge of his great mind, leading her to conclude with final authority: "c'est à moy d'en estre creue de bonne foy."[65]

Ridiculed for her hyperboles, she disavowed her 1595 preface in a letter to Justus Lipsius scarcely a year after its original publication, replacing it in the 1598 edition with a second abbreviated preface of some ten lines. It reappears nevertheless, with deletions, additions, and revisions, in the 1599 edition of the *Proumenoir de M. de Montaigne*, as well as in the 1617 and 1625 editions of the *Essais*.[66] The final and definitive version in the 1635 edition is considerably more confident, orderly, and cohesive than the original 1595 text, less emphatically intimate and personal in its reference to her relationship with

Montaigne, no doubt indicating increased self-assurance in her own literary standing. For example, the exuberance of the passage in which she registers her initial reaction to the *Essais* in the 1595 edition:

On estoit prest à me donner de l'hellebore lors que, comme ils me furent fortuitement mis en main au sortir de l'enfance, ils me transsissoient d'admiration, si je ne me fusse à propos targuée de l'eloge que ce personnage leur avoit rendu dez quelques annees, m'estant monstré lors que je vis premierement leur auteur mesme, que ce m'est tant de gloire d'appeller Pere[67]

is significantly moderated in the 1635 version:

L'admiration dont ils me transsirent, lors qu'ils me furent fortuitement mis en main au sortir de l'enfance, m'alloit faire reputer visionnaire: si quelqu'un pour me ramparer contre un tel reproche, ne m'eust descouvert l'Eloge tressage, que ce Flamand en avoit rendu depuis quelques annees à leur Autheur mon Pere.[68]

More important, however, is the fact that most of the passages excised from the 1595 preface could be considered impressionistic and, as such, identified with an unsophisticated, uncritical, unscholarly woman. In removing comments which she may subsequently have considered too obviously gendered, Marie de Gournay may have wanted to present a less personal and more objective introduction to the *Essais*. In any event, in the so-called short preface of 1598 she apologizes for the weakness and effusiveness of the 1595 text, attributing her fervor, among other things, to youthful enthusiasm:

Lecteur, si je ne suis assez forte pour escrire sur les Essais, aumoins suis-je bien assez genereuse pour advouër ma foiblesse, et te confesse que je me retracte de ceste Preface que l'aveuglement de mon aage, et d'une violente fievre d'ame me laissa n'aguere eschaper des mains.[69]

Her retraction coincides perfectly with the self-criticism implied in the revamped version of the 1595 passage of praise, providing an additional indication that both were dictated by a similar intention to modify her public image in conformity with the increased independence of her literary career. No longer Montaigne's "fille d'alliance," she had become his "friend" as well as an author and authority in her own right.[70] Thus in her 1595 preface, she appropriates the argument that Montaigne, as La Boétie's friend, was able to interpret his intentions, to authorize her own right, as Montaigne's friend, to edit and interpret the *Essais*. Montaigne, of course, argued that friendship was reserved to men, but Marie de Gournay considered herself, as La Boétie's legitimate successor, an exception, rewriting herself into Montaigne's friendship and, consequently, his thoughts.

How, finally, does Marie de Gournay situate herself in relation to Montaigne? When she refers to him in the 1595 preface, she remains deferential, reminding her readers of her formation through him ("Je ne suis moy-mesme que par où je suis sa fille").[71] Montaigne is her "père" and, as his "fille d'alliance," she acquires a measure of self-expression and a means of public recognition.[72] Her strategy of association gradually becomes one of assimilation, authorizing her move from a purely filial, and therefore marginal, relationship to a more central and autonomous position. When irony surfaces in her depiction of those readers who have failed to understand Montaigne and his book, it reflects positively on her own astuteness. Thus, initial modesty gives way to pride in her self-proclaimed equality with Montaigne: "Toy et moy nous rendons l'un à l'autre, par ce que nous ne sçaurions si bien rencontrer ailleurs."[73]

The question which arises finally is whether Marie de Gournay becomes more like Montaigne, or whether Montaigne becomes more like Marie de Gournay. Clearly, in her prefaces, she authorizes herself, as Montaigne's friend and intellectual heir, to interpret him as she would want him to mean. This is initially apparent in the fact that she reads his failure to acknowledge receipt of the *Proumenoir* as an inducement to publish it in his honor. Furthermore, in her *Egalité des hommes et des femmes*, she rewrites a passage from "De l'affection des pères aux enfans" to support her profeminist argument. Whereas Montaigne states his position unequivocally:

Revenant à mon propos, il me semble, je ne sçay comment, qu'en toutes façons la maistrise n'est aucunement deuë aux femmes sur des hommes, sauf la maternelle et la naturelle, si ce n'est pour le châtiment de ceux qui, par quelque humeur fievreuse, se sont volontairement soubmis à elles (II, viii, 398),

she is convinced that he means otherwise:

Il lui semble, dit-il et si ne sait pourquoi, qu'il se trouve rarement des femmes dignes de commander aux hommes. N'est-ce pas les mettre en particulier à l'égale contrebalance des hommes, et confesser, que s'il ne les y met en général, il craint d'avoir tort?[74]

With her various remarks on Montaigne and the *Essais*, Marie de

Gournay effectively displaces the ordinary masculine reader, moving him to the periphery of her literary world, while bringing herself, the exceptional reader, to the fore. In this respect, she reinforces the revisionist tactics of Louise Labé and Pernette du Guillet, who, in reconfiguring Petrarchan and Neoplatonic dialectics, similarly replace the masculine with the feminine. Although their collective printed voices may be relatively small in volume (with the notable exception of Marie de Gournay's), they modify significantly the monopoly entertained heretofore by their male counterparts, marking their presence in the revival of learning and literature which followed the invention of printing. Marie de Gournay remains exceptional, however, in that she operates within a broader, less confining or constraining intellectual reality, measuring and asserting herself more in the world of ideas than in ideologies, more through textual or critical concerns than gendered reconfigurations.[75] Montaigne is the means by which she is able to breach traditional margins, becoming more herself through her long experience with the *Essais*. In a very real sense, she finally becomes the friend she claims to be, providing Montaigne with another, sometimes disparate, voice in his dialogue with himself and others.

CHAPTER 5

Sexual marginality

However incongruous the association between homosexuality and pornography may seem, the manner in which both are perceived and represented in early modern French texts affords a common discursive denominator. Not surprisingly, there are no first-person accounts of deviant sexual preferences or practices. When the subject arises, it is related by others, primarily in ecclesiastical, legal, or scientific texts, where it is treated as an example of the kind of anomaly which nature occasionally produces. Whereas the Renaissance gives gradual rise to the voice of women, it fails to provide homosexuals of either gender with an equivalent means of self-expression, consigning them consequently to the margins of medical treatises, courtly gossip, or private journals. Further, while there is evidence of increased curiosity about homosexuals, whatever printed records exist on the subject are dictated from without, with little or no input from those most directly involved, and we come to see and know them almost exclusively through the eyes of indiscreet or detached observers.[1]

The appearance in print of the sexual other will be viewed first in the context of contemporary cultural and civil expectations. For example, Brantôme and Montaigne demonstrate curiosity about all kinds of irregular erotic behavior, including lesbianism, cross-dressing, homosexual marriages and practices. Their writings on the subject are dissimilar in intent and scope, however. Brantôme, as we will see, tends to exploit homosexuality for its sensational appeal, encouraged partly by the curiosity of his patron the Duke d'Alençon; for Montaigne, homosexuality affords a number of examples, generally anecdotal in character, of human divergence and difference. Where they concur, however, is in their secular reading of areas of human conduct which previously had been confined to the jurisdiction of ecclesiastical or civil works and courts, making them available to the general public through the medium of the printed page.

This chapter on marginal sex and its figurations is divided into four somewhat unequal parts. The first reviews various ways of reading writings on homosexuality; the second, cross-dressing in the theatre; the third, the androgyne myth. The final part examines the way in which Brantôme and a number of Renaissance medical treatises present women, their sexual organs and orientation. Whereas the first three parts are concerned with the place afforded various accounts of marginal sexual behavior, the concluding one deals more specifically with the subtle but purposeful exploitation of sexual material in literary and medical discourses of the day for its pornographic and promotional appeal, affording thereby a radicalization of the misogynist issues which characterized the *Querelle des femmes* from its inception. Renaissance antifeminism finally loses the playfulness of its rhetorical coefficient and takes on a darker hue as its arguments are transformed into fantasies of a different kind, with the sensual pleasure of the sexually curious reader firmly in mind.

Whereas literary historians have long attempted to rewrite the Renaissance along political or confessional lines, delimiting the parameters of the supposed personal, religious, and ideological propensities of various authors, both canonical and marginal, social historians, more recently, have been especially concerned with ways of recovering and interpreting the language of sexual otherness, overt as well as covert, before the advent, or at least the coming into consciousness, sometime in the late nineteenth century, of homosexuality as it has come to be understood and defined today, that is, more with an eye to its social and political repercussions than its discursive beginnings and rhetorical underpinnings.[2] The pages that follow will address the problem of reading early modern writings on homosexuality within a contemporary cultural and literary context. Once again, more questions will be raised than answers given, with the express intention of suggesting that while much has already been said on the subject, there is still much more to learn.

READING HOMOSEXUALITY

The word "homosexuality" did not exist in French much before 1891 – only the idea of sexual inversion, usually described as sodomy.[3] Moreover, there was no equivalent word for homosexuality in classical, biblical, or patristic Greek or Latin. As a phenomenon, however, its unrecognized and largely unwritten history is considerably longer and better known. While neither ancient Greeks, Romans, nor Renaissance French acknowledged it as a condition distinct from heterosexuality, all three had names for persons who practiced same-sex acts, most of which, however, applied to men rather than women. They included, in Greek, *paiderastés, pallakós, kínaidos, paidophthóros*; in Latin, *cinaedus, catamitus, pathicus, pedicator, fellator, tribas*; in French, *pédéraste, sodomite, catamite, bougre, lesbienne, tribade.*

In order to recognize and, it is to be hoped, circumvent the problem of anachronism in discussing past perceptions of marginal sexual orientation, we need first of all to realize that equivalent words in the Renaissance lexicon were used rather loosely and must be read differently. What writers and readers of the day understood by sodomy, for instance, was any form of "abnormal" sex. Particular meaning attached to the word was determined not only by reference to classical and biblical antecedents, but also rhetorical codes and satirical strategies. The charge of sodomy was frequently leveled for political reasons and conveyed a polemical and cultural context with which the postmodern reader may no longer be sufficiently familiar.[4] Whereas today sodomy is associated with anal or sometimes oral sex, to the Renaissance reader it had also a much more general meaning, covering civil or religious transgression of almost any kind.[5]

On the one hand, even if historians, especially since Foucault, have attempted to show that past proscriptions of a set of sex acts perpetrated by individuals, collectively subsumed under the category of sodomy, were displaced in the nineteenth century by the perception that homosexuality is a way of being, Renaissance texts seem at times to obviate this neat chronology. In fact, already in the sixteenth century, homosexuality as a concept, if not a word, seems to have existed in the minds of those who wrote about it. Thus, for example, even though Brantôme, Erasmus, or Montaigne were not concerned explicitly with its nature and causes, they provide a number of examples of individuals whose sexual identity is expressed in a way which seems consistent with the current idea that homosexuality is a condition in nature.

Thus, in an extensive list of strange customs intended to illustrate his conviction that "les miracles sont selon l'ignorance en quoy nous sommes de la nature, non selon l'estre de la nature" (I, xxiii, 112 c),

Montaigne refers to "bordeaux publicz de masles, voire et des mariages" as "natural" in certain people and places (ibid., B); actual cases of them, as we will see later, he was careful to record in his *Journal de voyage*. Equally pointed is his reference to Aristotle's remark in the *Nichomachean Ethics* (VII, v) that "autant par coustume que par nature les masles se meslent aux masles" (I, xxiii, 115 C), an affirmation he neither confirms nor denies.[6]

On the other hand, Montaigne's allusion to strange customs and Aristotle's authority notwithstanding, homosexual acts were generally considered unnatural in Renaissance France and, as such, designated as unspeakable sins. As sins, moreover, they were viewed as a momentary stepping beyond or across the bounds of nature: rather than the inevitable consequence or expression of a particular nature, a kind of malady which comes and goes. This being the case, it is surprising that there is little or no scientific Renaissance writing on sodomy, especially since there is a fairly large body of literature on the origins, symptoms, and treatment of syphilis, as well as on the incommensurability of divine and human justice where disease is concerned.[7]

Homosexuality never obtained a similar scientific or literary forum. Confined to theological or legal texts, sodomites and lesbians are summarily dismissed as figures of evil and depravity, perpetrators of a sin subject to divine punishment, regardless of class. In literary or political tracts, their practices were viewed as aristocratic vices, imported from Italy, and denounced as signs of the kind of moral corruption which prevailed at the French Court, especially during the reign of Henri III.[8] The charge of sodomite or lesbian was usually ideologically motivated, and it was leveled, more or less indiscriminately, to compromise or discredit anyone with whom one disagreed, assembling a somewhat disparate company under its banner, including Louise Labé, Jeanne Flore, Marot, Rabelais, Muret, and, more insistently, Henri III himself, along with his so-called "mignons," Quélus, Maugiron, Joyeuse, Epernon, Saint-Mégrin, d'O, Saint-Luc, Livarot, Grammont, and Bellegarde.[9]

Despite biblical prohibitions and legal restrictions, Renaissance writings consider lesbianism less subversive than sodomy. Whether through prosthesis or tribadism, a woman, in the gendered discourse of the day, becomes masculine and, as such, is considered less objectionable than the person, male or female, who, through penetration or its simulation, plays the part of a woman. Lesbianism becomes problematic when, as in Brantôme's paradoxical framing of the question in his *Vie des Dames galantes*, it threatens the integrity of marriage, or, as in cases reported by Montaigne, when cultural injunctions come into play.[10]

If, in fact, Brantôme's discussion reflects the discourse of a culture rather than the idiosyncrasies of an individual, then lesbianism did not necessarily fall into the category of sin in the eyes and judgment of the Renaissance male. Sodomy was another matter, and Church and State were considerably less indulgent or tolerant towards its perpetrators, reading male homosexuality from a legal rather than a worldly perspective. While the traditional condemnation had its primary basis in the interpretation of the Sodom and Gomorrah story in Genesis 19:4–11, the strongest New Testament argument was derived from Romans 1:26, where it is described as *parà phúsin*, usually translated as *praeter* or *contra naturam*, "against nature." The Church taught that the repetition of such unnatural offenses had from time to time provoked God's wrath in the form of earthquakes, floods, or famines. It was taken for granted, therefore, by both ecclesiastical and civil law, that appropriate punitive steps should be taken to preclude the fate that befell the cities of the plain.

When therefore Erasmus, in his *Paraphrases on Romans and Galatians*, writes a gloss on the Pauline condemnation of same-sex relations as a wandering from the truth of God's intended purpose for human sexuality and punishment for failing to honor him properly, his interpretation reflects and translates prevailing civil and religious reactions.[11] Nonetheless he entertains a double standard, and according as his frame of reference is biblical or classical, his perspective differs sharply. When, for instance, he chooses Virgil's second eclogue in the *De ratione studii* to illustrate pedagogic method, and neglects to comment (except indirectly) on the quality or propriety of Corydon's desire for Alexis or, elsewhere, on Socrates' penchant for Alcibiades, except, in the latter case, as a means of confirming the demands and persistence of virtue, his exclusion of classical prototypes from his condemnation of homosexuality is troubling.

Because its sexual and social systems were different from his own, Erasmus seems to believe that Antiquity, and especially its literature, should not be judged by contemporary standards and values. Although pederasty was acceptable to Greeks and Romans when it occurred within certain normative parameters, teachers should be prepared to anticipate and deflect their pupils' attention from homosexual elements in their readings, providing them with general themes of a moral character as a key to interpreting their meaning.[12] Thus, if the essence of friendship is similarity, the teacher could argue that while the relationship between Corydon and Alexis may be exemplary of a certain type of friendship, it is nevertheless disorderly from the outset, not because it would be considered deviant according to Christian standards, but because dissimilarity in upbringing, class, education, age, and physical appearance (Corydon is from the country, Alexis from the city; Corydon is a shepherd, Alexis a courtier; Corydon is unlearned, Alexis is cultivated; Corydon is advanced in years, Alexis is a youth; Corydon is deformed, the latter is finely formed) makes it unnatural and unsuitable as a model.[13]

The idea of natural and suitable affection informs the language of Montaigne's reflections on friendship as well. In "De l'amitié" he is careful to point out similarities between himself and La Boétie in age, temperament, and career, while criticizing the disparity which typifies the classical system of same-sex relationships. Yet while he abruptly dismisses "cet' autre licence Grecque" in the original 1580 essay on friendship, he treats it at considerable length in a manuscript "alongeail." Thus his deliberations remained marginal in both senses of the word during his lifetime, causing recent critics to wonder if they translate into a belated admission of a covert relationship with La Boétie.

In fact, both the text of "De l'amitié" and the addition on Greek love are problematic. First of all, the original version of the essay displays chronological hesitations and inconsistencies which require analysis and reconciliation. But is this evidence, as some have thought, of Montaigne's attempt to dissimulate the true nature of his relationship with La Boétie, or a result of the intensity of the emotion he felt on first writing of his death? What is clear from a consideration of the A B C strata is that the most moving and personal passages were added later, once distance and memory entered into play, which is an understandable human and literary phenomenon. Victor Hugo's "4 septembre 1843," written to mark the date of Léopoldine's tragic accident, provides a comparable example of troubled silence. Originally reduced by the weight of present grief to a series of suspension points, his usual eloquence returns in "A Villequier," once the passage of time had converted the fact of his daughter's death into the theme of universal death. Similarly Montaigne, upon rereading his chapter, is more lyric in his memory of La Boétie and more emphatic in his desire to isolate their friendship from contamination with other, more ordinary kinds. It is then that he completes the reference to Greek love, the one most different from, yet most closely resembling, his own.[14]

There would thus seem to be no reason, despite a number of recent attempts, for interpreting Montaigne's addition as deceptive or self-incriminating. In the first place, it falls under the rewriting category of other "alongeails", informed here by his rereading of Pausanias' intervention in Plato's *Symposium*.[15] Secondly, it is justified, and perhaps motivated, by the flood of printed pamphlets directed at Henri III and his Court "mignons," which gave sudden notoriety to the subject. With both League and Protestant propagandists multiplying accusations of homosexuality, Montaigne would have realized that his original text might appear ambiguous. Thus, while in the 1580 essay he casually dismissed "cet' autre licence Grecque" as irrelevant, he described it at length some twenty years later in the changed and charged context print and politics had brought about, drafting an "alongeail" which differentiated it once and for all from the relationship he had known with La Boétie.

The Greek system of masculine love, Montaigne explains in his manuscript addition, was predicated on a crucial difference in age and social position:

[A] Et cet' autre licence Grecque est justement abhorrée par nos moeurs. [C] Laquelle pourtant, pour avoir, selon leur usage, une si necessaire disparité d'aages et difference d'offices entre les amants, ne respondoit non plus assez à la parfaicte union et convenance qu'icy nous demandons. (I, xxviii, 187 c)

Contrary to his relationship with La Boétie, who, as Montaigne informs us in another manuscript addition, was far from being handsome,[16] Greek friendship required physical beauty and sexual attraction, conditions which did not obtain in his friendship with La Boétie and to which a quotation from Cicero allows him to object: "*Quis est enim iste amor amicitiae? Cur neque deformen adolescentem quisquam amat, neque formosum senem?*" (I, xxviii, 187, c).[17] Another quotation, also from Cicero, underscores the necessity of intellectual compatibility, a quality which could be judged only once age and mind were fully formed and affirmed: "*Omnino amicitiae, corroboratis jam confirmatisque ingeniis et aetatibus, judicandae sunt*" (I, xxviii, 188 c). In multiplying differences between Greek love and his friendship with La Boétie, Montaigne's "alongeail" effectively counters any possibility of suspicion or confusion in the minds of his readers on a topic which recent events had politicized and sensationalized.

Although Montaigne condemns Greek love in this chapter, he shows himself to be considerably more tolerant and curious about irregular or controversial sexual behavior elsewhere in the *Essais*, even though his remarks always remain equally discreet. Not infrequently he entrusts to a Latin quotation the task of alluding to homosexual practices, either because the polite or learned words needed to describe them were not yet current in the French of his day (*pédérastie*, for instance, dates from 1581), or because he felt it more tasteful to express himself on such matters in a language reserved for the educated reader. At times, he extrapolates the contents of Latin quotations, irrespective of their original meaning, translating, as the occasion requires, homosexual allusions into heterosexual ones.

In "Sur des vers de Virgile," for example, he truncates a notoriously graphic passage from Juvenal, in which Nevolus complains that his master, whose lover he is, does not remunerate him sufficiently for his services: despite his huge penis, he is unable to make a living from it. Montaigne reproduces only that part of Juvenal's text which concerns those who, like himself, are able both to "se rendre aux efforts de l'amour, et ce neantmoins reserver quelque devoir envers le mariage," incorporating it into a larger commentary on Virgil's depiction of Venus' passionate display of love for her husband.[18]

Elsewhere, he takes a line from an epigram in which Martial evokes a number of pederastic fantasies:

> Mollia quod nivei duro teris ore Galaesi
>   basia, quod nudo cum Ganymede iaces,
> (quis negat?) hoc nimium est, sed sit satis; inguina saltem
>   parce fututrici sollicitare manu.
> levibus in pueris plus haec quam mentuia peccat
>   et faciunt digiti praecipitantque virum:
> inde tragus celeresque pili mirandaque matri
>   barba, nec in clara balnea luce placent.
> divisit natura marem: pars una puellis,
>   una viris genita est. utere parte tua

diverting it from its original homosexual context and personalizing it with the addition of *meae* to refer to his own sexual, presumably heterosexual, precociousness: "Et peut on marier ma fortune à celle de Quartilla, qui n'avoit point memoire de son fillage. *Inde tragus celeresque pili, mirandaque matri / Barba meae*" (III, xiii, 1087 B).[19]

Should one read Montaigne's reappropriation back into Martial's text and consider it as a veiled reference to his own youth, education, and times? Is there, as has been suggested, some allusion here to Marc-Antoine Muret, his professor and tutor at the Collège de Guyenne?[20] While it is true that Muret was notorious for his involvement with pupils and fled to Italy in 1554, ostensibly for this reason, it is not clear that his sexual proclivities had anything to do with Montaigne.[21] In the first place, Muret's reputation for pederasty postdates his brief tenure at Bordeaux, originating from public accusations, undoubtedly for political reasons, while he was professor at Toulouse and Paris. Admittedly, the alleged practice could have begun earlier, but this is merely speculation.[22] Nevertheless, Montaigne's attitude towards Muret is problematic. He omits his name from his list of preceptors in the 1580 version of "De l'institution des enfans," adding it in the 1582 edition of the *Essais* after their meeting in Rome at a dinner given by the French ambassador, where their discussion revolved harmlessly around the accuracy of Amyot's translation of Plutarch.[23] Thus there is much for conjecture but little that is actually compromising to be inferred from these allusions.

On the other hand, Renaissance reactions to homosexuality remain curiously ambivalent. Examples found in Greek and Latin texts were usually appreciated by humanist pedagogues according to classical principles, as we have seen in Erasmus. If and when they occur in a contemporary context, Christian concepts and criteria are brought into play. Several entries in Montaigne's *Journal de voyage* confirm a worldly, even a detached, amused perspective on such matters, dictated in great part by his interest in human behavior of every sort. The first occurs in his story of a woman, originally called Marie Garnier who, quite unexpectedly and accidentally, found "herself" to be a man, and was now known as Germain.[24] Montaigne recalls that Ambroise Paré, in his *Des monstres et prodiges* (1573), tells of seeing Germain, known by some as Germain Marie because she was called Marie as a child, but that he himself, on his circuitous way to Rome some years later, was only able to hear the story of *Marie la barbue*, as she was known familiarly, during a stopover at Vitry-le-François: "Nous ne le sceumes voir, parce qu'il estoit au village" (p. 7).[25]

In the revised version of the incident in "De la force de l'imagination," Montaigne claims, on the contrary, that his account is not based on hearsay, but that he had seen Germain in person: "Passant à Victry le Françoys, je peuz *voir* un homme que l'Evesque de Soissons avoit nommé Germain en confirmation, lequel tous les habitans de là ont cogneu et veu fille, jusques à l'aage de vingt deux ans, nommée Marie" (I, xxi, 99 B). Further, he deletes the journal reference to Paré and omits the nickname "la barbue" – details which were no longer essential to the point he wished to make in printed and public form, namely the role imagination played in such occurrences. Whereas the entry in the *Journal de voyage* is essentially the record of a "memorable" story, its reprise in the 1588 edition of the *Essais* serves to confirm and actualize a number of exemplary cases of sexual transformation: "Pline dict avoir veu Lucius Cossitius de femme changé en homme le jour de ses nopces. Pontanus et d'autres racontent pareilles metamorphoses advenües en Italie ces siecles passez."[26] After these "real" metamorphoses, Montaigne recounts Ovid's fiction of Iphis, who prayed her goddess mother to change her into a man so that she could consummate her love for Ianthe, quoting the line that Iphis the boy fulfilled the vow made when he was a girl: "*Vota puer solvit, quae foemina voverat Iphis*" (I, xxi, 98–9 A). In retelling Germain Marie's story immediately after Ovid's, Montaigne casts it in a different and more meaningful light, making it read like a wry commentary on classical myth or one of Joubert's "popular errors."

These instances of curiosity and speculation about genital organs and sexual change provide a marginal complement to more scientific deliberations on the matter. Medical and anatomical treatises, from the time of Galen until the Renaissance, maintained that the female genitals were simply the male organ inverted. Sexual experience was conceived to be the same in both; both were said to ejaculate during coitus, and female seed was deemed necessary for conception. A foetus was thought to develop into a male if the man's seed was dominant and generated enough heat to press the genital organs outward.[27] Many cases were recorded of women becoming men through the pressure of excitement or some great activity, as in the case reported by Montaigne; but the contrary, namely men turning into women, was thought to be impossible, the alleged transformation operating in only one direction, from female to male, towards gendered perfection,[28] a sexual teleology with which Montaigne's ironic conclusion to the story of Germain Marie seems to concur:

Ce n'est pas tant de merveille, que cette sorte d'accident se rencontre frequent: car si l'imagination peut en telle choses, elle est si continuellement et si vigoureusement attachée à ce subject que, pour n'avoir si souvent à rechoir en mesme pensée et aspreté de desir, elle a meilleur compte d'incorporer, une fois pour toutes, cette virile partie aux filles (I, xxi, 99 B).

There are two other accounts of sexual reorientation in the *Journal de voyage*, the first female, the second male, both of a voluntary nature this time rather than accidental. The first, in which transvestism and dildos play a role, concerns seven or eight women from around Chaumont-en-Bassigny who dressed as men. One of them came to live at Vitry under the surname of Mary, earning her living as a weaver, and became engaged to a woman from the town.[29] Because of some unspecified disagreement between them, their marriage did not take place. She then moved to Montirandet, continued her trade as a weaver, fell in love with another woman, married her, and lived four or five months with her, reportedly to their mutual satisfaction. Recognized by someone from Chaumont, brought to justice and condemned to be hanged, she said that she preferred to suffer death rather than become a woman once again. And she was hanged, Montaigne adds, "pour des inventions illicites à supplir au defaut de son sexe" (p. 6), implying that her condemnation was brought about, not because of lesbianism or transvestism, but for having had recourse to dildos, a crime punishable by death.[30]

Montaigne's final story concerning marginal sex is one which he heard at Rome. It concerns a strange confraternity, founded a few years before by a group of Portuguese men who initiated and entered into homosexual marriage, simulating the ritual of the sacrament of heterosexual marriage: "Ils s'espousoient masle à masle à la Messe, avec mesmes ceremonies que nous faisons nos mariages, faisoient leurs pasques ensemble, lisoient ce mesme evangile des nopces, et puis couchoient et habitoient ensemble" (p. 118).[31] His appreciation of the reasoning of the "clever people" who authorized this ceremony is obviously ironic:

Les esprits Romains disoient que, parce qu'en l'autre conjonction, de masle et femelle, cette seule circonstance la rend legitime, que ce soit en mariage, il avoit semblé à ces fines gens que cette autre action deviendroit pareillement juste, qui l'auroit de ceremonies et mysteres de l'Eglise. (p. 118)[32]

Eight or nine Portuguese of this "fine" sect, he concludes with equal irony, were eventually burned. Curiously, whereas a fair amount of the material contained in the *Journal de voyage* found its way into later editions of the *Essais*, this particular entry, despite its relatively sensational character, did not.

While historians are beginning to fill in the gaps retrospectively, detecting and deciphering covert signs of homosexual discourse in texts of the past, Montaigne's interest in such matters seems to have little to do with himself, except perhaps as a means for situating his own sexuality and defining his own ideas on love, marriage, and friendship for La Boétie. Nevertheless, his commentary indicates what kind of sexual behavior was considered noteworthy by both him and the people he encountered during his travels. Since he heard the first two stories at Vitry, and has nothing further to report from his stay there, it can be assumed, first, that they were repeated to visitors as a matter of course, thereby providing him and us with a glimpse into the cultural and sexual gossip of an early modern French village; secondly, that homosexuality, the sin too vile to be named, was nevertheless frequently discussed and committed; and lastly, that Montaigne, as well as his contemporaries, was curious about its practices and practitioners. His observations seem dictated by a conscious desire to collect and record anecdotes concerning various examples, both ancient and contemporary, of deviant behavior, and they continue to provide useful information for a study of sexual history and culture in early modern France. Nevertheless, his manuscript commentary and Latin quotations on Greek love are marginal, even marginalized, in relation to the primary body of the text, as are the anecdotes recorded in the *Journal de voyage* which, except for an occasional and much modified rewriting, remained confined to the periphery of the *Essais*. Montaigne may have felt that material fit for Latin or confidential notes was not necessarily fit for printing in French, which, in itself, is an indication either of personal or contemporary cultural preference and prejudice.

CROSS-DRESSING

In the scientific literature of the day, one is either a man or woman, and any combinations or variations of the two are feats or freaks of

nature. Medical and theological treatises stress this difference,
portraying women as less intelligent than men, less in control of their
passions, colder, more illogical, and so forth, justifying thereby a
whole range of demonstrations of male superiority and domination
over women. This distinction explains the disdain felt, in comments
on sodomy or lesbianism, for the "effeminate" partner, the one who
assumes the passive role, as well as awe of the hermaphrodite, a
"monster" of another kind, half woman, half man. A woman does
not become a man, or vice versa; but a man who was thought
originally to be a woman may finally prove to be a man. Sex is given,
but gender may be simulated, and the question which arises is
whether a boy or man could play a woman, in life or on the stage,
without producing gender anxiety or change in the minds of those
who recount or witness the event.[33]

French Renaissance authors regularly subvert the established
order of literary codes in order to represent marginal dress or
regender sexual mores. The *Description de l'isle des Hermaphrodites*, for
instance, recounts the progressive discovery and exploration of a
terra incognita, patiently described by a narrator who, like Alcofrybas
in Pantagruel's mouth, never ceases to wonder at the unfamiliarity of
the systematically reversed familiar he encounters on this strangest
of islands.[34] This anonymous satire of aristocratic dandyism affords
a striking example of rewriting the cultural signs of gender, language,
dress, gesture, manners, and morals, as required by the art of
depicting a man who is also a woman and for which there are no
adequate words in French:

> En ceste ruelle allerent les trois personnes que je disoy ci-dessus, &
> commencerent à invoquer ceste idole par des noms qui ne se peuvent pas
> bien representer en nostre langue, d'autant que tout le langage, & tous les
> termes des *Hermaphrodites* sont de mesmes que ceux que les Grammariens
> appellent du genre commun, & tiennent autant du masle que de la femelle
> . . ."[35]

Similarly, Louise Labé, acting and dressing like a man in arms,[36]
inspired by the gift of Apollo's lyre to sing of Lesbian love:

> Il m'a donné la lyre, qui les vers
> Souloit chanter de l'Amour Lesbienne[37]

seemingly invites Calvin's denunciation of her as a transvestite and
plebeia meretrix. In fact, her referents are Ariosto's Bradamante and
Catullus' Lesbia. Bradamante was a woman who dressed and fought

as a man and who vowed she would marry only the man capable of defeating her in combat; but Lesbia recalls Lesbos and its poet, whose reputation for homosexuality was already established in Antiquity. On the one hand, Labé means to locate in Sappho, whose work was first printed early in the sixteenth century, classical antecedent and authority for her own inspiration. On the other, she adapts the familiar asymmetrical model of intersexual love, involving desire on one side and indifference on the other, inverting the themes and metaphors of the prevailing Platonic-Petrarchan poetics to reflect and translate a feminine perspective.[38] Further, Ronsard, in imitating classical, especially bucolic, poetry, readily converts homosexual individuals and situations into heterosexual norms.

While the proper reception of a regendered literary text is relatively unproblematic insofar as the author is able to direct the reader's reaction, it is difficult for dramatists to anticipate the effect of transvestism on their immediate audience. It was an accepted convention for boys to play the part of women on the Elizabethan stage, but it is not certain that this was true in France. Who, for instance, played Cléopâtre in Jodelle's *Cléopâtre captive*, Amital and the Jewish Women in Garnier's *Les Juifves*, or Mary Queen of Scots in Montchrétien's *Reine d'Ecosse*? Were the roles attributed to women, men, or boys? If to men or boys, what was the effect of cross-dressing on the public? Did such practice feminize and eroticize the actors? Or was this looked upon as a plausible substitution in the theatre, much as it was considered an acceptable refinement at Court?

Stephen Orgel has argued that women were banned from the stage in the English Renaissance theatre, but that such was not the case in continental Europe.[39] To be sure, most Spanish companies included both women and transvestite boys at the end of the sixteenth century and beginning of the seventeenth; and women were members of French companies at the same time, playing the part of women in classical tragedies and comedies. However, there is no clear evidence that either was allowed on the stage in Renaissance France.[40] Historians have studied individual authors and plays for their sources, structure, and influence, but they have paid almost no attention to questions of casting and performance. The obvious and most immediate reason for this discrepancy is that while the texts themselves exist, there are few contemporary references to the circumstances of their production. Exceptionally, we have Estienne Pasquier's statement that Jodelle's *Cléopâtre captive* and *La Rencontre* were successfully played before an illustrious audience, first at the Hôtel de Rheims, then at the Collège de Boncourt. He says little about the actors however, but what little he says is troubling:

Cette comedie et la Cleopatre furent representées devant le Roy Henry à Paris en l'hostel de Reims, avec un grand applaudissement de toute la compagnie, et depuis encore au college de Boncourt, où toutes les fenestres estoient tapissées d'une infinité de personnages d'honneur, et la cour si pleine d'escolliers que les portes du college en regorgeoient. Je le dis comme celuy qui y estois present, avec le grand Tornebus en une mesme chambre. Et les entreparleurs estoient tous hommes de nom: car mesme Remy Belleau et Jean de La Peruse jouoient les principaux roullets.[41]

If, as Pasquier reports, the actors were all men of renown, and if Belleau and La Péruse played the principal roles along with Jodelle, how were they distributed? The masculine parts are L'Ombre d'Antoine, Octavian, Séleuque, Proculée, and Agrippe. Inasmuch as L'Ombre is alone on the stage in Act I, Octavian, Agrippe, and Proculée in Act II, Octavian and Séleuque in Act III, and Proculée in Act V, the same actor could have played more than one character. On the other hand, there are no male characters in Act IV and the "principaux roullets" of *Cléopâtre captive* are, without question, Cléopâtre herself, Octavian, and, finally, either Agrippe or Proculée. Who then played Cléopâtre or the other female parts, namely Eras, Charmium, and the Chorus of Alexandrine Women?[42] Is it possible, as would seem to be the case, that there were no women in this original production of the first classical tragedy in France, and that all of the roles were interpreted by men?

Gillian Jondorf has speculated on the presence and placement of the Chorus on the stage, but she says nothing about the gender of its participants. She suggests that the Chorus may have come on to replace the Shade with which the play begins, marking the shift from the supernatural to the human level; but she has nothing to say about Pasquier's claim that all of the *entreparleurs* in the cast were men of renown. Can we assume that by *entreparleurs*, Pasquier meant only the principal actors, and that consequently the Chorus could have been made up of women or, perhaps, boys? Since he is not specific on this point, we can only conclude that either there were no women, as his words imply, or if there were, it must have seemed sufficiently natural to him not to require notice or comment. In either case, his silence has broad implications, both for the history of the early French theatre and for the role gender played in its organization and development.[43]

Much has been made recently of Stephen Gosson's 1579 observation that the theatre "effeminates" the mind, that boy actors who wear women's clothing literally "adulterate" male gender. Furthermore, and seemingly in conjunction with this anxiety, there followed a series of antitheatrical pamphlets expressing the belief that costume defines its wearer. "Garments are set down for signes distinctive betwene sexe and sexe," writes Gosson, reiterating Deuteronomic prohibition against cross-dressing.[44] Although historians have been prone to read these caveats as proof of the fear that a boy or man who played the part of a woman could actually be turned into a woman, that the theatre, in its reliance on boy actors, is no more than a forum for male homosexuality, they would seem to be concerned less with a loss or change of gender identity than with the traditional question of the possible or potential effects of imitation on actor and audience.[45]

Plato had argued in the *Republic* that poetry has a terrible power to corrupt and that dramatists, in order to win a popular reputation, tend to exploit material that is unstable and provocative. When therefore we hear Homer or one of the dramatists representing the suffering of a great man and making him lament at length, we allow ourselves to be carried away by our feelings. Impersonation requires that author and actor enter into the character speaking, think the same thoughts and feel the same emotions. Indulgence in any form of literature leaves its mark on our moral nature, affecting not only the mind but also physical poise and intonation. It is for this reason that Plato will not allow his guardians to take the parts of women, young or old (for they are men), nor to represent improper behavior or words.[46]

In France, there would seem to have been no equivalent apprehension, and the 1548 decree banning the performance of *mystères* by the Confrérie de la Passion was brought about by the unruliness of the audience and the intrusion of the profane into the sacred. There is no mention of male youths playing female parts, nor is there any condemnation of the theatre on moral grounds, with the notable exception of Calvin's Geneva, until Bossuet's notorious dispute with Caffaro or Rousseau's *Lettre d'Alembert sur les spectacles*. Here we have to deal with the unwritten history of the French stage, with problems of casting and performance which remain outside of the printed record. Based on available information, it is impossible to know whether silence indicates shame or lack of concern; but is does point out a lacuna in a crucial area of dramatic and cultural history.

THE ANDROGYNE MYTH

On the other hand, the ideal of sexual and cultural harmony promoted by Plato's myth of the androgyne, that enigmatic figure both uniting and distinguishing masculine and feminine, is revived by Ficinian Neoplatonists and propagated by writers as diverse as Marguerite de Navarre and Montaigne, finding its earliest literary expression in Rabelais's chapter on how the infant Gargantua was dressed. After a systematic description of various items of apparel,[47] Rabelais turns to the emblem portrayed on Gargantua's extravagant golden medallion:

Pour son image avoit en une platine d'or pesant soixante et huyt marcs, une figure d'esmail competent: en laquelle estoit pourtraict un corps humain ayant deux testes, l'une virée vers l'aultre, quatre bras, quatre piedz, et deux culz telz que dict Platon *in Symposio*, avoir esté l'humaine nature à son commencement mystic. Et au tour estoit escript en lettres Ioniques

ΑΓΑΠΗ ΟΥ ΖΗΤΕΙ ΤΑ ΕΑΥΤΗΣ.[48]

The prolonged debate this passage has generated revolves essentially around the purported interrelation between image and motto. Most readers view it as a serious representation of Renaissance syncretism, with the pagan myth of Eros assimilated and remotivated by the Christian ideal of Charity or Love. Others have interpreted it as a humorous rewriting of Aristophanes' already humorous description of our original nature in Plato's *Symposium*.[49] Still others argue that it explains the genesis of homosexuality.[50] In any case, it would seem that Rabelais was the first to reappropriate Plato's passage in Renaissance France and, even more significant, that his reading of it is decidedly idiosyncratic.

Whereas the figure Plato's Aristophanes depicts is a circular being with four hands and four legs, two faces (identical in every way) on a circular neck, with a single head for the two faces which looked in opposite directions, four ears and two sets of genitals, the figure Rabelais's Alcofrybas describes, with two heads turned toward one another, four arms, four feet, two rumps, and, significantly, no genitals, is a much more abbreviated, even truncated, being. As a comic rewriting of Plato's text, it is relatively coherent, but its allegorical relation to the motto from Paul's first epistle to the Corinthians is not immediately evident. In the first place, it is already difficult to reconcile Plato's self-seeking halves with Paul's idea of "Charity which seeketh not its own." Calvin, in his *Commentary* on Paul's epistle, infers how very far we are from having Charity implanted in us by nature, for we are naturally prone to have love and care for ourselves, and aim at our own advantage.[51] How then would Rabelais's readers have understood Paul's Charity, which supposedly "non quaerit sua ipsius," when it is rendered with two heads turned one towards the other, fixed therefore seemingly in solipsist contemplation? Viewed separately, image and motto are coherent; juxtaposed, they are contradictory, perhaps purposely so, creating a composite and ludic image.

Originally, Aristophanes claims in the *Symposium*, our nature was by no means the same as it is now. In the first place, there were three kinds of human beings: not merely male and female as at present, but a third kind as well, which was a combination of these two. Its name has survived, he adds, though the phenomenon itself has disappeared. This single combination, comprising both male and female, was, in form and name alike, hermaphrodite. Now, he concludes, it survives only as a term of abuse. Their separation, and division into male and female entities by Zeus in punishment for pride and arrogance in attempting to overthrow the gods, is intended to recount – and account for – the origin and subsequent development of sex and sexuality, as the etymology, the "true meaning" of the word "sex" confirms,[52] since, although cut apart by Zeus and reconfigured by Apollo, the two halves immediately sought to come together once again and reform the lost perfection of their circular whole.

Aristophanes' speech on the origin of human nature has some elements that are obviously derived from Empedocles' account of the formation of the cosmos, in which he pictures the primeval monsters which peopled the world before Charity or Love entered into it to create an ordered universe out of the turmoil brought about by Strife.[53] His bisexual or asexual creatures, like Aristophanes' double creatures, are similarly split apart into men and women as a result of their sin against the gods.[54] In general, the underlying idea in Aristophanes' speech is that Love is not simply an immediate delight, as the other speakers of the *Symposium* suppose, but a desire that can find complete fulfillment only beyond the present world. This idea is basically Empedoclean, though it belongs to the whole Greek world from which he drew his religious inspiration. In this sense, Gargantua's motto, with its informing closure of Christian Love, becomes consistent with the symbolism implied by the double creature of pagan cosmology, suggesting the desired emergence of order from chaos.

Not unexpectedly, however, Rabelais's image is significantly different from Plato's. Mystifying rather than mystical, it affords an example of the way in which he rewrites and displaces classical texts. With two heads turned toward one another, four feet, and two rumps, it may be suggestive of erotic sameness or ideal sexual harmony; it is difficult to imagine, however, that it represents copulation, either homo or hetero.[55] On the contrary, without genitals, it is genderless as well as sexless. Thus, despite reference to Plato, Rabelais's figure is not properly Platonic, nor even androgynic.

Could it be Ovidian and hermaphroditic? Whereas Plato's being is conjoined in body and separate in sex, Ovid's hermaphrodite, according to Alcithoë's story in Book 4 of the *Metamorphoses*, is the result of a violent and mutilating merging of the two sexes into a new body, neither fully masculine nor fully feminine.[56] The son of Hermes and Aphrodite, whose joined names he bore, came one day upon a pool of crystal-clear water called Salmacis, the abode of a nymph of the same name. She happened to be gathering flowers nearby, and when she saw the boy, she longed to possess him. But when she attempted to seduce him, she was rejected. Pretending to depart, she waited in hiding until he, charmed by the inviting waters, undressed and dived into the pool. Casting off her clothing, she plunged in after him and embracing him tightly, prayed to the gods that they might never be separated. The gods heard her prayer, and their two bodies were merged into one, with one face and form for both. When the son of Hermes and Aphrodite saw that he had become but half-man, he asked his parents to grant that, henceforth, anyone who went into this pool as man be similarly transformed, thereby explaining the origin of the evil reputation of the fountain Salmacis, believed to render soft and weak all men who bathed in its enervating waters, and of the hermaphrodite, the man-woman.

Early modern medical literature did not distinguish between the androgyne and the hermaphrodite. Thus in a chapter on the subject in his *Des Monstres et prodiges*, Ambroise Paré writes that "les hermafrodites ou androgynes, sont des enfans qui naissent avec double membre genital, l'un masculin, l'autre feminin."[57] Since the two coexist within the same body, some of them, he explains, through mutual and reciprocal use, take their pleasure first with one set of sex organs and then with the other, because they have the natures of man and woman suitable to such an act. But Rabelais's spherical, sexless figure is different from Plato's "man-woman," who possessed both sexes, and from Ovid's Hermaphroditus, who, no longer man or woman, merged both into one.

Lucretius, on the other hand, in his account in *De rerum natura* of the origin and development of vegetable and animal life, describes a similarly sexless "man-woman":

> multaque tum tellus etiam portenta creare
> conatast mira facie membrique coorta,
> androgynum, interutrasque nec utrum utrimque remotum[58]

who, lacking "those instruments whereby the females with male can unite" ("feminaque ut maribus coniungi possit." v. 853), and unable therefore to propagate, are condemned from the outset to death and disappearance, clearing the way for the development, as Empedocles had argued, of harmony out of strife. Although reminiscent of Lucretius' primeval sports of nature, the image on Gargantua's medallion is a composite creature of Rabelais's own invention, designed to symbolize and prefigure the spiritual and intellectual unity which culture and civilization will eventually impart to Gargantua, the predestined victor of the Picrocholine war and founder of the Abbey of Thélème. With two heads turned toward one another in sexless, selfless contemplation, it is consistent finally with the idea of Pauline Charity, "which seeketh not its own," while confirming the Platonic idea that love which seeks its own is contrary to the nature of love. Love which has found another does not need to look elsewhere for fulfillment, physical or spiritual, in Rabelais, Plato, or Paul. Thus Gargantua's androgyne is neither properly sexual nor homosexual, but rhetorical, designed to be read as a figure of peace and harmony.

The truly androgynous or hermaphrodite creature, at least in the literary and political imagination, emerges more distinctly in the polemically inspired depictions of Henri III, "roi femme" or "homme reine," as D'Aubigné would have it, and his circle of favorites and friends:

> Non les hermaphrodits, monstres effeminez,
> Corrompus, bourdeliers, et qui estoyent mieux nez
> Pour valets des putains que seigneurs sur les hommes . . .[59]

In fact, accusations of sodomy and homosexuality were part of the repertory of political satire throughout the Renaissance and especially at the time of the League. So much so in fact that Henri III's reputation for monstrous dress and sexual behavior, fueled by conservative Catholic and reactionary Protestant pamphlets, entered into legend before it became history.[60] His favorites have not fared much better. The entry *mignon* in the *Dictionnaire Robert* reads: "*Les mignons d'Henri III*, favoris du roi, très effeminés." The charge of effeminacy, however, distorts the true meaning of *mignon*. From its introduction into French in the middle of the 15th century, *mignon* designated a "serviteur des Grands" or "homme de Cour en faveur auprès de son maître," without any pejorative connotation whatever, and such was the real status of Henri's so-called *mignons*.[61]

Much of D'Aubigné's satire is directed against the dress of Henri and his Court, as if clothing rather than behavior translated the nature and affected the ability of its wearer to rule or to fight. In the *Tragiques* as well as in the *Confession du sieur de Sancy*, he presents and interprets the extravagant dress and manners of king and courtiers as transparent signs of effeminacy and corruption. But when he reports that Henri de Navarre and the duc de Guise "couchoyent, mangeoyent, et faisoyent ensemble leurs mascarades, balets et carousels,"[62] he draws no negative conclusion from their physical promiscuity. It was common of course in Renaissance France for men to share the same bed, and the rank or distinction of the person with whom one slept provided an indication of the degree of favor, that is, of social or political intimacy, which one enjoyed with one's betters or suitors. Moreover, when men kissed and embraced in public, it was a sign of friendship that was familiar and acceptable to Renaissance eyes and minds.[63] But refined dress and manners were another matter, at least in the eyes of military men in the closing years of the sixteenth century.

It is not to be denied that Henri III's behavior was in no way designed to modify or dispel the rumors that circulated about him, and that his enemies, both Protestants and Leaguers, found in his and his favorites' notoriously elaborate dress, perfumes, and cosmetics, their affected manners and language, ready material for their attacks which, in the main, were directed towards illustrating their immorality and questioning their virility – and therefore their unsuitability for the positions they held.[64] Jules Quicherat, in his *Histoire du costume en France,* gives a detailed description of the King's vestimentary extravagances compiled, one can only assume, from various prints and paintings of the time:

> Il avait un goût invincible pour tout ce qui était le propre des femmes, à ce point que pas une des nouveautés qu'il introduisit dans le costume ne lui vint d'autre part que de ses études sur la garde-robe de la reine; car c'était là une chose qu'il connaissait mieux que toutes les dames d'atour réunies.
> . . .
> Il rejeta les chausses bouffantes pour n'en porter plus que d'étroites, taillées et froncées comme les caleçons des femmes. Il prit les chapeaux d'homme en horreur, jusqu'à les bannir absolument du Louvre; et il les remplaça par un bonnet à aigrette, calqué sur l'escoffion des dames du règne précédent
> . . .
> Pour les bijoux il avait une faiblesse plus que féminine. Il en achetait toujours, et il ne les avait pas plutôt, qu'il s'ingéniait à trouver d'autres façons de les monter . . . Il fit triompher la mode des boucles d'oreilles, qui était commune aux deux sexes de l'autre côté des Pyrénées.[65]

Quicherat's depiction concurs with a number of contemporary accounts, such as one in L'Estoile's *Journal*; but, surprisingly, there is no attempt on his or their part to explain the origin or the reasons of this extraordinary, even revolutionary change in dress and taste, nor to reconcile the reported effeminacy of the clothing and conduct of the King and his *mignons* with the documented record of their conquests in love and war.[66] Rightfully, one can only suspect a prejudice motivated by political and confessional antagonism, but heightened and compounded by marked hostility to foreign fashions and tastes.

Whereas the Court was increasingly under the influence of Italian, particularly Florentine, ideas of dress and good breeding, an earlier, more provincial generation, accustomed to the rudimentary exercises of hunting, jousting, and military encounters, remained essentially conservative, even reactionary in its ideas of personal hygiene and acceptable clothing. Thus the opinion, promulgated by D'Aubigné and other detractors of the monarchy, both Catholic and Protestant, that life at Court sapped the physical stamina and military skills expected of the nobility was rejected summarily by

Brantôme who, not unexpectedly, found no incompatibility whatsoever between the two.

A gallant man, according to him, is versatile, able at once to appreciate the leisure and pleasure of Court and the rigors of the battlefield:

car, quand tout est dict, je voudrois bien sçavoir que nuist à un homme de guerre d'aymer la court, d'aymer les gentillesses, d'aymer les dames et tous autres beaux plaisirs et esbattemens qui y sont? Tant s'en faut, que je croy, et l'ay ainsi veu et tenir à des plus gallans, qu'il n'y a rien qui doive plus animer un homme de guerre que la court et les dames.

Recalling the criticism of an older generation of soldiers:

Ah! ce sont des mignons de court, des mignons de couchette, des fardez, des pimpans, des douilletz, des frisez, des fardez, des beaux visages. Que scauroient-ilz faire? Ce n'est pas leur mestier d'aller à la guerre: ils sont trop delicatz, ils craignent trop les coups,

he counters that they are the gallant men

qui se sont battuz si bravement en combatz singuliers, et les ont mis si honnorablement en usage. Ce sont eux qu'à la guerre ont esté les premiers aux assaulz, aux batailles, et aux escarmouches et que, s'il y avoit deux coups à recevoir ou donner, ilz ne vouloient avoir un pour eux, et mettoient la poussiere ou la fange à ces vieux capitaines qui causoient tant.[67]

Finally, the metamorphosis of the androgyne, first from a rhetorical to a sexual, generally caricatural figure, and later to a medical phenomenon, represents a turning point in its connotative history. No longer a curious, but noble classical symbol, it becomes a grotesque deviant in political propaganda, then a monster or freak of nature in the writings and illustrations of medical textbooks. Since the figure remains the same but its meaning varies, it has produced a number of different readings. Cultural historians have tended to pay more attention to political and ideological implications than to rhetorical or literary specificity, but the polemics of gender would seem to have little to do with either marginal subjects in the texts under review, whether misogynistic or homosexual, or the way in which they should be read. Generally speaking, there are many more words than things in these writings, more discursive display and posturing than philosophical or scientific reasoning. On the other hand, it is culturally significant and relevant that authors of the day increasingly identify gender with dress and manners, making it inevitable and seemingly legitimate, through outward signs, to distinguish and ridicule sexual marginalities. Furthermore, it is equally clear that printers gradually come to realize the potential commercial value of sexual exploitation in the books they choose to publish, making their proper reading unexpectedly problematic.

BRANTÔME, MEDICAL DISCOURSE, AND THE MAKINGS OF PORNOGRAPHY

While printing facilitated the spread of culture, the culture it spread was affected in turn by print. Thus as writers and their works become increasingly subject to the economic realities of the market-place, sexuality acquires a decidedly pornographic cast. In response to a perceived demand from a wider and more worldly reading public, publishers begin to replace works in Latin on such scientific or pseudo-scientific topics as human reproduction, venereal disease, lesbianism, hermaphrodism, and erotic melancholy with more accessible versions in the vernacular. In this sense, Laurent Joubert's *Traité des erreurs populaires*, Ambroise Paré's *Des Monstres et prodiges*, Jacques Duval's *Traité des hermaphrodites, parties génitales, accouchemens des femmes*, or Jacques Ferrand's *Traité de l'essence et guérison de l'amour ou De la mélancholie érotique* share rhetorical strategies with Rabelais's *Gargantua* and *Pantagruel*, Marguerite de Navarre's *Heptaméron*, Montaigne's *Sur des vers de Virgile*, or Brantôme's *Les Dames galantes*, in playing to the sexual curiosity and erotic sensibility of an ever larger body of potential readers, both male and female.[68]

In literary texts dealing with deviant sexual practices, a curious or prurient stance prevails, as though authors and printers alike were determined to exploit the potential appeal of such novel and sensational material to attract the attention of the ever-expanding reading and buying public. Thus, while accusations and instances of sodomy are common and relatively conventional in Renaissance civil, religious, and polemical writings, they are characteristically succinct, limited to facts or names. References to lesbianism, on the other hand, are extensively detailed, even pornographic, in response no doubt to masculine curiosity about the subject. In *Les Dames* (baptized *galantes* by the Dutch Sambix, his first editor),[69] Brantôme writes about lesbianism at length, detailing its history and practices more fully and plainly perhaps than any other writer of the day – ostensibly in answer to the unusual, and fundamentally rhetorical, question whether two women who are in love with one another, as has happened in the past and is often seen now, sleeping together in

one bed and doing what is called *donna con donna* (imitating in this
that learned poetess Sappho of Lesbos) can commit adultery and,
between them, cuckold their husbands.[70] The pretext for Brantôme's
inquiry may have to do with perennial misogynistic doubts about the
fidelity of women, but his presentation shows him to be much more
interested in describing lesbianism as a common, yet relatively
unexplored, social and sexual phenomenon.[71] Although he concludes that, in most instances, lesbianism is resorted to only as an
expedient substitute for heterosexual congress, he intimates that
lesbians, more generally speaking, constitute a race apart, with their
own sexual preferences, practices, and history.

In keeping with customary Renaissance methods, Brantôme
begins his inquiry with reference to classical authority, quoting
Martial's epigram to Bassa, a woman who, because men were never
seen to visit her, had acquired a reputation for chasteness. It was
soon discovered however that she was constantly welcoming beautiful women and girls, with whom she assumed a masculine role,
leading Martial to conclude, seemingly paradoxically, that here,
where there was no man, still there was adultery: "Hic, ubi vir non
est, ut sit adulterium."[72]

Brantôme then gives other examples of women who, even after
they were married, continued their lesbian practices, quoting Lucian
to the effect that those who devote themselves to other women are
called tribads, from the Greek, and, in Latin, *fricatrices*, that is, those
who rub one another.[73] After reference to the authority of Antiquity,
he moves from contemporary Italy, where lesbianism was said to be
common in aristocratic circles, to France, with a number of anecdotes designed to illustrate how women are able to make love
together. What emerges from these pages is that while men were
being denounced and prosecuted for sodomy, lesbianism and tribady
were openly acknowledged and tolerated at Court.

After recounting a number of incidents and examples, Brantôme
alludes to different means by which lesbians obtain mutual satisfaction: "les unes par fricarelles, et par (comme dit le poete) *geminos
committere cunnos*. Cette façon n'apporte point de dommage, ce disent
aucuns, comme quand on s'ayde d'instruments façonnez de . . . ,
mais qu'on a voulu appeler des *godemichis*."[74] Whereas Montaigne
expresses distaste for such "unnatural" devices and reports instances
of capital punishment incurred by their rural users, Brantôme
mentions them almost casually, as if they were inevitable concomi-

tants of courtly lesbianism. Anxiety about the fidelity of women, on the other hand, does seem to concern him. In fact, his preoccupation with cuckoldry betrays a conventional masculine mentality towards woman and marriage.

Conceding that many of the women who engage in homosexual acts are deprived of the company of men, Brantôme contends that there are some who refuse to have anything at all to do with men, even when and if the chance and opportunity arose, leading him to distinguish between habitual, bisexual, and occasional lesbians. As an example, he recounts how Louis-Béranger du Guast and he, upon reading one day in a little Italian book by Agnolo Firenzuola,[75] fell upon a passage saying that women were made by Jupiter so that some are set to love men, but others the beauty of one another. These, he adds, "de nature haïssent à se marier, et fuyent la conversation des hommes tant qu'elles peuvent."[76] Such was Sappho herself, he concludes, the mistress of them all, who, nevertheless, in later life, according to the legend entertained and developed by Ovid in his *Heroides*, fell in love with Phaon, as yet a somewhat ambiguous youth sexually – "nec iuvenis nec iam puer" (xv 93), and reproached herself for the feelings she formerly held for women – "non sine crimine amavi" (xv 19).[77] Sappho's example provides Brantôme with confirmation of his theory that husbands should not make the mistake of tolerating lesbianism on the grounds that it is less dangerous than adultery because women, as her case demonstrates, can become dissatisfied with other women and turn eventually to male lovers, thereby making them cuckolds.

Even though Sappho may have wavered in her lesbianism, this is not always the case of the "gallant" women in Brantôme's annals. Thus he recounts an anecdote about a gentleman who, desiring one day at Court to seek in marriage a certain lady, consulted one of her relations as to the likelihood of his success. She told him quite frankly that he would be wasting his time, for a lady whom his chosen beloved knew would never allow her to marry. Instantly realizing what this meant,[78] the gentleman thanked her for her good advice, but not without accusing her of speaking from self-interest, since, he remonstrated, she also enjoyed the lady surreptitiously from time to time.

What emerges from Brantôme's account is, first of all, that lesbianism was far from being an isolated phenomenon, and, secondly, that it provoked more curiosity – erotic, even prurient –

than anxiety or indignation in him or his contemporaries. Of course, Brantôme's idea of lesbianism is informed by classical authors and authorities (here Martial and Juvenal) rather than religious or legal thinking; and it echoed a popular view of female sexuality within a society which punished sodomy and adultery while admitting lesbianism, provided it did not attempt to legitimatize itself through same-sex marriage. The fact remains that allusions to marginal sex and descriptions of its practices were exceedingly rare at the time, which accounts in part for the huge success Brantôme's work was to enjoy when it was finally published.

Brantôme was not unaware of the popular appeal of the subject matter of his work on "gallant ladies," anticipating that printers would have no difficulty in selling it and that readers would be eager to buy it. Thus, in recounting the story of Pietro Aretino's success, he could easily have been reflecting on his own:

J'ai cogneu un bon imprimeur venetien à Paris, qui s'appeloit Bernardo, parent de ce grand Aldus Manutius de Venise, qui tenoit sa boutique en la rue de Sainct-Jacques, qui me dit et jura une fois qu'en moins d'un an il avoit vendu plus de cinquante paires de livres de l'Aretin à force gens mariés et non mariés, et à des femmes, dont il m'en nomma trois de par le monde . . . et me dit davantage qu'une autre dame luy en ayant demandé, au bout de quelque temps, s'il en avoit point un pareil comme un qu'elle avoit veu entre les mains d'une de ces trois, il luy respondit: *Signora, si, e poggio*; et soudain argent en campagne, les acheptant tous au poids de l'or . . .[79]

Without being overtly pornographic, Brantôme's work is intentionally provocative in its revelations of sexual excesses at Court, the account of which was designed to satisfy the curiosity not only of his protector the duc d'Alençon, but of the general reading public as well.

Vernacular scientific works on women and their sexuality were to prove similarly sensational. Thus Joubert's 1578 *Erreurs populaires* caused a major scandal in that it revealed in the vulgar tongue, and to a mixed audience, sexual information previously reserved in Latin for learned men. The longest chapter in the book, "Whether There is Certain Knowledge of the Virginity of a Maiden" (v, iv), accounted for much of the scandal as well as much of the success of the work. The fact that Joubert anticipated a public reaction is spelled out in his apologetic "Letter to His Friends and Those Who Speak Well of Him" in the following terms:

How well did I foresee that I would be calumniated because of a few words contained in my *Erreurs populaires*, and especially because I dedicated it to the most illustrious and excellent queen of Navarre, one of the most chaste and virtuous princesses in the world. As if the explanation of natural matters such as conception, pregnancy, birth, and lying-in – all things that people wish to know about and that they seek out every day, men as well as decent women – ought not to be presented to such a lady and true model of virtue.[80]

The fact that he realized the potential appeal of the scandalous nature of his work is confirmed by his (and Montaigne's) printer Simon Millanges who, in a letter to the reader, lists the very topics which were denounced as scandalous – namely conception, reproduction, childbirth, lying-in, reckoning of virginity – with the caveat that the author "was often forced, in discussing the errors committed in such acts, to use words and expressions that seem a little obscene, and that it would be good if only married people were to read the interesting information that is put there for them in these books." Moreover, as if to make sure that readers would not miss the contentious passages, he marked them typographically with asterisks in the 1579 edition, making them all the more certain to be noticed: "As for others, who do not care to hear about the shameful parts, they can skip over the chapters and passages marked with this sign: * "[81]

Clearly, both author and printer anticipated the commercial appeal that the publication of such controversial medical material would have for the public. Nor were they disappointed in their expectations, as the great popularity of Joubert's work would prove. It was reportedly printed in four different places within six months, in Bordeaux, Paris, Lyons, and Avignon, and in each place no fewer than sixteen hundred copies were made available. In fact, the work enjoyed such a great reputation that it started out selling for ten or twelve sous and then for an écu and eventually even four francs, in much the same way that the price of wheat goes up every day in time of famine.[82] Moreover, in dedicating the work to Marguerite de Valois, Joubert was successful in creating something of a literary happening. Those who thought it inappropriate, even indecent, to propose such a vile subject to such a noble person remonstrated in a series of letters, provoking a veritable debate on the issue by the author and his readers. Criticized for speaking too openly about reproduction and reproductive organs, but also for making medical

knowledge public and in French, undermining thereby the professional privilege of reserving such matters to writings in Latin,
Joubert defended himself against his colleagues and apologized to
the Queen, explaining that it was not his intention to offend.[83] As
Louis Dulieu aptly put it: "On est en droit de penser que le succès
littéraire de ce livre ne fut pas non plus étranger à tout cela! Jalousies
d'auteurs, jalousies de confrères, c'était bien suffisant pour créer tout
ce bruit."[84]

Out of the hundreds of plates and figures of surgical instruments
and procedures with which Ambroise Paré illustrated his works,
"quoy qu'auec frais excessifs, que i'estimeray bien employez,
pourueu que cela soit agreable aux gens de bien, & que ceux de ma
nation en puissent tirer quelque proffit,"[85] the seventy-seven representing monsters and prodigies had a different, more sensational,
less rigorously scientific vocation. Combined with exemplary stories
and personal anecdotes, they were intended to provide the author
with diversion from his more serious work and to stimulate the erotic
imagination of his readers.[86] In providing graphic evidence for tales
of extraordinary birth and the sexual organs of hermaphrodites,
these illustrations possessed a tangible reality that was more forceful
than words, contributing to the charge, leveled on July 9, 1575 by the
Faculté de Médecine of the University of Paris that the work was
"nuisible aux bonnes moeurs et à l'Etat." Since Paré felt constrained
in his reply to justify both the decency of what he had to say about
the sodomitic practices of hermaphrodites and androgynes "qui
couchent ensemble, exerceans alternativement acte de masle et de
femelle" with reference to Pliny, and the description of the anatomy
of the "parties génitales de la femme" with reference to Galen, it
would appear that, among other recriminations, his censors had
called him to task for flagrant obscenity.[87]

In defense of his discussion of lesbianism, Paré argued that he was
dispensing useful information as well as discouraging sinful behavior.
In advising that parents marry off girls quickly so that they do not
corrupt one another, he felt that he was performing a useful service
to both. Moreover, he concluded, the information he provided was
already in the public domain. But even this defense, with its explicit
commentary on stimulation of the clitoris and recommendation that
it be excised, displays a fascination with female sexuality which, if
not morally reprehensible, remains psychologically suspect,
especially when translated into French:

Les excroissances viennent si grandes presqu'à toutes les femmes d'Egypte, et à quelques ieunes des nostres, que comme elles se trouuent en la compagnie des autres femmes, ou que leurs habillements encheminant les frottent, ou quand leurs maris les veulent approcher, elles se dressent comme la verge de l'homme, voire qu'elles s'en iouent avec les autres femmes, comme feroyent leurs maris. Pour ceste cause en Egypte on la coupe à toutes les filles, comme tesmoigne Galien en son introduction.

Quand à ceste exemple dangereux de Sodomie, que vous dictes estre indigne, leu, recité et entendu des Chrestiens, Hippo. liu. 2., de la maladie des femmes. Paul Egineta, liu. 6. chap. 70. AEce 4. sermo. 4. ch. 30. en fait mention.

Et quand à l'histoire, Leon l'Africain la descrit liu. 3 de son historie, dediee au Pape Leon son parrain. Mesmes le bon et docte Maistre Iean Papon, Conseiller du Roy, nous en a laissé vn arrest en termes François, en son recueil des arrests notables, liu. 22. titre 7. arrest 2. en telles paroles comme il s'ensuict:

Deux femmes se corrompans l'une l'autre, etc.

De ma part, ie suis d'opinion, et ay escrit qu'on coupe ceste carnucule, à fin que l'on n'en abuse . . ."[88]

Somewhat later, an ecclesiastical tribunal condemned Jacques Ferrand's *Traité de l'essence et guérison de l'amour ou De la mélancholie érotique* (1610) because he had written it in the vernacular: "ce qui est d'autant plus perilleux."[89] This was a reminder to specialists like Joubert or Paré that, while the Church might be willing to allow for works written for other specialists in Latin, it would not tolerate works in French which discussed sperm, human reproduction, male impotency, and female infertility in crude but necessary terms, making delicate information available to the reading public at large.

In his 1623 recasting, *De la maladie d'amour ou mélancholie érotique*, Ferrand offers the following apology for his language: "This is an appropriate moment for me to certify to my reader that I wish to speak as modestly as possible, but that I must also express certain medical concepts that are often in disaccord with polite discourse." The words themselves, he maintains, cannot be objectionable, because the parts of the anatomy they stand for are "natural, useful, and necessary – parts, moreover, that are now dissected and demonstrated in public in order to understand their substance, number, figure, placement, connection, action and function."[90]

Jacques Duval's prefatory remarks to his *Traité des hermaphrodites* are even more self-consciously and pointedly promotional. As if the subject matter and the use of French were not already sufficiently daring and sensational in themselves, he takes pains to point out its pornographic interest.[91] Thus in the "Advertissement au lecteur," he excuses himself halfheartedly for using "propos qui paroissent lascifs, ou ressentent quelque gayeté," explaining that the subject requires them, and that, moreover, such words and thoughts afford pleasure both to those who write and those who read them:

> Dont ayant à faire mention, et des parties destinées à l'acte de génération, que cette excellent ouvrière la puissante Nature, désirant beaucoup favoriser, pour tousjours de plus en plus ayder et promouvoir les hommes à la propagation de leur espèce, elle ne s'est contentée d'exciter une grande délectation, lors que on descend à l'usage d'icelles: mais aussi elle a, par je ne sçay quel instinct, concédé une tant voluptueuse titillation et libidineuse amorce, lors que par la nomination, ou seule signification, l'esprit est attiré à s'y encliner, que quand j'userois de lettres Hiérogliphiques empruntées des Égyptiens, ou seulement de signes expressifs répétés de l'Anglois Taumaste, pour les désigner, sans autrement les nommer: encore ne pourrois-je rescinder cette naifve gayeté dont Nature a voulu décorer et orner leur commémoration.[92]

What is clear, then, is that in matters of sexuality, Brantôme and his century increasingly blur the line between eroticism and pornography. Furthermore, contemporary manifestations of sexual deviations or social differences become troubling only in proportion as they are conceived as a public rather than a private phenomenon, transgressing religious and/or civil laws. No one seems primarily concerned with the possibility that such behavior may be more than a momentary, sometimes even an amusing, aberration; although there is some peripheral evidence, mainly in Montaigne and Brantôme, that habit, being second nature, may also translate an exclusive inclination. In any event, sexual rhetoric remains conventionally aesthetic in early modern French prose and poetry, unless charged with vindictive, propagandistic, or pornographic purpose. It is then that it becomes less meaningful as the language of literature or, at least, that it acquires a polemical, displaced, meaning, similar in intent and effect to indiscriminate accusations of heresy or atheism. When, therefore, print culture becomes commercially motivated or politicized and rhetoric is thought to be opposed to truth and reason, one can be sure that the play of Renaissance texts is slowly drawing to a dramatic and disappointing close.

Conclusion

In many ways, the early modern period in French literature begins with the feminization of writers and readers, at once provoking and promoting what we have come to call the *Querelle des femmes*, which, originally at least, concerned the proper place of women in life and letters. At the outset, as we have seen, this exchange is exclusively between men, who take opposite sides, either as detractors or praisers of women, on what had become increasingly a rhetorical question, one already raised in classical treatises as appropriate for the training of students in the art of argumentation *in utramque partem*, and recently renewed through the medium of printing.

Feminist or antifeminist arguments advanced and defended by male protagonists were generally ready-made, catalogued and codified by centuries of tradition. Rather than conveying original reasons or personal prejudices, they were essentially indefinite and derivative display pieces. Conceived to impress and convince, their point of view depended more on commonplace than on psychological or philosophical exploration. It is not until Christine de Pisan's reply to Jean de Meun's *Roman de la rose* that misogynistic discourse was transformed momentarily into the discourse of misogyny, structured by differences in gender as well as perspective, and that the age-old debate about the vices and virtues of women finally developed into the *Querelle des femmes*, which was to become one of the principal literary events of early modern France.

One of the main purposes of this study has been to provide a rereading of this gradual process along with an analysis of its consequences on a number of prominent texts. The first lesson derived from the preceding pages is that the expression, even the very idea, of marginality was variously inflected by the rule and practices of rhetorical performance, and that literary truth and social conditions do not always coincide. In fact, without the formal training in the formulation of arguments for or against a given topic that was an integral part of Renaissance education, it is unlikely that such a self-conscious proliferation of pro and antifeminist texts would have occurred. When, therefore, we are concerned with the place and interpretation of marginalizing discourses in early modern works, we need to consider not only words, but also the writer, the occasion, the audience, that is, the context of the text. In short, rhetorical writing requires rhetorical reading, and this practice has not always prevailed in recent cultural criticism.

Secondly, without the intermediary of the printed word which recorded and propagated their proceedings, there is every reason to believe that these treatises would have had little repercussion beyond the limited confines of a select group of learned readers. Printers were not unaware of the market potentiality of the books they published, and it is partially through their influence that marginal and marginalizing authors and subjects finally obtained a prominence and audience they could not have enjoyed otherwise. Fictionalized or poeticized, the matter of the *Querelle des femmes* gradually permeated a variety of texts, usually in a somewhat perfunctory or parodic manner, gradually becoming part and parcel of the cultural context of the day. Whenever, therefore, women are praised or blamed in a given text, it is not sufficient to conclude from this fact alone that Renaissance society actually viewed them in this particular way, at least not without taking into consideration the protocol of traditional rhetoric which regulated the ordering and arguing of a given topos. In addition, print culture required new acts of reading arising out of the new way of reproducing writing; and one of the most outstanding of these, as we have seen, was a sense and appreciation of textual performance in the formulation of topical material. Finally, since a topos is a fragment of discourse which is constantly rewritten, its repetition in successive texts causes a replacement or displacement of its meaning, making a cultural reading theoretically problematic.

Since rhetoricians considered *imitation* to be the equivalent, or at least a part, of *invention*, it was perhaps inevitable that misogynistic writing would eventually turn parodic. Parody inflects Neoplatonic and Petrarchan discourses as well, either undermining their original seriousness or readjusting them from a different standpoint. Parody is originally "parallel writing," with negative and positive connotations: negative, when the stylistic peculiarities of the appropriated text are assumed in a derogatory or emphatic fashion, and a noble or serious original is recast in a self-consciously ludic mode; positive, when one text competes with another, rewriting it in a different but equivalent language. In both senses of the word, much of the literature of the *Querelle des femmes* is parodic, making it difficult to determine where and to what extent it is socially or politically relevant, and, consequently, whether it is to be interpreted as diatribe or literary exercise. One sure thing is that it becomes a distinctly recognizable factor in the shaping of the cultural landscape of the day, reflecting the kind of writing that was of obvious interest to printers and readers alike.

Once the novelty of traditional rhetoric wore thin and imitation became increasingly perfunctory, a reaction inevitably occurred, promoting the development of a counter-rhetoric which, as we have seen, became equally imitative and standardized in its language. Thus after exploiting indiscriminately the profeminist thematics and imagery of Petrarchism and Platonism in *L'Olive*, Du Bellay turned to parody in *Contre les pétrarquistes*. And with the appearance of similar palinodes in other works by other writers, both male and female, the languages of antiplatonism and antipetrarchism become, in turn, equally parodic. Suddenly *Amours* and *Contr'amours* proliferate, alternating arguments and images which subsequently become the discursive models of other texts. Once again, the place and perspective of the author in relation to theme is not always evident. At times, in fact, it would seem as though rhetoric rather than meaning came to determine the ultimate end of writing.

It is in this sense that rhetorical works are self-contained and self-critical, commenting on their own method and limitations, with little concern with reality or for practical solutions. Thus Renaissance women may have been marginalized in life, but the degree or the terms of their marginalization cannot be properly resolved by reference to the body of literature for or against them. Furthermore, all writing, especially rhetorical writing, is a reordering and therefore a distortion of reality. When, therefore, women become the subject of debate in the so-called *Querelle des femmes*, they occupy the discursive center of a generation of literary texts which privilege their merits as well as their faults. This fact alone should make us resistant to the lure of anachronistic interpretation, based on prejudicial ideologies which extrapolate from literature to social conditions.

More and more, printing allowed for the extension and expansion of the written domain and its functions. In Montaigne's case, it served as a means for filtering the sexual information recorded in the *Journal de voyage*, making it proper and fitting for public instruction and consumption. For Brantôme, it provided a way of exposing and exploiting the intimate lives of the noble and famous. Literature no longer addressed only the learned, but the larger public; in fact, various and varied publics. On the one hand, writing was meant to explain, fascinate, and persuade; on the other, to popularize, proliferate, even corrupt. For men of learning, as well as for men and women of different social and cultural standings, information about sex and sexuality became much more readily available through the printing of classical, popular, scientific, and pseudo-scientific works on the subject, eroticizing the senses, forming public attitudes, and fixing sexual stereotypes.

Gender aside, sexual discourses appear, superficially at least, difficult to read. Homosexuality was a real marginality at the time, which it is not easy (but correspondingly important) to evaluate on the historical and literary evidence at hand, mostly because it never becomes the center of contemporary investigation or debate. Even though women had little opportunity to speak about their own sexuality, it was a subject which was frequently described and sometimes decried by men. Homosexuals, on the other hand, were completely voiceless and effectively marginalized in the few texts, theological, medical, anecdotal, which refer to their existence or describe their practices. Thus the absence of homosexual discourse in Renaissance France modifies or ought to modify our sense of what marginality and its discourses are. Applied to women in letters and society, it is perhaps not a particularly effective concept, especially in an age when women and women writers were the order of the day. It becomes so, however, when sex or sexuality, whether dominant or deviant, is exploited by writers and printers alike, seemingly for subversive or prurient effect.

Pornography is decidedly a Renaissance phenomenon, another by-product of print culture.[1] Sexually explicit writing and images can be found in all times and places, but the invention of printing not only afforded humanists the opportunity to disseminate their texts and learning to a wider audience, but also generated a growing industry which capitalized on the formation of an urban reading public and the demand for political, scientific, and erotic works in the vernacular.

The desire of readers to purchase certain books contributed greatly to the kind of subject printers encouraged authors to pursue in order to ensure their own economic stability. This was certainly a significant factor in the sudden proliferation of vernacular texts, which had the effect of fomenting a lasting separation between learned and worldly cultures. Ironically, it was the printing press that gave censorship its technological basis. With the power to prevent the printing of certain books and to restrict their distribution, ecclesiastical and secular authorities found themselves in an ideal position to monitor reading material and manipulate public opinion.

The play between rhetoric and reading has been another of the underlying themes of the present study: more precisely, the problematic relation between writing practices and meaningfulness. There is a tendency, especially in contextual or cultural criticism, to read literally, and consequently to confuse words with reality. Renaissance literature is much more rhetorically devised and publicly oriented. It is conceived and designed to exert the author's authority over the reading public, to persuade, but also to please. French Renaissance literature is not play; but it requires, in order to operate successfully, the playful manipulation of words and ideas in conjunction with the expected and necessary participation of the complicit reader.

Obviously, context is anything and everything outside the text, which means that the principle of context, in order to be useful, must itself be contextualized. What constitutes context? Can one distinguish text from context? To what extent is meaning the perception of a relationship between discourse and its context? Can a text supply, through textual means, a contextual situation that gives pertinence and meaning to what is written? Is not right reading textual reading, that is, reading in which context is integrated into the text itself? Political and cultural circumstances both reflect and effect certain kinds of writing, but literary texts are redundant in that they are responsible for their own contexts. The way we come to read them, when we read them in relation to the reality they represent, is the way they were conceived and written. To read them otherwise is to ignore their way with words while acknowledging their effect on meaning, which is precisely the illusion rhetoric is designed to promote and perpetuate.

Notes

INTRODUCTION

1 Inasmuch as "feminism" as a concept is of fairly recent origin, the designations "feminist" and "antifeminist" are used here in a general and generic sense.

2 The text of this anonymous preamble to the 1526 edition of the *Roman de la rose*, long attributed to Marot, was republished by Bernard Weinberg, *Critical Prefaces of the French Renaissance* (Evanston: Northwestern University Press, 1950), pp. 59–64. For the passage in question, see p. 61.

3 Contrary to a rigidly structured dialectical system founded on evidence and fact, rhetoric introduces into discourse an element of chance and personal inclination, a principle Erasmus recognizes explicitly with numerous exercises in his seminal and widely diffused *De copia*. "Context," in this sense, is produced and determind by the "weaving together of words" (*contexere*).

I DISCOURSES OF MISOGYNY

1 For a useful list of works by and on sixteenth-century women writers, see Kirk D. Read, "Bibliography," *L'Esprit Créateur* 30.4 (1990), 106–11. Gisèle Mathieu-Castellani's *La Quenouille et la lyre* (Paris: José Corti, 1998), which touches on most of the authors studied here, appeared after the present work was completed.

2 For a detailed survey of this complex question, see Evelyne Berriot-Salvadore, who argues that "la littérature qui alimente le débat autour de la 'querelle' des femmes n'est évidemment pas à lire comme une traduction littérale d'un statut social effectif." *Les Femmes dans la société française de la Renaissance* (Geneva: Droz, 1990), p. 15.

3 Print culture, as Roger Chartier reminds us, refers not only to the profound transformations that the invention and extended use of printing brought to all domains of life, but also to the set of new acts of reading arising out of the production of writing in a new form. See *The*

Culture of Print: Power and the Uses of Print in Early Modern Europe, ed. Roger Chartier (Oxford: Polity Press, 1989), pp. 1–10.

4 See, for example, Rabelais's prologues. For a pertinent account of the differences between classical and Renaissance rhetorical theory and pratices, see Wayne A. Rebhorn, *The Emperor of Men's Minds: Literature and the Renaissance Discourse of Rhetoric* (Ithaca and London: Cornell University Press, 1995). William J. Kennedy's *Rhetorical Norms in Renaissance Literature* (New Haven and London: Yale University Press, 1978) stresses the notion of rhetoric through the speaker's interrelationship with the audience.

5 For an introduction to this vast and complex question, see the articles by various authors in *Renaissance Eloquence: Studies in the Theory and Practice of Renaissance Rhetoric*, ed. James J. Murphy (Berkeley, Los Angeles, London: University of California Press, 1983), and *Renaissance Humanism: Foundations, Forms and Legacy*, vol. 3, *Humanism and the Disciplines*, ed. Albert Rabil, Jr. (Philadelphia: University of Pennsylvania Press, 1988).

6 According to Quintilian, there are three things which the orator should always have in mind: he must inform, move, and charm his audience. *Institutio oratoria*, ed. H. E. Butler (London: William Heinemann; Cambridge, MA: Harvard University Press, 1963), III.5.2, p. 396.

7 Quintilian distinguishes between two kinds of speech: "the continuous which is called rhetoric, and the concise which is called dialectic (the relation between which was regarded by Zeno as being so intimate that he compared the latter to the closed fist, the former to the open hand)." *Institutio*, II.20.7, p. 353.

8 In Renaissance Italy, Lorenzo Valla (*Respastinatio dialecticae et philosophiae*, c. 1439) and Mario Nizolio (*De veris principiis*, 1553) subordinated dialectic to rhetoric and logic to language. In France, Ramus (*Aristotelicae animadversiones, Dialecticae disputationes*, 1543) proposed the union of rhetoric (for style) and dialectic (for all the other needs of discourse). See Eugenio Garin, Paolo Rossi, and Cesare Vasoli, *Testi umanistici su la retorica* (Rome and Milan: Fratelli Bocca, 1953) and Erika Rummel, *The Humanist–Scholastic Debate in the Renaissance and Reformation* (Cambridge, MA: Harvard University Press, 1995). Most of the arguments in the quarrel between philosophers and rhetoricians in Antiquity as well as the Renaissance are adaptations of points made by Plato.

9 In Renaissance thinking, rhetoric was not limited to just these traditional varieties; it had already become part of poetics in the Middle Ages and the Renaissance continued to conflate the two. See Peter Mack, *Renaissance Argument: Valla and Agricola in the Traditions of Rhetoric and Dialectic* (Leiden and New York: Brill, 1993), pp. 1–21, 244–56, 356–72.

10 Cicero has an exhaustive list of places of invention in his treatise on the *Topica*, dividing them into intrinsic and extrinsic topics. Renaissance students used this type of scheme as a basic guide for the proper

method to follow in developing or "inventing" a given argument. Francis Goyet, *Le Sublime du "lieu commun": l'invention rhétorique dans l'Antiquité et à la Renaissance* (Paris: Champion, 1996), provides a comprehensive history of the commonplace in the art of rhetorical invention. See also Christian Plantin, *Lieux communs: topoï, stéréotypes, clichés* (Paris: Editions Kimé, 1993).

11 *Prisciani Grammatici Caesariensis de Praeexercitamentis Rhetoricae ex Hermogene Liber.* Priscian of Caesaria taught Latin in Constantinople around 515 AD. For a comprehensive study of Hermogenes' stylistics, see Michel Patillon, *La Théorie du discours chez Hermogène le rhéteur: Essais sur les structures linguistiques de la rhétorique ancienne* (Paris: Les Belles Lettres, 1988).

12 Donald Leman Clark identified 114 printings of Aphthonius from 1507 to 1689 ("The Rise and Fall of Progymnasmata in Sixteenth and Seventeenth Century Grammar Schools," *Speech Monographs* 19, 1952, 259–63). For the use of Aphthonius in Renaissance schools, see William G. Crane, *Wit and Rhetoric in the Renaissance: The Formal Basis of Elizabethan Prose Style* (Gloucester, MA: Peter Smith, 1964), pp. 61–70; 136–38.

13 In the *De partitione oratoria*, which Cicero wrote for the instruction of his son Marcus Tullius, there is a brief but detailed discussion on *quaestio* (XVIII sq.). Cf. Cicero, *De inventione. De optimo genere oratorum. Topica*, ed. H. M. Hubbell (Cambridge, MA: Harvard University Press, London: William Heinemann, 1968); [Cicero], *Ad C. Herennium de ratione dicendi*, ed. Harry Caplan (Cambridge, MA: Harvard University Press, London: William Heinemann, 1989).

14 Already in the *Gorgias*, Plato's Socrates establishes an opposition between *res* and *verbum*, between the dialectic of the philosopher which deals with things and the rhetoric of the sophist which deals with words.

15 To render *res* as "idea" is to simplify matters. See Terence Cave, *Cornucopian Text: Problems of Writing in the French Renaissance* (Oxford: Clarendon Press, 1979), p. 19.

16 Through etymology, the original, therefore the "true" meaning of words was revealed.

17 Joachim Du Bellay, *Deffense et Illustration de la langue françoyse*, ed. Henri Chamard (Paris: Didier, 1948), I, 1, p. 12.

18 "C'est abus dire que ayons languaige naturel. Les languaiges sont par institutions arbitraires et convenences des peuples; les voix (comme disent les dialecticiens), ne signifient naturellement, mais à plaisir." Rabelais, *Tiers Livre*, ed. Abel Lefranc (Paris: Champion, 1931), p. 148.

19 See Helen Solterer's chapter on "Christine's Way: The *Querelle du Roman de la rose* and the Ethics of a political response" in her *The Master and Minerva: Disputing Women in French Medieval Culture* (Berkeley, Los Angeles, London: University of California Press, 1995), pp. 151–75. As Solterer demonstrates, although Christine de Pisan's polemic shares the form of the standard clerical *disputatio*, it takes the issue of the defamation of women to a larger public forum.

20 Misogynistic and feminist arguments were dialectically interrelated, as Joan Kelly argues in "Early Feminist Theory and the *Querelle des Femmes, 1400–1789*," *Signs: Journal of Women in Culture and Society* 8 (1982), p. 27. The static quality of the genre, she adds in her reprise of this article, should not mislead us into accepting the commonly held notion that the *querelle* was a kind of literary game. "Did Women Have a Renaissance?" in her *Women, History and Theory* (Chicago: The University of Chicago Press, 1984), p. 74. There is, however, an element of play in the systematic way in which opposing arguments are made to confront one another, as Madeleine Lazard argues in her *Images littéraires de la femme à la Renaissance* (Paris: Presses Universitaires de France, 1985), p. 11.

21 For a convenient and comprehensive review of relevant literature, see *Woman Defamed and Woman Defended: An Anthology of Medieval Texts*, ed. Alcuin Blamires, Karen Pratt, and C. W. Marx (Oxford: Clarendon Press, 1992). The editors of this anthology rightly point out that the sayings and anecdotes comprising the antifeminist corpus are rarely interpreted with critical rigor or in the light of original context, and that the same arguments and the same examples keep turning up over and over again (p. 7).

22 Ruth Kelso, *Doctrine for the Lady of the Renaissance* (Urbana: University of Illinois Press, 1956), counts 891 texts dealing with the question. For a detailed, chronological table, see Maïté Albistur and Daniel Armogathe, *Histoire du féminisme français du moyen âge à nos jours* (Paris: Editions des femmes, 1977).

23 For a survey of the modes and practices of paradoxical argumentation, see Rosalie Colie, *Paradoxia epidemica: The Renaissance Tradition of Paradox* (Princeton University Press, 1966). Although Linda Woodbridge (*Women and the English Renaissance: Literature and the Nature of Womankind, 1540–1620*, Urbana and Chicago: University of Illinois Press, 1984, p. 59) overstates somewhat the point, she is right in seeing the formal controversy as a kind of sophisticated game for *literati*.

24 Dedicatory epistle to Maximilian of Transylvania, councillor of the Emperor Charles V, in Henri Corneille Agrippa, *De nobilitate et praecellentia foeminei sexus*, ed. R. Antonioli (Geneva: Droz, 1990), p. 47, and to Marguerite, p. 49. While "paradox" is not in the original, Agrippa's translators interpreted it as such. Thus the anonymous edition of 1537 was reprinted by S. de Gueudeville in 1726 with the following modification in the dedicatory letter: "De plus, si j'ai mis le beau sexe au-dessus du nôtre, j'espère que le public me fera grâce, en faveur de l'auguste princesse, à l'honneur de qui j'ai avancé un si grand *paradoxe*."

25 See Charles Estienne's *Paradoxes, ce sont propos contre la commune opinion: debatus, en forme de Declamations forenses: pour exerciter les ieunes aduocats, en causes difficiles* (Poitiers: Au Pelican par Ian de Marnef, 1553), which is a translation, with additions of his own, of Ortensio Lando's *Paradossi cioè, sententie fuori del commun parere*. The title and subject of one of these

paradoxes is "Que l'excellence de la femme est plus grande que celle de l'homme" (*Declamation* XXIII, pp. 177–87). See also Alexandre de Pont-Aymery, *Paradoxe apologique, où il est fidellement démonstré que la femme est beaucoup plus parfaite que l'homme en toute action de vertu* (Paris: A. L'Angelier, 1594).

26 This is the case, for instance, in Marconville's 1564 *De la bonté et mauvaiseté des femmes* (Paris: Côté-femmes, 1991), where one position is played against the other. See Evelyne Berriot-Salvadore, *Un Corps, un destin: la Femme dans la médecine de la Renaissance* (Paris: Champion, 1993), p. 1.

27 See Lefranc's introduction to the critical edition of the *Tiers Livre* (Paris: Champion, 1931), pp. I–LV and Emile Telle, *L'Œuvre de Marguerite d'Angoulême, reine de Navarre, et la querelle des femmes* (Toulouse: Lion, 1937).

28 See, for instance, Kelly, "Did Women Have a Renaissance?", pp. 65–109, and Constance Jordan, *Renaissance Feminism: Literary Texts and Political Models* (Ithaca: Cornell University Press, 1990), pp. 86–105.

29 See Charles Oulmont, "Gratian du Pont sieur de Drusac et les femmes," *Revue des Etudes Rabelaisiennes* 4 (1905), 22–3. Marc Angenot provides a survey of sixteenth-century misogynistic and feminist writings in *Les Champions des femmes: Examen du discours sur la supériorité des femmes 1400–1800* (Montréal: Presses de l'Université du Québec, 1977).

30 There are very few studies on the *Querelle des femmes* as such. One of the earliest, although somewhat desultory and tangential, is René Doumic's "Le féminisme au temps de la Renaissance," *Revue des Deux Mondes* 149 (1898), 921–32. Dating from the same year is R. de Maulde la Clavière's diffuse *La Femme de la Renaissance* (Paris: Perrin, 1898). Telle (*Œuvre de Marguerite d'Angoulême*, pp. 9–68) regards the *Querelle des femmes* as a pretext for the demonstration of rhetorical virtuosity. Similarly, Arthur Piaget writes: "Nous avons vu jusqu'à présent des poètes prendre parti nettement pour ou contre les femmes. Les uns comme les autres écrivent des panégyriques ou des invectives qui dépassent généralement toute mesure, et dans lesquels ils ne manquent pas de s'injurier réciproquement," *Martin Le Franc Prévot de Lausanne* (Lausanne: F. Payot, 1888, p. 150). Finally, in the introduction to his edition of François de Billon's *Le Fort inexpugnable de l'honneur du sexe Femenin* (printed in Switzerland: S. R. Publishers Ltd, Johnson Reprint Corporation, Mouton éditeur, 1970), M. A. Screech contends: "Dès ses plus lointaines origines – et au moins depuis le *Contra Jovinianum* de saint Jérôme, la *Querelle des Femmes* a été fortement empreinte de rhétorique" (p. XI).

31 *Molestiae nuptiarum* was already a topos in Antiquity. For an early Christian attitude, see, for instance, Paul's First Epistle to the Corinthians, Tertullian's three treatises, *Ad uxorem*, *De exhortatione castitatis*, *De monogamia*, and Jerome's *Adversus Jovinianum*. Although Calvin considers marriage remedial, his argument is not directed against women: "le Seigneur nous a donné remède en cest endroit, en instituant le mariage, lequel après l'avoir ordonné de son auctorité, l'a sanctifié de sa

bénédiction" (*Institution de la religion chrestienne*, Paris: "Les Belles Lettres", 1961), vol. I, p. 216.

32 Misogamy is distinct from misogyny, but the two are frequently combined, both in works of celibate propaganda and literary entertainment. Jerome's *Adversus Jovianum* (*Patrologia Latina*, vol. 23, Paris: Vrayet, 1845, pp. 211–338) falls into the first category, whereas Walter Map's "Dissuasio Valerii Rufino ne ducat uxorem" (in *De nugis curialium. Courtiers' Trifles*, ed. and trans. M. R. James, revised by C. N. L. Brooke and R. A. B. Mynors, Oxford: Clarendon Press, 1983, pp. 289–315) typifies the second.

33 Paul Meyer established a useful list of medieval poems for or against women. See his "Plaidoyer en faveur des femmes," *Romania* 6 (1877), 499–503. For a more complete survey, see Georges Ascoli, "Essai sur l'histoire des idées féministes en France du xvie siècle à la Révolution," *Revue de Synthèse Historique* 13 (1906), 25–57, and, by the same author, "Bibliographie pour servir à l'histoire des idées féministes depuis le milieu du xvie jusqu'à la fin du xviiie siècle," *Revue de Synthèse Historique* 13 (1906), 99–106.

34 See Jean Lecointe, *L'Idéal et la différence: la perception de la personnalité littéraire à la Renaissance* (Geneva: Droz, 1993), especially "De l'exercice scolaire à la pratique littéraire," pp. 88–99.

35 Thus the master narrator of Jean de Meun's *Roman de la rose* (ed. Ernest Langlois, Paris: Champion, 1922, vol. 4, pp. 94–5, vv. 15198–210) asks his female readers not to blame him for words which may seem biting and offensive or to defame his writing, since he means to instruct. Further, Jean de Meun's defenders claimed that it was wrong to attribute the opinions of fictional characters to the author, and that the *Roman de la rose* was an ironic and consequently a moral work. Gerson addressed this issue in his treatise against the *Roman de la rose*. See Joseph L. Baird and John R. Kane, *La Querelle de la Rose: Letters and Documents* (Chapel Hill: North Carolina Studies in the Romance Languages and Literatures, 1978), pp. 79–83.

36 For these dates, see Jehan Le Fèvre, *Les Lamentations de Matheolus et le Livre de Leesce*, ed. A.-G. van Hamel (Paris: Librairie Emile Bouillon, 1905), vol. 2, pp. cxxvi; clxxxii. Others date Le Fèvre's translation from between 1380 and 1387, and the original Latin from about a century earlier. See Alfred Schmitt's critical edition of the *Lamentationes Matheoluli* (Bonn: Philosophischen Fakultät der Universität Bonn, 1974), pp. 19–21. As translator of Matheolus' *Lamentations*, Le Fèvre was largely responsible for its popularization; as author of the *Livre de Leesce*, he recants its misogynistic stance.

37 In the opening lines of his poem, Le Fèvre apologizes for having translated Matheolus (1–11). His turnabout was professionally as well as politically motivated, as Van Hamel points out (Jehan Le Fèvre, *Les Lamentations*, p. cxcv).

38 Aside from Christine de Pisan, whose *Cité des dames* has been called the most important feminist text in the *Querelle des femmes,* these early "feminists" were not generally woman. It should be noted that Christine's role was perhaps not quite as radical as it has sometimes been made out to be. See F. Douglas Kelly, "Reflections on the Role of Christine de Pisan as a Feminist Writer," *Sub-Stance* 2 (1972), 63–71. Moreover, her work was known in manuscript copies only from 1405, the date of its composition, until 1986, when it was first printed.

39 It is most probably Le Fèvre's text that Christine had in mind when she refers at the beginning of the *Cité des dames* to a book which treats its subject frivolously.

40 When the *Querelle* became a dialogue, then it truly resembled a *quarrel* in its juridical sense of a debate with alternating accusation and retort (*querella*: a complaint or accusation).

41 See *La Femme dans la littérature française et les traductions en français du XVIe siècle,* ed. Luce Guillerm-Curutchet, Jean-Pierre Guillerm, Laurence Hordoir-Louppe, and Marie-Françoise Piéjus (Lille: Publication de l'Université de Lille III, 1971), p. 109.

42 "Iay dit Pantagruelistes . . . Car se sont tous gens de myse Satirique, qui pour vous denigrer Dames, en propos & écritz, Suyuent volontiers le Guidon d'vn gros Rabelier, qui (comme Rondibilis qu'il est) ne courut onc en Guerre, mais y mene ses Supos en roullant" (1970 reprint of 1555 text, ed. Screech), p. 19.

43 M. A. Screech has shown that the mass of examples in François de Billon's *Fort inexpugnable* is built very largely about a skeleton of argument taken from Agrippa's *De nobilitate*. See his "Rabelais, De Billon and Erasmus (A re-examination of Rabelais's attitude to women)," *Bibliothèque d'Humanisme et Renaissance* 13 (1951), 241–65. Of course, Agrippa's arguments were already highly derivative, which makes the case for direct borrowing less likely or convincing.

44 First in *The Rabelaisian Marriage: Aspects of Rabelais's Religion, Ethics and Comic Philosophy* (London: Edward Arnold, 1958), then in his critical edition of the *Tiers Livre* (Geneva: Droz; Paris: Minard, 1964), and finally in his comprehensive *Rabelais* (London: Duckworth, 1979).

45 "Deliberationes partim sunt eiusmodi ut quaeratur utrum potius faciendum sit, partim eiusmodi ut quid potissimum faciendum sit consideratur," *Ad C. Herennium,* III.II.2, p. 157.

46 For an English translation of the model in Aphthonius on the thesis "Whether One Should Marry," see Ray Nadeau, "The Progymnasmata of Aphthonius," *Speech Monographs* 19 (1952), 280–3. In 1627, John Brinsley refers as follows to Aphthonius for the rules of theme writing on both sides of the question of marriage: "The Declamation being nothing else but a Theame of some matter, which may be controverted, and so handled by parts, when one taketh the Affirmative part, another the Negative, and it may be a third moderateth or determineth

betweene both; we have very good Presidents in the *Thesis* in *Aphthonius*: as in that question handled both Affirmative and Negative, viz. *Uxor est ducenda, Uxor non est ducenda*." See John Brinsley, *Ludus literarius or The Grammar Schoole*, ed. E. T. Campagnac (Liverpool: University Press, 1917), p. 184.

47 Richard Rainolde, *The Foundacion of Rhetorike* (New York: Scholars' Facsimiles & Reprints, 1945), folio liiij.

48 "*Definite* questions involve facts, persons, time and the like. The Greeks call them *hypotheses*, while we call them *causes*. In these the whole question turns on persons and facts. An *indefinite* question is always the more comprehensive, since it is from the *indefinite* question that the *definite* is derived. I will illustrate what I mean by an example. The question 'Should a man marry?' is *indefinite*; the question 'Should Cato marry?' is *definite*, and consequently may be regarded as a subject for a *deliberative* theme." Quintilian, *Institutio*, III.v.7–8, p. 401. Thus, there is a kind of continuity between Socrates (the name Greek rhetoricians used as an example), Cato (the Latin substitute), and Rabelais's Panurge.

49 Thomas O. Sloane writes that this exercise was so standard that one could center an entire history of two-sided argument on it and find a host of examples, extending from the *controversiae et suasoriae* of Seneca, and the declamatory exercises of Aphthonius, to Erasmus and beyond. See his *On the Contrary: The Protocol of Traditional Rhetoric* (Washington: Catholic University of America Press, 1997), p. 121.

50 Erasmus, *De conscribendis epistolis*, ed. Jean-Claude Margolin in *Opera omnia Desiderii Erasmi Roterodami* (Amsterdam: North Holland Publishing Co., 1971), vol. 1, part 2.

51 It was translated and adapted as "An Epistle to Persuade a Young Gentleman to Marriage, Devised by Erasmus in the Behalf of His Friend" by Thomas Wilson in *The Arte of Rhetorique* (1560), ed. Peter E. Medine (University Park: Pennsylvania State University Press, 1994), pp. 79–100.

52 Screech gives no reason for locating this practice in Aphthonius rather than in Quintilian or contemporary humanist works. Giovanni Nevizzano, for instance, treats the question negatively in the first two books of his *Sylvae nuptialis libri sex* (Lyons: A. de Harsy, 1572): *Non est nubendum*; then, in the following two, positively: *Est nubendum*. Moreover, both Quintilian and Agricola (*De inventione dialectica*, II.x, Cologne: I. Gymnicus, 1539) describe the same rhetorical practice and give the same sample questions as Aphthonius. Of course, whether or not a man should marry remained a distinct preoccupation in the minds of Rabelais's contemporaries. No longer simply a rhetorical matter, it became part of a concerted effort, initiated by Luther and Erasmus, to rehabilitate the seventh sacrament, over and against the opposition of monks and theologians. Cf. Emile V. Telle, *Erasme de Rotterdam et le septième sacrement* (Geneva: Droz, 1954), p. 196.

53 See Roland Antonioli, *Rabelais et la médecine* (Geneva: Droz, 1976), pp. 244–56.
54 Lawrence D. Kritzman has studied the question of male subjectivity in the Rondibilis episode. See *The Rhetoric of Sexuality and the Literature of the French Renaissance* (Cambridge University Press, 1991), pp. 29–44.
55 Rabelais, *Œuvres complètes*, ed. Pierre Jourda (Paris: Garnier, 1991), vol. 1, p. 537.
56 When similarly privileged, digression is not specially marked as structurally disruptive. On the contrary, rather than threatening the unity or cohesion of the *Tiers Livre*, it provides its distinctive rhetorical energy, subjecting it to a certain predictability. Thus, in successive episodes, the dynamics of repetition and reversal are substituted for narrative progression. The text revolves constantly around its own axis, tracing a succession of concentric circles, with Panurge at its center.

2 IRONY AND THE SEXUAL OTHER

1 Especially if, as Jean-François Marmontel proposes in his *Elémens de littérature*, "une excellente *parodie* serait celle qui porterait avec elle une saine critique." See *Œuvres complètes* (Geneva: Slatkine Reprints, 1968), vol. 4, p. 828). Moreover, these stories include large excerpts, even translations, recast in a different mode of, among others, Francesco Bello's *Menbriano*, Francisco Colonna's *Hypnerotomachia Poliphili*, Ovid's *Metamorphoses*, Boccaccio's *Decameron*, Boiardo's *Orlando innamorato*, and Petrarch's *Trionfi*.
2 Since we know nothing about Jeanne Flore's identity, we can only speculate on the background of her life and her probable association with Lyons. It is most likely, however, that the author's name is a pseudonym. Significantly, François de Billon includes Marguerite du Bourg, Claudine and Jeanne Scève, Jeanne Gaillarde, Pernette du Guillet, and Hélisenne de Crenne in his list of women authors in *Le Fort inexpugnable*, but the name of Jeanne Flore is conspicuously and inexplicably absent. Claude Longeon advances a series of circumstantial arguments to bolster his contention that the final version of the *Comptes* should be attributed to Etienne Dolet. See his "Du nouveau sur les *Comptes Amoureux de Madame Jeanne Flore*," in *Hommes et Livres de la Renaissance* (Université Jean-Monnet Saint-Etienne: Institut Claude Longeon, 1990), pp. 259–67.
3 "Puis tout soubdain je me suis advisée que je feroys chose tres agreable et plaisante aux jeunes Dames amoureuses, lesquelles loyaulment continuent au vray service d'Amour, et lesquelles se delectent de lire telz joyeulx comptes, si je les faisois tout d'ung train gecter en impression." Jeanne Flore, *Contes amoureux*, ed. Gabriel-A. Pérouse (Lyon: Presses Universitaires de Lyon, 1980), p. 24. Further references,

incorporated into the text, are to this edition. Note that *Comptes*, rather than *Contes*, was the original spelling of the title (p. 97).

4 "Madame Melibée après que la jeune Salphionne eust mist fin à son compte, où receut assez plaisir toute la compaignie, print parolle, et dit . . ." (p. 101). In addition, the reader is not made privy to Madame Cebille's "acerbe accusation à l'encontre de la sacrosaincte divinité d'Amour" (p. 101) which Madame Melibée mentions as the reason for her own story. Madame Cebille is punished at the end of the sixth story. She is caught by her husband with "ung vilain et sale palefrenier" (p. 215); he ties the two of them together and exposes them naked in public for all to see their shame.

5 Régine Reynolds-Cornell argues for the collective nature of the work, with Clément Marot as one of the participants. See her "Madame Jeanne Flore and the *Contes amoureux*: A Pseudondym [*sic*] and a Paradox," *Bibliothèque d'Humanisme et Renaissance* 51 (1989), 123–33.

6 "Ce que j'ay faict presentement: neantmoins soubs espoir que vous, et les humains lecteurs excuserez le rude et mal agencé langaige. C'est oeuvre de femme, d'où ne peult sortir ouvraige si limé, que bien seroit d'ung homme discretz en ses escriptz" (p. 97).

7 "Si vous liséz ceste oeuure toute entiere, / Arrestéz vous, sans plus, à la matiere: / En excusant la Rhyme, et le langaige, / Voyant que c'est d'une femme l'ouuraige, / Qui n'a en soy science, ne sçauoir . . .". "Au Lecteur," *Le Miroir de l'âme pécheresse*, ed. Renja Salminen (Helsinki: Suomalainen Tiedeakatemia, 1979), p. 165. Similarly, Christine de Pisan speaks of herself with pretended modesty and humility, disclaiming learning and ability in her reply to the treatise of Jean de Montreuil. For a discussion of the "affected modesty" topos, see Ernst Robert Curtius, *European Literature and the Latin Middle Ages* (New York: Harper and Row, 1953), pp. 83–5.

8 There are numerous allusions to the fact that her stories take place in the distant past: "Icy fine mon compte tel qu'il est veritablement jadiz advenu" (p. 154); "vous toutes icy moult eslongnées du temps que cela advint" (p. 158); "jà a longtemps y eust en ceste ville" (p. 158); "Et celle merveille veoit on encores en la forestz Garboniere jusques à aujourd'huy, et si a plus de cinq cens ans que cela premierement advint" (p. 184).

9 Quite obviously, such descriptions are literary, as a Renaissance reader would have immediately realized. This one conflates Virgil's evocation in the *Aeneid* of the divine grace of Venus's measured step (1, 405) and Jean Lemaire de Belges's display of her charms in the judgment of Paris episode (*Les Illustrations de Gaule et Singularitez de Troie*, in *Œuvres*, ed. J. Stecher, Geneva: Slatkine Reprints, 1969, vol. 1, pp. 255–6).

10 Although onomastics suggest ardor for both, only Pyrance lives up to his name.

11 The portrait of the *senex amans* is a classical set-piece. See, for example,

Erasmus' bridegroom, "with his snub nose, dragging one leg after him, but not as easily as the Swiss were wont [the allusion to the "Suiseri" in the Latin original is not clear], with itchy hands, a stinking breath, heavy eyes, a bound-up head, with pus running from his nose and ears." *Opera omnia Erasmi Roterodami*, ed. Jean-Claude Margolin (Amsterdam: North Holland Publishing Company, 1972), vol. 1, part 3 p. 593).

12 For the classical theorist, *amplificatio* was a device used in judicial and demonstrative rhetoric to give weight and substance to an argument or to praise a person or an act. In the Renaissance, *amplificatio* is conflated with *copia*, the search for linguistic and semantic abundance.

13 Dilwyn Knox's *Ironia: Medieval and Renaissance Ideas on Irony* (Leiden: Brill, 1989) provides a detailed review of the meaning and applications of the term. For an equally useful study, from a more literary standpoint, see C. Jan Swearingen, *Rhetoric and Irony: Western Literacy and Western Lies* (New York: Oxford University Press, 1991).

14 Lemaire de Belges, *Œuvres*, vol. 1, p. 255.

15 See Roberta Kay Binford, "The *Comptes amoureux* of Jeanne Flore: A Critical Study" (Diss. University of Iowa, 1972), p. 179.

16 Ovid, *Metamorphoses*, ed. Frank Justus Miller (Cambridge, MA: Harvard University Press, and London: William Heinemann, 1984), vol. 1, Book III, vv. 339–510, pp. 148–61.

17 For a deconstructive reading of Ovid's text, see John Brenkman, "Narcissus in the Text," *Georgia Review* 30 (1976), 293–327. For a detailed discussion of Brenkman's analysis of the disruption of narrative schemes in Ovid's story, see Jonathan Culler, *On Deconstruction: Theory and Criticism after Structuralism* (Ithaca: Cornell University Press, 1982), pp. 251–7.

18 Ovid gives 45 lines to Echo and 108 to Narcissus. Flore reverses the ratio, devoting 7 pages to Echo and only 5 to Narcissus. Does more interest in Echo imply that the author is a man? Contemporary cultural and literary conventions relegate the female author to the role of Echo in relation to her male counterpart, and this is a situation which our author seems to accept without anxiety.

19 Cf. Ronsard's mythological regendering in "Je vouldroy bien . . . / Estre un Narcisse, & elle une fontaine / Pour m'y plonger une nuict à sejour" (*Les Amours* 1552–3, xx).

20 The motif of Love's revenge and victory is strongly emphasized in the metamorphosis of Narcissus in the medieval *Ovide moralisé*. Narcissus' fate is mainly looked upon as a warning against pride in physical beauty, or even pride in general. Cf. Louis Vinge, *The Narcissus Theme in Western European Literature up to the Early 19th Century* (Lund: Skånska Centraltryckeriet, 1967), pp. 92–93. Vinge, unfortunately, was not aware of Flore's treatment of the theme.

21 "ne vueillez, dis je, despriser vos serviteurs: ne vous esjouyssez de leurs martyres, sur tant que vous aymez le ciel, et vous mesmes. Que vous les

debvez aymer de mutuelle amour, l'exemple que j'ay recité vous le montre assez: vous souvienne, je vous pry, que de peu sert le repentir" (p. 181). Curiously, her injunction echoes the *sententia* with which Guillaume de Lorris ends his version of the Narcissus myth: "Dames, cest essample aprenez, / Qui vers voz amis mesprenez; / Car, se vos les laissiez morir, / Deus le vos savra bien merir" (*Roman de la rose*, ed. Ernest Langlois, Paris: Firmin-Didot, vol. 2, 1920, p. 78, vv. 1507–9).

22 See Gabriel-André Pérouse, *Nouvelles françaises du xvie siècle. Images de la vue du temps* (Geneva: Droz, 1977), pp. 84–5.

23 See Marcel Tetel, *Marguerite de Navarre's Heptaméron: Themes, Language and Structures* (Durham, NC: Duke University Press, 1973), and Gisèle Mathieu-Castellani, *La Conversation conteuse: Les Nouvelles de Marguerite de Navarre* (Paris: Presses Universitaires de France, 1992).

24 For variant readings of the tenth story, see Lucien Febvre, *Autour de l'Heptaméron: Amour sacré, amour profane* (Paris: Gallimard, 1944); Marcel Tetel, "Une réévaluation de la dixième Nouvelle de l'*Heptaméron*," *Neuphilologische Mitteilungen* 72 (1971), 563–9; Carla Freccero, "Rape's Disfiguring Figures: Marguerite de Navarre's *Heptaméron*, Day I: 10," in *Rape and Representation*, ed. Lynn A. Higgins and Brenda R. Silver (New York: Columbia University Press, 1991), 227–47.

25 Marguerite de Navarre, *L'Heptaméron*, ed. Michel François (Paris: Garnier Frères, 1964), p. 9. Further references will be to this edition.

26 "Et si je vous en nommois une, bien aymante, bien requise, pressée et importunée, et toutesfois femme de bien, victorieuse de son cueur, de son corps, d'amour et de son amy, advoueriez-vous que la chose veritable seroit possible?" (p. 54)

27 "car mon histoire est si belle et si veritable, qu'il me tarde que vous ne la sachiez comme moy. Et, combien que je ne l'aye veue, si m'a-elle esté racomptée par ung de mes plus grands et entiers amys, à la louange de l'homme du monde qu'il avoit le plus aymé" (p. 54).

28 Patricia Cholakian, *Rape and Writing in the Heptaméron of Marguerite de Navarre* (Carbondale and Edwardsville: Southern Illinois University Press, 1991), p. 96.

29 Ibid., p. 99.

30 Cholakian reads Amadour's character as sinister and his story as the history of the formation of a rapist: "From the beginning, Amadour is depicted as a maker of devious plots" (ibid., p. 89). Or "Meanwhile, the wily Amadour has wormed his way more and more into the countess's confidence" (p. 91).

31 *Couverture* means both "garment" and "the art of covering with a garment." Randle Cotgrave gives "apparell, rayment, attire" and "an arraying, cloathing, cladding, attiring." See his *A Dictionaire of the French and English Tongues* (reproduced from the first edition, London, 1611, with intro. by William S. Woods. Columbia: University of South Carolina Press, 1950).

32 In the sixteenth century, the word *froidement* "n'est plus en usage au sens concret; il s'emploie au figuré avec le sens de 'avec calme'." Paul Robert, *Dictionnaire historique de la langue française* (Paris: Le Robert, 1992).

33 Remembering perhaps Briçonnet's instruction in a letter dated February 26 (1522): "et ne doibt le chrestien plus vivre que vie spirituelle, laquelle ne congnoisse raison, par ce qu'elle luy est contraire." Guillaume Briçonnet and Marguerite d'Angoulême, *Correspondance (1521–1524). Années 1521–1522*, ed. Christine Martineau and Michel Veissière, with Henry Heller (Geneva: Droz, 1975), vol. I, p. 172.

34 "Ramené à la formule la plus simple, l'*Heptaméron* peut être considéré comme une suite d'histoires relatant la lutte entre les passions et la raison." Henri Vernay, *Les Divers Sens du mot raison autour de l'œuvre de Marguerite d'Angoulême reine de Navarre (1492–1549)* (Heidelberg: Carl Winter, 1962), p. 123.

35 "La relative apparaît donc comme un élément important de la structure narrative de l'*Heptaméron*; c'est notamment par elle que les différents thèmes s'enchaînent et que le récit progresse, par étapes, vers sa fin." Eliane Kotler, "Syntaxe et narration. Le rôle des relatives dans les passages narratifs de l'*Heptaméron*," in *Colloque Marguerite de Navarre 15–16 février 1992*, Université de Nice-Sophia Antipolis: Faculté des Lettres, Arts et Sciences Humaines, 1998, p. 89. See also Alexandre Lorian, whose statistics show that, out of twenty-one authors considered, only Marguerite and Monluc exceed the norm. *Tendances stylistiques dans la prose narrative française au XVIe siècle* (Paris: Klincksieck, 1973), p. 246.

3 ANONYMITY AND THE POETICS OF REGENDERING

1 For an excellent study of the increasingly prominent paratextual intrusion of the author in the late medieval period, see Cynthia J. Brown, *Poets, Patrons, and Printers: Crisis of Authority in Late Medieval France* (Ithaca and London: Cornell University Press, 1995). See also Elizabeth Armstrong, *Before Copyright: The French Book-Privilege System 1498–1526* (Cambridge University Press, 1990).

2 "Raisonné," modifying "dérèglement," gives both terms exceptional force.

3 Arthur Rimbaud, *Œuvres complètes. Correspondance* (Lausanne: Henri Kaeser, 1948), pp. 29–30.

4 "Vatibus Aoniis faciles estote puellae; / Numen inest illis, Pieridesque favent. / Est deus in nobis, et sunt commercia caeli." ("Be affable to Aonian poets, young ladies: a divinity inhabits them, and the Pierides favor them. A god is in us, we have commerce with the sky" (*Ars amatoria* III.547–9). Although Ovid's evocation of *furor poeticus* is meant, in its original context, to be humorous, Renaissance theoreticians and poets refer to it as if it were not. The "Platonic" theory of inspiration in the Renaissance is a later, essentially Florentine, construct which has

little to do with Plato. His description of the poet possessed by the god in the *Ion*, which, together with two passages from the *Phaedra* and *Symposium*, is the principal source of the Ficinian concept of the four divine furies – the amorous, poetic, mystic, and prophetic, attributed successively to Venus, the Muses, Dionysos, and Apollo – is actually intended to discredit the poet or rhapsode in favor of the philosopher. Ronsard, in his ode *A Calliope*, remembers Ovid's claim to divine inspiration: "Dieu est en nous, et par nous fait miracles" (*Odes*, Livre II, 31).

5 For a fuller discussion, see the chapter on "Poetry as Divine Fury" in Grahame Castor, *Pléiade Poetics: A Study in Sixteenth-Century Thought and Terminology* (Cambridge University Press, 1964), pp. 24–36.

6 See the documentation provided by Gérard Defaux in his critical edition of Marot's *Œuvres poétiques* (Paris: Garnier, vol. 1, 1990; vol. 2, 1993). Further references will be to this edition.

7 "L'expression qui désigne les 'Grands Rhétoriqueurs' provient d'une erreur de lecture de D'Héricault qui, en 1861, la tira d'un texte du XVᵉ où elle qualifie en réalité . . . les gens de justice!" Paul Zumthor, *Anthologie des Grands Rhétoriqueurs* (Paris: Union Générale d'Editions, 1978), p. 7.

8 Jean Molinet, *Les Faictz et dictz*, ed. Noël Dupire (Paris: Société des Anciens Textes Français, 1937), vol. 2, p. 30. For a comprehensive study of Molinet, his professional obligations, works, and political thought, see Jean Devaux, *Jean Molinet indiciaire bourguignon* (Paris: Champion, 1996).

9 While Cretin plays on the meaning of the word *cretin* (a woven basket carried on the back), Molinet (*moulin nect*) is a mill which grinds out verse. Lemaire signed his works with "De peu assez," and Marot with "La Mort n'y mord."

10 Molinet, *Les Faictz et dictz*, vol. 2, p. 597.

11 The *Plainte* appeared in 1509 together with the *Regretz de la Dame infortunée*, a *déploration* written in honor of Philippe le Beau, Marguerite's only brother, deceased at Burgos in 1506.

12 "Lequel alteré de grand chaud, et querant refrigere à sa soif extreme, se reiouit assez de lofferte de sa mesauenture . . . Si but par trop grand auidité de ceste liqueur aquatique infortunee, congelatiue et mortifiant . . ." (Lemaire de Belges, *Œuvres*, vol. 4, p. 26). Marguerite died in 1530 and the *Couronne margaritique* was not published until 1549. One can assume, however, that she knew it in manuscript form.

13 "Dont, comme je feusse prouchain de mettre fin à l'impression du premier livre des Illustrations et Singularitéz, je me suis advisé que ce ne seroit point chose malsëant ne desagrëable aux lecteurs de aussi faire imprimer ladicte epistre, attendu qu'elle est favorisée par l'approbation de ladicte tresouveraine princesse, et encoires y adjouster la seconde, pour estre ensemble publiées soubz la tresheureuse guide et decoration

du nom de sa haultesse et majesté tresclere, à la quelle (s'il te plait) pourras faire ung petite et humble present de la lecture du tout" (*Les Epîtres de l'Amant vert*, ed. Jean Frappier, Lille and Geneva: Droz, 1948, pp. 3–4). Further references will be to this edition.

14 See Chartier, *The Culture of Print*, p. 5.

15 Obviously, there is a deeply serious, sincere, and religious Marot, but his inevitable recourse to rhetoric makes a definitive reading of his *moi* problematic. To what extent is the other Marot another Marot, intent upon convincing his audience of the moment? Gérard Defaux locates the problem succinctly in the introduction to his edition of Marot's *Œuvres*: "En effet, comme le mensonge, la vérité – non pas la vérité qui est, mais celle qu'il s'agit de communiquer – se fabrique. Elle est le fruit d'une technique" (vol. 1, p. CXXXVII).

16 Marot, *Œuvres*, vol. 2, pp. 30–1.

17 Ibid., vol. 1, "La dixseptiesme elegie," p. 261.

18 Ibid., vol. 2, p. 84. Addressed to a *lector* rather than an *auditor*, the Renaissance prose letter was designed to give a sense of presence to one who is absent, according to the oft-quoted definition derived from Sextus Turpilius: "Sola res est quae homines absentes, praesentes facit." See Justus Lipsius, *Epistolica institutio*, ed and trans. R. V. Young and M. Thomas Hester (Carbondale and Edwardsville: Southern Illinois University Press, 1996), p. 8. Since Marot intends his *epistres* to be "heard" as well as read, he seeks to convey through their familiar language and conversational style the immediacy and informality of a personal voice, assuring through writing the presence of the absent subject.

19 For a pertinent study, see Natalie Zemon Davis, "Protestantism and the Printing Workers of Lyons: A Study in the Problem of Religion and Social Class During the Reformation" (Diss., University of Michigan, 1959).

20 See V.-L. Saulnier, "Etudes sur Pernette du Guillet et ses *Rymes*," *Bibliothèque d'Humanisme et Renaissance* 4 (1944), 9, and Ann Rosalind Jones, *The Currency of Eros: Women's Love Lyric in Europe, 1540–1620* (Bloomington and Indianapolis: Indiana University Press, 1990), pp. 79–103. It is significant that much women's writing appears anonymously or posthumously. Thus Pernette's poetry and most of Marguerite de Navarre's works in prose and verse were published after their deaths and by male editors, whereas Louise Labé and Hélisenne de Crenne apologized for their audacity in going public on their own.

21 One time valet de chambre at the Court of Marguerite de Navarre, Antoine Du Moulin left her service and came to live in Lyons in 1544, where he worked as corrector-editor for the celebrated printer Jean I de Tournes. See Alfred Cartier and Adolphe Chenevière, "Antoine Du Moulin: valet de chambre de la reine de Navarre," *Revue d'Histoire Littéraire de la France* 2 (1895), 469–90; 3 (1896), 90–106. Du Moulin's motives for publication may have included the potential commercial

success of a work written by a woman, especially in the cultural climate of mid-century Lyons.

22 Joseph Buche was probably the first to propose such a personal relationship. See his "Pernette du Guillet et la 'Délie' de Maurice Scève," in *Mélanges de philologie offerts à Ferdinand Brunot* (Paris: Société nouvelle de Librairie et d'Edition, 1904), 33–9. Scève's name appears in the *Rymes* in anagram (p. 12) and puns (pp. 54, 55), as well as in abbreviated form in the first of the four accompanying *épitaphes*, but this is flimsy evidence on which to base a claim for anything other than the poetic relationship assumed here.

23 Platonism and Petrarchism, despite certain similarities, are fundamentally, even radically, different in their philosophical orientations. They have in common a number of formulas – supreme beauty, sovereign good – which the Petrarchists borrowed from the Platonists, but without their doctrinal implications.

24 Pernette du Guillet, *Rymes*, ed. Victor E. Graham (Geneva: Droz, 1968), p. 45. Further references will be to this edition.

25 Since Scève's *Délie* first appeared in 1544 and Pernette died in 1545, she either read his work prior to publication (presumably in manuscript form) or wrote her *Rymes* quickly, in the few months before her death.

26 Especially Saulnier, "Etudes," and in even greater detail, Gisèle Mathieu-Castellani, "La Parole chétive: les *Rymes* de Pernette du Guillet," *Littérature* 73 (1989), 46–60.

27 See Gisèle Mathieu-Castellani, "Parole d'Echo? Pernette au miroir des *Rymes*," *L'Esprit Créateur* 30.4 (1990), 63.

28 Saulnier mentions XIII, XVII (*sic*), XVIII, XLIII, XLIV ("Etudes," 60).

29 *Délie*, ed. I. D. McFarlane (Cambridge University Press, 1966), *dizain* 136, p. 193.

30 This text, published for the first time in the 1552 edition, is considered authentic by both Saulnier and Graham. It is given as "Epître II" in Graham's edition, pp. 119–20.

31 Subsequent editions read "Comme Caton" or "Comme de nom, severe."

32 William J. Kennedy's *Authorizing Petrarch* (Ithaca and London: Cornell University Press, 1994) affords a compelling analysis of the way in which Pernette fashions her union with Scève through language and rhetorical conventions. For his remarks on the anagram of Scève's name, see p. 150.

33 Saulnier, "Etudes," 59.

34 In an insightful reading with a psychoanalytic cast, Robert D. Cottrell concludes that Pernette's poetry "anatomizes" the texts it inherits from tradition, reinscribing them in a text gendered differently, becoming thereby "an expression of the aggressivity that informs every identificatory gesture." "Pernette du Guillet and the Logic of Aggressivity," in *Writing the Renaissance: Essays on Sixteenth-Century French Literature in Honor*

of Floyd Gray, ed. Raymond C. La Charité (Lexington: French Forum, 1992), p. 112.

35 Saulnier, "Etudes," 106. Similarly, Albert-Marie Schmidt: "Pernette du Guillet, réduisant doucement en ses vers la distance qui séparerait leur fond de leur forme, tend à appauvrir son vocabulaire, à l'exténuer, à l'abstraire. Il en résulte une œuvre singulièrement décantée . . .". *Poètes du xvie siècle* (Paris: Gallimard, 1953), p. 228.

36 According to Ann Rosalind Jones: "The women poets . . . wrote within but against the center of the traditions that surrounded them, using Neoplatonic and Petrarchan discourse in revisionary and interrogatory ways." See her "Assimilation with a Difference: Renaissance Women Poets and Literary Influence," *Yale French Studies* 62 (1981), 135.

37 See I. D. McFarlane's pertinent observations in the introduction to his edition of Maurice Scève, *Délie,* pp. 23–43.

38 The designation *Lyonnaise* is significantly restrictive (especially in view of the appeal to the "Dames Lionnoises" in *Elégie III*), indicative of an intended localized, even local, audience. Anne R. Larsen reminds us that early women writers exploited the preface to legitimize their venue into the world of the printed book, framing it as a letter addressed by one woman to another. See her " 'Un honneste passetems': Strategies of Legitimation in French Renaissance Women's Prefaces," *L'Esprit Créateur* 30.4 (1990), 12.

39 Louise Labé, *Œuvres complètes,* ed. François Rigolot (Paris: Garnier-Flammarion, 1986), p. 43. Further references will be to this edition.

40 Labé reminds her female reader that in addition to public recognition, learning affords personal satisfaction: "S'il y ha quelque chose recommandable apres la gloire et l'honneur, le plaisir que l'estude des lettres a acoustumé donner nous y doit chacune inciter" (p. 42).

41 See François Rigolot, "Quel 'genre' d'amour pour Louise Labé?," *Poétique* 55 (1983), 303–17.

42 Deborah Lesko Baker argues that Labé does not mean to align herself with the position of either defender, but rather to expose Amour and Folie in their plenitude and ambiguity as dramatic characters and affective concepts. See *The Subject of Desire: Petrarchan Poetics and the Female Voice in Louise Labé* (West Lafayette: Purdue University Press, 1996), p. 67. Of course, Folly is no more a real woman than Cupid (a mere boy) is a man. On the contrary, both represent vital forces present in various forms of human acts and aspirations. This makes a gendered reading of their respective behavior and language problematic.

43 See Erwin Panofsky, *Essais d'iconologie* (Paris: Gallimard, 1967), p. 179, and Jean Delumeau, *La Civilisation de la Renaissance* (Paris: Arthaud, 1967), pp. 462–66.

44 See Christiane Lauvergnat-Gagnière, "La Rhétorique dans *Le Débat de Folie et d'Amour,*" in *Louise Labé: les voix du lyrisme,* ed. Guy Demerson (Paris: Editions du CNRS, 1990), p. 65. See also the collection of articles

in *Mercure à la Renaissance. Actes des Journées d'Etude des 4–5 octobre 1984, Lille,* ed. M.-M. de La Garanderie (Poitiers: P. Oudin, 1988).

45 In her debate between Folly and Reason, Labé may be remembering the conceit of the two horses in Plato's *Phaedrus,* the black one symbolizing the waywardness of sensual appetite and the white, aspiration towards good.

46 Mercury's irony is directed against Apollo's idealism, especially in the passages which contrast the reception women afford the wise, and the foolish lover: "Et quand ce viendra à faire comparaison des deus, le sage sera loué d'elles, mais le fol jouira du fruit de leurs privautez" (Labé, *Œuvres,* p. 91).

47 In the opening exchange, Folly is not cast in a particularly favorable or sympathetic role. On the contrary, she is depicted as self-centered, impulsive ("A ce que je voy, je seray la derniere au festin de Jupiter, ou je croy que lon m'atent. Mais je voy, ce me semble, le fils de Venus, qui y va aussi tart que moy. Il faut que je le passe," p. 49) and impolite ("Qui est cette fole qui me pousse si rudement? quelle grande háte la presse?" p. 49). In a word, Labé depicts Folly acting foolishly and expecting Cupid to have enough sense to understand that it would be shameful to attempt to reason with a woman ("Laisse moy aller, ne m'arreste point: car ce te sera honte de quereler avec une femme," p. 49).

48 Ibid., pp. 41–2.

49 Pontus de Tyard distinguishes between *furie* and *fureur,* physical madness and celestial furor, the first producing babble, the second, poetry: "fureur . . . contient sous soy deux especes d'alienations. La premiere procedant des maladies corporelles, dont vous avez parlé, et de son vray nom l'avez bien appellée follie et vice de cerveau; la seconde, estant engendrée d'une secrette puissance divine . . . et la nommons, fureur divine, ou, avec les Grecs Enthusiasme" (*Solitaire premier ou Discours des Muses, et de la fureur Poëtique,* ed. Silvio F. Baridon, Geneva: Droz, 1950, p. 10).

50 The quatrains of sonnet LV in Olivier de Magny's *Les Soupirs* are identical with Labé's; but since it is impossible to assign chronological priority, it is difficult to decide who is quoting whom, and with what degree of irony. In any event, they use the same words to say completely different things.

51 As linguistic analysis has demonstrated. See Nicolas Ruwet, "Un sonnet de Louise Labé," in *Langage, Musique, Poésie* (Paris: Seuil, 1972), pp. 176–99.

52 In this sonnet, Labé provides a summary, in interrogative form, of various Petrarchan conceits, raising thereby the question of criteria for judging them. See Keith Cameron, *Louise Labé: Renaissance Poet and Feminist* (New York, Oxford, Munich: Berg, 1990), p. 82.

53 Elizabeth Schulze-Witzenrath remarks on the irony with which Labé

quotes Petrarchan clichés in sonnet 23: "dem Vergleich des Haares mit Gold, der Augen mit Sonnen, aus denen Amor seine Pfeile schiesst, dem Tod aus Liebe und den 'ewigen' Tränen – all das ist gängigster Petrarkismus, dessen Banalität seine Unglaubwürdigkeit nur unterstreicht." *Die Originalität der Louise Labé: Studien zum weiblichen Petrarkismus* (Munich: Wilhelm Fink, 1974), p. 115.

54 Following the example of Petrarch's evocation of his *primo giovenile errore* (*Rime*, I, 3), poets such as Scève and Pontus de Tyard referred to their *erreurs amoureuses*, which, to them, implied *deviation* from a more reasoned course, and, in Petrarch's case at least, a turning from the love of God. Labé, however, in assuming the *jeune erreur de [s]a fole jeunesse* (p. 115), does not hesitate to acknowledge the place of Folly in her experience with Love.

55 *Carmina*, ed. Robinson Ellis (Oxford: Clarendon Press, 1911). Even more hyperbolically, Ariosto writes in sonnet 13 that his pleasures will culminate in "dolci baci, dolcemente impressi, ben mille et mille e mille e mille volte" (*Lirica*, ed. Giuseppe Fatini, Bari: Gius Laterza e Figli, 1924). Both Jean Second ("Centum basia centies, / Centum basia millies, / Mille basia millies, / Et tot millia millies . . .", *Les Baisers*, ed. Maurice Rat, Paris: Garnier, 1938, p. 10) and Olivier de Magny ("Je ne me contenteray pas / De cent baisers pris d'une fille, / Mais en prendray plus de cent mille . . .", *Les Odes d'Olivier de Magny*, ed. E. Courbet, Paris: Lemerre, 1876, vol. 2, p. 137) exploit the same theme, but neither with Labé's strategic distancing.

56 "Quod quantum aduertentibus ingessit admirationis, tantum mulieris maiestatem inclitam ampliauit." Boccaccio, *De claris mulieribus*, ed. Herbert G. Wright (London: Oxford University Press, 1943), p. 13.

57 François Rabelais, *Pantagruel*, ed. Floyd Gray (Paris: Champion, 1997), pp. 107–8.

4 THE WOMEN IN MONTAIGNE'S LIFE

1 *Les Essais de Michel de Montaigne*, ed. Pierre Villey and V. L. Saulnier (Paris: Presses Universitaires de France, 1965), III, ii, 811 B. Further references, included in the text, will be to this edition.

2 Benvenuto Cellini, *La Vita*, ed. Lorenzo Bellotto (Parma: Ugo Guanda, 1996); Gerolamo Cardano (Jérôme Cardan), *Ma vie*, trans. Jean Dayre (Paris: Champion), 1936; Marguerite de Valois, *Mémoires et autres écrits*, ed. Yves Cazaux (Paris: Mercure de France, 1986).

3 In addition, Montaigne had three sisters, Jeanne (mother of his sainted niece), Léonor, and Marie (whose date of birth he recorded in his *Ephémérides*), none of whom is mentioned in the *Essais*.

4 An earlier version of these pages appeared in *Montaigne Studies* 8 (1996), pp. 9–22.

5 According to the *Essais*, Montaigne thought it unnecessary and unseemly to arouse sexual passion in his wife (I, xxx, 198 C). See also his

remarks in "Sur des vers de Virgile" (III, v, 849–50 B). For opposite sides of the debate on his wife's purported infidelity, see Maurice Rat, "Le ménage de Montaigne," *Bulletin de la Société des Amis de Montaigne* 2/15 (1949–52), 14–23; Ferdinand Duviard, "A la trace du vrai Montaigne: Montaigne en ménage," *Revue des Sciences Humaines* Fasc. 81 (1956), 5–18.

6 See the article by Natalie Zemon Davis, "Boundaries and the Sense of Self," in *Constructing Individualism: Autonomy, Individuality, and the Self in Western Thought*, ed. Thomas C. Heller, Morton Sonsa, and David E. Wellbery (Stanford University Press, 1986), pp. 53–63.

7 "Ung bon mariage, s'il en est, refuse la compaignie et conditions de l'amour. Il tache à representer celles de l'amitié. C'est une douce societé de vie, pleine de constance, de fiance et d'un nombre infiny d'utiles et solides offices et obligations mutuelles" (III, v, 851 B).

8 For example, he regrets that his wife had to lose a long-awaited first baby, named Toinette, in its *second year*, when, in fact, the child was *two months* old at her death. See "A Mademoiselle de Montaigne ma femme" prefacing his publication of La Boétie's translation of the "Lettre de consolation de Plutarque à sa femme." Etienne de La Boétie, *Œuvres complètes*, ed. Paul Bonnefon (Geneva: Slatkine Reprints, 1967), p. 185.

9 These twenty-three letters were written over a ten-year period, from 1617 to 1627. Twenty of them were dictated and almost always signed by Françoise de La Chassaigne. When she was too ill to sign, her signature was imitated by one of her secretaries; the other three are in the hand of Montaigne's grand-daughter, Marie de Gamaches. For the text of these letters, see Gabriel Richou, *Inventaire de la collection des ouvrages et documents réunis par J.-F. Payen et J.-B. Bastide sur Michel de Montagne* [sic] (Paris: Téchener, 1878), pp. 275–324. In his introduction, Jean Delpit characterizes these letters as the "correspondance d'une vieille femme, préoccupée de pratiques de dévotion et du soin d'assurer l'exécution de ses dernières volontés . . ." (p. 276).

10 Roger Trinquet concludes from a reading of these letters that Françoise "devait surtout lasser son spirituel mais peu indulgent époux par la médiocrité constante de ses préoccupations et une sorte de manque d'humour congénitale." See his "Sur un texte obscur des *Essais* éclairé par une lettre de Madame de Montaigne," *Bulletin de l'Association des Amis de Montaigne* 17 (1955), pp. 45–46. The letters to Saint-Bernard have a curious complement in a dedicatory text in which Charles de Gramaches paints a peculiar picture of Françoise's relationship with her husband: "A vous Madame, qui non seulement estes d'une naissance très-spirituelle, mais encore avez couché vingt-huict ans aux costez de feu Monsieur de Montaigne . . . Car encore que vostre excellente beauté l'occupast souvent à vos caresses, néantmoins durant les grandes remises et ennuyeuses relasches, à quoy la loy de la vigueur mesme abstrainct les plus allumez; il s'employait je m'asseure à mesler ses oppinions avec les vostres, et vos esprits se marioyent à leur tout."

Text reproduced in Olivier Millet, *La Première Réception des Essais de Montaigne (1580–1640)* (Paris: Champion, 1995), p. 203.

11 Her grandfather and father were presidents in the Parlement de Bordeaux.

12 "Ma fille (c'est tout ce que j'ay d'enfans) est en l'aage auquel les loix excusent les plus eschauffées de se marier; elle est d'une complexion tardive, mince et molle, et a esté par sa mere eslevée de mesme d'une forme retirée et particuliere; si qu'elle ne commence encore qu'à se desniaiser de la nayfveté de l'enfance" (iii, v, 856 b).

13 According to a stipulation in her will and testament, dated March 4, 1615, which reads as follows: "Item j'ay donné et donne par ce testament et veux et entens quil soict donné à Monsieur de Rochefort, grand vicaire daux entièrement tous les livres de la librairie de Montaigne pour estre par luy transportée ou lhuy plaira et en disposer à sa vollonté lesquels livres je veux et entens quil luy soit donnés et que luy mesme les prenne par ses mains et advenant quilz y fassent la moindre opposition je luy donne tout pouvoyr et puissance duser pour les avoir de toutes voix et rigueurs de justice." See J. R. Marboutin, "La librairie de Michel de Montaigne léguée à un Vicaire Général d'Auch," *Revue de Gascogne*, Nouvelle Série 21 (1926), p. 64. The terms of the will are very elaborate and seem designed to prevent other branches of the Montaigne family (referred to as "ilz," without being named directly) from getting their hands on the library or other property.

14 See Françoise Charpentier, "L'absente des *Essais*: quelques questions autour de l'Essai ii–8, 'de l'affection des pères aux enfans'," *Bulletin de la Société des Amis de Montaigne* 17–18 (1984), 7–16.

15 For the pertinent passage, see Montaigne's *Journal de voyage*, ed. François Rigolot (Paris: Presses Universitaires de France, 1992), p. 139.

16 Théophile Malvezin, *Michel de Montaigne: son origine, sa famille* (Bordeaux: Charles Lefebvre, 1875), pp. 101–11.

17 Roger Trinquet, *La Jeunesse de Montaigne: ses origines familiales, son enfance et ses études* (Paris: Nizet, 1972), pp. 42–5, effectively discredits Dr. H. Bertreux's assertion in "Les ascendances et les hérédités juives de Montaigne" (*Revue Hebdomadaire* 12, February 1938, 220–8) that the Eyquems were Jewish rag merchants, also from Spain or Portugal.

18 Paul Bonnefon, *Montaigne: l'homme et l'œuvre* (Bordeaux: G. Gounouilhou; Paris: J. Rouam, 1893), p. 22.

19 "La goutte de sang juif est aussi sensible dans le mobilisme de Montaigne que dans celui de Bergson et celui de Proust." Albert Thibaudet, *Montaigne*, ed. Floyd Gray (Paris: Gallimard, 1963), p. 18.

20 Trinquet, *La Jeunesse*, p. 158.

21 Montaigne himself suggested a possible English connection: "les miens se sont autres-fois surnommez Eyquem, surnom qui touche encore une maison congneuë en Angleterre" (ii, xvi, 627 a).

22 See Thibaudet, "Portrait français de Montaigne," *Nouvelle Revue Française* 40 (1933), 646–53.

23 Just as Rousseau introduced *green* into French literature (according to Sainte-Beuve), Proust introduced mothers.

24 "il est accordé et entendu entre les parties ladicte clause ne se pourroit estendre à autre surintendance et maistrise que honoraire et maternelle" (p. 298); "ladicte damoiselle y sera nourrie suyvant ledict testament avec tout honneur, respect et service filial, ensemble deux chambrières et un serviteur" (p. 299); "le commandement et maistrise dudict chasteau de Montaigne en général, de ses préclostures et de ses entrées et yssues, demeure entièrement audict sieur de Montaigne" (p. 299). Quotations from Malvezin, *Michel de Montaigne*, pp. 197–300.

25 Lawsuits in the Montaigne family are a very large area that has not yet yielded all its secrets. It does seem clear that the members of the family were litigious against each other. See, for example, the suit brought (and nearly won) by Thomas de Montaigne, sieur de Beauregard, against his mother and sister, for the "chasteau de Montaigne avec ses préclotures, mesteries, héritages, rentes et autres apartenences" together with the right to the "nom, surnom et armes de ladicte maison." Ibid., pp. 321–3.

26 In his *Sexuality/Textuality: A Study of the Fabric of Montaigne's Essais* (Columbus: Ohio University Press, 1981), p. 7.

27 Two of the three quotations from this satire in "Sur des vers de Virgile" (pp. 849, 854, 869) refer to women's inordinate wiles and sexual appetite. For contemporary examples, see Laurent Joubert's *Popular Errors*, trans. Gregory de Rocher (Tuscaloosa: University of Alabama Press, 1989).

28 For an interesting overview of the question of "masculine" style and its "feminine" or "effeminate" counterpart, see Patricia Parker, "Virile Style," in *Premodern Sexualities*, ed. Louise Fradenbury and Carla Freccero (New York and London: Routledge, 1996), pp. 201–22. For Montaigne's reconciliation of the two, see Richard L. Regosin, "Rhétorique de la femme: 'de farder le fard'," in *Montaigne et la rhétorique. Actes du Colloque de St Andrews 28–31 mars 1992*, ed. John O'Brien, Malcolm Quainton, and James Supple (Paris: Champion, 1995), pp. 228–9.

29 Similarly, Justus Lipsius, in his *Epistolica institutio*, recommends the works of Sallust, Seneca, and Tacitus, saying that contact with that kind of concise and subtle writer will cut back the luxuriance of your style, making it terse, strong, and truly masculine ("Sed imprimis suadeam Sallustium, Seneca, Tacitum, et id genus brevium subtiliumque scriptorum jam legi, quorum acuta quasi falce luxuries illa paullisper recidatur; fiatque oratio stricta, fortis, et vere virilis" (pp. 38–41).

30 The imagery of ravishment translating the gendered notion that effective language is potentially agressive, penetrating, and conse-

quently masculine appears regularly in Renaissance rhetorical treatises. See Rebhorn, *The Emperor of Men's Minds*, chapter 3, especially pp. 155–64.

31 "J'entends que la matiere se distingue soy-mesmes. Elle montre assez où elle se change, où elle conclud, où elle commence, où elle se reprend, sans l'entrelasser de paroles, de liaison et de cousture intro-duictes pour le service des oreilles foibles ou nonchallantes, et sans me gloser moymesme" (III, ix, 995 B).

32 "ingenieuse contexture de parolles" (II, x, 414 A).

33 See Kelso, *Doctrine for the Lady*, for a compendium of contrasting views on women and their place in the world.

34 "Moulant sur moy cette figure, il m'a fallu si souvent dresser et composer pour m'extraire, que le patron s'est fermy et aucunement formé soy-mesmes. Me peignant pour autruy, je me suis peint en moy de couleurs plus nettes que n'estoyent les miennes premieres. Je n'ay pas plus faict mon livre que mon livre m'a faict . . ." (II, xviii, 665 c).

35 Marie de Gournay, "Préface à l'édition des *Essais* de Montaigne (Paris: L'Angelier, 1595)," ed. François Rigolot, *Montaigne Studies* I (1989), 45–6.

36 For example, the passage in "De la vanité" (III, ix, 972–3 B) in praise of Paris as a place of unity in a country divided by civil war. See Floyd Gray, *La Balance de Montaigne: exagium/essai* (Paris: Nizet, 1982), pp. 39–43.

37 "De la praesumption," II, xvii, 661–2 C. Significantly, in the auto-biographical *Copie de la Vie de la Damoiselle de Gournay* (1616), she describes her initial encounter with Montaigne in much the same language as he describes his with her: "Environ les dix-huit ou dix-neuf ans, cette fille lut les *Essais* par hasard: et bien qu'ils fussent nouveaux encore et sans nulle reputation qui pust guider son jugement, elle les mit non seulement à leur juste prix, trait fort difficile à faire en tel aage, et en un siecle si peu suspect de porter de tels fruits, mais elle commença de desirer la connaissance de leur auteur, plus que toutes les choses du monde." See Elyane Dezon-Jones, *Fragments d'un discours féminin* (Paris: Corti, 1988), p. 138.

38 Some 1595 additions not in the Bordeaux Copy can be attributed to Montaigne's use of paste-on slips when there was no more room in the margins, which, of course, is not the case here. However, it is possible that this addition existed in a copy of the Bordeaux Copy that Mme de Montaigne and Pierre de Brach sent to Paris, which Marie de Gournay used for her edition, and which is now lost.

39 Marie de Gournay admits her editorial license in both the 1625 and 1635 preface: "En ce seul poinct ay-je esté hardie, de retrancher quelque chose d'vn passage qui me regarde: à l'exemple de celuy qui mist sa belle maison par terre, affin d'y mettre avec elle l'enuye qu'on luy en portoit. Ioinct que je veux dementir maintenant & pour l'advenir,

si Dieu prologne mes années, ceux qui croient; que si ce Liure me loüoit moins, je le cherirois et servirois moins aussi" (*Essais*, Paris: chez la veufve Dallin, 1625, p. 7, ɪv–2r; 1635, p. ij). See R. A. Sayce and David Maskell, *A Descriptive Bibliography of Montaigne's Essais 1580–1700* (London: Oxford University Press, 1983), pp. 103, 118, 121.

40 *Les Essais de Michel, Seigneur de Montaigne, édition nouvelle* (Paris: Jean Camusat, 1635), p. 517. Sayce and Maskell's *A Descriptive Bibliography* omits reference to the copy (second issue) of this edition in the University of Michigan Harlan Hatcher Graduate Library.

41 See Paul Bonnefon, "Une Supercherie de Mlle de Gournay," *Revue d'Histoire Littéraire de la France* 3 (1896), 71–89.

42 Guillaume Colletet, *Pierre de Ronsard "ses juges et ses imitateurs,"* ed. Franca Bevilacqua Caldari (Paris: Nizet, 1983), p. 74. His *Vie de Ronsard* dates from 1648.

43 For this manuscript addition, see *Essais*, reproduction en phototypie (Paris: Hachette, 1906–1931), vol. ɪ, planche 42.

44 Estienne Pasquier confirms this information in a 1619 letter to Monsieur de Pelgé: Montaigne "faisant, en l'an 1588, un long sejour en la ville de Paris, elle le vint expres visiter, pour le cognoistre de face. Mesmes que la Damoiselle de Gournay sa mere et elle le menerent en leur maison de Gournay, où il séjourna trois mois en deux ou trois voyages . . ." See Villey, in *Essais*, p. 1210.

45 Thus she requested and was denied a perpetual "privilège" for her 1635 edition. Paul Bonnefon is convinced that the discrepancies or variants between the printed text of 1595 and the manuscript text of the *Exemplaire de Bordeaux* should be attributed to Montaigne's "éditeurs posthumes," particularly Marie de Gournay. See his *Montaigne et ses amis* (Paris: Armand Colin, 1898), vol. ɪɪ, p. 378.

46 For a detailed analysis, see Cathleen M. Bauschatz, "'L'oeil et la main'": Gender and Revision in Marie de Gournay's 'Préface de 1595,'" *Montaigne Studies* 7 (1995), 95–6. Comparing the revisions in the ɪɪ, xvii passage with those in the 1595 preface, Bauschatz concludes that Gournay's hand is at work in both (p. 96).

47 Marie de Gournay, "Préface de 1595," p. 27. Further reference will be to this edition. When, in 1598, Marie de Gournay replaced the 1595 preface with a shorter one, this passage became, with a few modifications, the beginning of the *Grief des Dames* (1626), a feminist retort to misogynistic prejudice against her and her works. Symbolically and in fact, this transfer signifies the inception of an autonomous literary vocation, no longer dependent on her desire to explain and defend Montaigne.

48 For a perceptive reading of this work, see Domna C. Stanton, "Woman as Object and Subject of Exchange: Marie de Gournay's *Le Proumenoir* (1594)," *L'Esprit Créateur* 23.2 (1983), 9–25. See also her "Autogynography: The Case of Marie de Gournay's 'Apologie pour celle qui

escrit,'" *Autobiography in French Literature*, French Literature Series 12 (Columbia, SC, 1985), pp. 18–31.

49 According to the explanatory note "L'Imprimeur au lecteur," as follows: "Il y a quelques annees que ce liuret fut enuoyé à feu monseigneur de Montaigne par sa fille d'alliance: dont ayant esté depuis son decés trouué parmi ses papiers, messieurs ses parens me l'ont faict apporter, pource qu'ils l'ont iugé digne d'estre mis en lumiere, & capable de faire honneur du deffunct: s'il se peut adiuster quelque chose à la gloire d'un si grand & si divin personnage." *Le Proumenoir de Monsieur de Montaigne (1594)*, ed. Patricia Francis Cholakian (Delmar, New York: Scholars' Facsimiles and Reprints, 1985), p. 2.

50 In an article on "Marie de Gournay éditrice des *Essais*," Claude Blum writes: "Il apparaît clairement que Mlle de Gournay utilise Montaigne pour devenir femme de Lettres, pour se faire un nom. Nous ne voulons pas dire par là que ses sentiments sont feints, nous analysons une stratégie de promotion littéraire; les deux choses, la sincérité d'une admiration et l'ambition de faire carrière, peuvent d'ailleurs s'associer et la première servir éventuellement la seconde," *Bulletin de la Société des Amis de Montaigne* 7/1–3 (1996), 33.

51 She inserted a revised version of the 1595 preface in the 1599 edition of *Le Proumenoir*.

52 Gournay, "Préface de 1595," p. 23.

53 "Je rends un sacrifice à la fortune qu'une si fameuse et digne main que celle de Justus Lipsius ayt ouvert les portes de louange aux *Essais*," ibid., p. 24).

54 Montaigne, "Consideration sur Cicéron," I, xl, 251 C.

55 Gournay, "Préface de 1595," p. 29.

56 Ibid., p. 30.

57 Ibid., p. 41.

58 Montaigne, "De l'institution des enfans," I, xxvi, 152 C.

59 Gournay, "Préface de 1595," p. 46.

60 See Richard L. Regosin's remarks on "Montaigne's dutiful Daughter" in *Montaigne's Unruly Brood: Textual Engendering and the Challenge to Paternal Authority* (Berkeley, Los Angeles, London: University of California Press, 1996), pp. 48–79.

61 Gournay, "Préface de 1595," p. 31.

62 Ibid., p. 46.

63 Ibid., p. 51.

64 Tilde A. Sankovitch, *French Women Writers and the Book: Myths of Access and Desire* (Syracuse University Press, 1988), p. 81.

65 Gournay, "Préface de 1595," p. 34.

66 See Cathleen M. Bauschatz, "Marie de Gournay's 'Préface de 1595': A Critical Evaluation," *Bulletin de la Société des Amis de Montaigne* (7/3–4, 1986), 73–82; Mary McKinley, "An Editorial Revival: Gournay's 1617 Preface to the *Essais*," *Montaigne Studies* 8 (1966), 193–201.

67 Gournay, "Préface de 1595," p. 24.

68 *Essais*, 1635, p. iij.

69 Quoted by Rigolot in his introduction to Gournay, *Préface de 1595*, p. 12. Although David Maskell attributes the two to three thousand differences between the *Exemplaire de Bordeaux* and Gournay's 1595 edition to Montaigne himself, there is still good reason to suspect her editorial hand at work. See his "Quel est le dernier état authentique des *Essais de Montaigne?*" *Bibliothèque d'Humanisme et Renaissance* 40 (1978), 85–103.

70 In a sense, she rewrites, in the preface, Montaigne's "De l'amitié," recasting it so as to include herself as his other self: "C'est à moy d'en parler; car moy seulle avois la parfaicte cognoissance de cette grande ame, et c'est à moy d'en estre creue de bonne foy" (*Préface de 1595*, p. 34). Thus, when she speaks of him, she speaks *for* him, not as a woman, but as his other self, and with the authority which their friendship – as unique in its way as Montaigne's for La Boétie – confers.

71 Gournay, "Préface de 1595," p. 25.

72 "Marie de Gournay poursuit le double objectif d'une recherche en paternité: à la fois faire reconnaître son 'père' et se faire reconnaître elle-même comme la 'fille' de son 'père'." François Rigolot, "L'amitié intertextuelle: Etienne de La Boétie et Marie de Gournay," in *L'Esprit et la Lettre: Mélanges offerts à Jules Brody*, ed. Louis van Delft (Tübingen: Günter Narr, 1991), p. 58.

73 Gournay, "Préface de 1595," p. 52.

74 See Dezon-Jones, *Fragments*, pp. 71, 118.

75 Antagonism is no longer centered solely on questions of gender. With Marie de Gournay especially, aesthetic considerations come to the fore. See Jean Rousset's "La Querelle de la métaphore," in *L'Intérieur et l'extérieur: Essais sur la poésie et sur le théâtre au XVIIe siècle* (Paris: Corti, 1968), pp. 57–71.

5   SEXUAL MARGINALITY

1 Pierre de L'Estoile's *Journal du règne de Henri III, 1574–1589*, ed. L.-R. Lefèvre (Paris: Gallimard, 1943), provides an example of personal and popular reactions to the subject.

2 The division of acts and people into categories – heterosexual, bisexual, homosexual – coincides with the assumption that sexual practice expresses something fundamental about a person's identity. A growing body of historical research, most of it inspired by Michel Foucault, contends that it is only in the very recent past that we began to view sexuality in this way and that we need, consequently, to separate premodern sexual acts from modern sexual identities and sexualities in order to avoid anachronism. See, e.g., Alan Bray, *Homosexuality in Renaissance England* (London: Gay Men's Press, 1982), and the authors represented in *Queering the Renaissance*, ed. Jonathan Goldberg (Durham,

NC and London: Duke University Press, 1994). The view that homo-sexuality is a relatively new historical "invention" has been questioned by Joseph Cady. See his "'Masculine Love,' Renaissance Writing, and the 'New Invention of Homosexuality'," in *Homosexuality in Renaissance and Enlightenment England: Literary Representations in Historical Context*, ed. Claude J. Summers (New York: Harworth Press, Harrington Park Press), 1992, pp. 9–40, and "The 'Masculine Love' of the 'Princes of Sodom.' 'Practising the Art of Ganymede' at Henri III's Court: The Homosexuality of Henri III and His *Mignons* in Pierre de L'Estoile's *Mémoires-Journaux*," in *Desire and Discipline: Sex and Sexuality in the Premodern West*, ed. Jacqueline Murray and Konrad Eisenbichler (Toronto, Buffalo, London: University of Toronto Press, 1996), pp. 123–54.

3 The date of the introduction of the word "homosexual" into the language has yet to be resolved. It was probably first used in French by a certain Dr. Chatelain who, in a review of the sixth German edition of Richard von Krafft-Ebing's medical handbook of sexual deviance, the *Psychopathia sexualis mit besonderer Berücksichtigung conträren Sexualempfindung* (Stuttgart, 1886), refers to both *homosexualité* and *homosexuels*. For the text of this review, see *Annales Médico-Psychologique* 14 (Sept.–Oct. 1891), 330–1. Thus both words enter French a year earlier than English, where their first occurrence, according to the *Oxford English Dictionary*, is in Charles Gilbert Chaddock's 1892 translation of Krafft-Ebing's work. However, Joan DeJean informs us that the dictionary is wrong, that John Addington Symonds speaks of "homosexual relations" in *A Problem of Greek Ethics*, a text which, she suggests, was available at least as early as 1883. See her *Fictions of Sappho 1546–1937* (Chicago and London: University of Chicago Press, 1989), p. 213. She adds in a note (p. 346) that she has not been able to locate any trace of this 1883 edition, but that Symonds uses "homosexual" in his 1891 *A Problem in Modern Ethics*, and that according to an undocumented reference in the *Dictionnaire de la langue du dix-neuvième et du vingtième siècle*, the word first appeared in German in 1869 and in French in 1809.

4 Thus in a chapter entitled "Du péché de sodomie et du péché contre nature en nostre temps," Henri Estienne attributes its modern, Chris-tian resurgence to contact with Italy and Italian influence. See his *Apologie pour Hérodote*, ed. P Ristelhuber (Paris: Isidore Liseux, 1879), tome I, pp. 174–78.

5 Renaissance notions of sodomy are varied, covering a wide range of sex acts. Gilles de Rais, for instance, was accused and accused himself of committing the "shameful sin of sodomy" on countless children. According to the dispositions of various witnesses, however, his crime did not involve sexual penetration, only seminal discharge: "He said and confessed that he had emitted his spermatic seed in a most guilty manner onto the belly of said children." *Laughter for the Devil: The Trials*

of Gilles de Rais, Companion-in-arms of Joan of Arc (1440), introduction and translation from Latin and French by Reginald Hyatte (London and Toronto: Associated University Presses, 1984), pp. 84; 93; 113. See also Guy Poirier, *L'Homosexualité dans l'imaginaire de la Renaissance* (Paris: Champion, 1996), pp. 25–59.

6 The relevant passage in Aristotle's text is less precise, leading one to suspect either that Montaigne has adapted it to fit his purposes or that he is quoting from a translation. Both Pierre Villey (*Les Sources et l'évolution des Essais de Montaigne*, Paris: Hachette, 1908, vol. 1, p. 69) and Albert D. Menut ("Montaigne and the 'Nicomachean Ethics'," *Modern Philology* 31, 1934, 227–8) conjecture that he read the *Ethics* in Bernardus Felicianus' Latin translation, first published at Venice in 1541. In a more recent study, Edilia Traverso confirms that Montaigne read this particular work of Aristotle: "L'*Etica Nicomachea* è l'unica opera di Aristotele di cui i critici, unanimemente, danno per certa la lettura da parte di Montaigne. La maggior parte di essi concorda nel collocare tra il 1588 ed il 1592 il periodo in cui essa sarebbe avvenuta" (*Montaigne e Aristotele*, Florence: Felice Le Monnier, 1974, p. 97) and, most probably, in Felicianus' version, "che, al momento, sembra costituire ancore l'unica fonte accertata" (p. 98). Significantly, however, when we compare Montaigne's text: "Par coustume, dit Aristote, aussi souvent que par maladie, des femmes arrachent le poil, rongent leurs ongles, mangent des charbons et de la terre; et autant par coustume que par nature les masles se meslent aux masles" (I, xxiii, 115, c) with Felicianus' translation: "Alii item morbosi sunt vel ex consuetudine: ut pilorum evulsiones unguinum soriones, carbonum etiam et terrae comestiones: praeterea venereorum usus cum maribus; id quod tum natura, tum consuetudine evenit" (Traverso, pp. 101–2), we find not only that Montaigne attributes specifically to *femmes* customs which Felicianus and Aristotle ascribe indiscriminately to *alii*, but that he distinguishes as well between what women do *par maladie* and men *par nature*.

7 For example, Jean Fernel, *De luis venereae curatione perfectissima liber* (1579), Laurent Joubert's *De peste liber unus* (1567), and, for its theological implications, Théodore de Bèze's *De peste quaestiones duae explicatae* (1529). Nancy G. Siraisi's *Medieval and Early Renaissance Medicine: An Introduction to Knowledge and Practice* (Chicago and London: The University of Chicago Press, 1990) provides a comprehensive introduction to various aspects of medieval and Renaissance medical education, knowledge, disease, and treatment.

8 Lesbianism *per se* was not prosecuted in Renaissance Venice. It is difficult to argue from silence, but the fact that this was a form of sexuality that did not threaten the family may have made it a noncrime. See Guido Ruggiero, *The Boundaries of Eros: Sex Crime and Sexuality in Renaissance Venice* (New York and Oxford: Oxford University Press, 1985), note 21, pp. 189–90.

9 Cf. Pierre Champion, "La Légende des mignons," *Bibliothèque d'Humanisme et Renaissance* 6 (1939), 494–528. See also Poirier, *L'Homosexualité,* pp. 129–45.

10 Montaigne's *Journal de voyage* sheds some light on lesbians in working-class or rural circles, while Brantôme is more interested in their presence and activities at Court: "En notre France, telles femmes sont assez communes; et si dit-on pourtant qu'il n'y a pas longtemps qu'elles s'en sont mêlées, même que la façon en a été portée d'Italie par une dame que je ne nommerai point." Pierre de Bourdeille, Sieur de Brantôme, *Les Dames galantes,* ed. Maurice Rat (Paris: Garnier, 1960), p. 122.

11 *New Testament Scholarship; Paraphrases on Romans and Galatians,* ed. Robert D. Sider, vol. 42 of *Collected Works of Erasmus* (Toronto, Buffalo, London: University of Toronto Press, 1984), p. 18. Homosexuality for Paul illustrates a theological error, namely the exchanging of something authentic for something counterfeit. It exemplifies better than any other sin the very nature of sin, which is the perversion of an original good, a disorientation leading to confusion and error.

12 "Veluti si quis praelecturus secundam Maronis aeglogam, commoda praefactione praeparet, vel potius praemuniat auditorum animos ad hunc modum, vt dicat: amicitiam non coire nisi inter similes, similitudinem enim esse benevolentiae mutuae conciliatricem, contra dissimilitudinem odii dissidiique parentem." ("If for instance someone were going to read Virgil's second eclogue, he should prepare or rather protect the minds of his listeners with an appropriate preface in this way, and say: do not enter into friendship except among equals, for similarity promotes mutual good will, while dissimilarity on the other hand is the parent of hate and dissension.") Erasmus, *De ratione studii,* ed. Jean-Claude Margolin, in *Opera omnia,* vol. 2, p. 139. My translation. It should be pointed out that the full title of the work, *De ratione studii ac legendi interpretandique auctores liber,* gives a clearer idea of Erasmian concern with the problem of Christian interpretation of classical culture.

13 "Corydon rusticus, Alexis vrbanus; Corydon pastor, Alexis aulicus; Corydon indoctus . . . , Alexis eruditus; Corydon aetate prouectus, Alexis adolescens; Corydon deformis, hic formosus" (*De ratione studii,* p. 142). See Forest Tyler Stevens, "Erasmus's 'Tigress': The Language of Friendship, Pleasure, and the Renaissance Letter," *Queering the Renaissance,* pp. 132–34, and Jonathan Goldberg, "Colin to Hobbinol: Spencer's Familiar Letters," in *Displacing Homophobia: Gay Male Perspectives in Literature and Culture,* ed. Ronald R. Butters, John M. Clum, and Michael Moon (Durham, NC and London: Duke University Press, 1989), p. 113.

14 Moreover, in the interim, Calvinist propagandists had converted the *Servitude volontaire* into the *Contr'un,* transforming La Boétie's "exercita-

tion" (*Essais*, I, xxviii, 194 A) into a revolutionary pamphlet against the "tyranny" of King and Church, making it necessary for Montaigne to defend his religious and political orthodoxy.

15 For a detailed analysis of Montaigne's rereading of Pausanias' speech, see Gabriel-André Pérouse, " 'Cette autre licence grecque . . .': Montaigne et le Pausanias du *Banquet* de Platon," in *Montaigne et l'histoire des Hellènes, Actes du Colloque de Lesbos*, ed. Kyriaki Christodoulou (Paris: Klincksieck, 1994), pp. 184–94. In adapting the classical and humanist practice of marginalia to the *Essais*, Montaigne derives much of his most personal commentary from a reconsideration of his own words.

16 "Mais nous appellons laideur aussi une mesavenance au premier regard, qui loge principalement au visage, et souvent nous desgoute par bien legeres causes: du teint, d'une tache, d'une rude contenance, de quelque cause inexplicable sur des membres bien ordonnez et entiers. La laideur qui revestoit une ame tres-belle en La Boitie estoit de ce predicament" (III, xii, 1057 C).

17 "What indeed is this love of friendship? Why does no one love a deformed adolescent or a beautiful old man?" Cicero, *Tusculan Disputations*, IV.xxxiii (my translation). Cicero speaks with severity of the education given to young boys in Greece and of the disorders arising from their nudity in the gymnasia: "Mihi quidem haec in Graecorum gymnasiis nata consuetudo videtur; in quibus isti liberi et concessi sunt amores." Cf. Cicero, *De Republica*, Book IV.

18 For a more detailed analysis of citational reappropriation, see my *Montaigne bilingue* (Paris: Champion, 1991), pp. 77–98.

19 *Epigrammata*, XI.xii. Although most editors refrain from providing a translation, one is required if we are to have an idea of the original context of the passage from which Montaigne quotes as well as of the way in which he alters its meaning: "That with your hard mouth you rub the soft lips of snow-white Galaesus, that you lie with naked Ganymede (who denies it?), this is too much. But let it be enough; refrain at least from stimulating his groin with copulating hand. This sins more than your penis where beardless boys are concerned and, moreover, your fingers fashion and hasten manhood: thence a goatish odor and fast-growing hair and a beard at which mothers wonder, nor do baths in the clear light of day please. Nature has divided the male: one part is provided for girls, one for men. Use your part."

20 See William John Beck, "Montaigne face à l'homosexualité," *Bulletin de la Société des Amis de Montaigne*, 6/9–10 (1982), 47–48.

21 The reasons for his flight to Italy are not totally clear. According to Colletet and Scaliger, the charge of sodomy was leveled against him on more than one occasion, a charge diversely appreciated by Catholic and Protestant polemicists. Moreover, the warrant of arrest issued at Toulouse condemned him as a sodomite, but also as a Huguenot. Cf. Charles Dejob, *Marc-Antoine Muret: un professeur français en Italie dans la*

seconde moitié du xvie *siècle* (Paris, Ernest Thorin, 1881), pp. 46–52; 56. It is possible therefore that these accusations were politically motivated, made without much, if any, basis in fact.

22 Roger Trinquet has shown that Muret was in Bordeaux only from the first months of 1547 until the summer of 1548. See his "Recherches chronologiques sur la jeunesse de Marc-Antoine Muret," *Bibliothèque d'Humanisme et Renaissance* 27 (1965), 278–81.

23 "Disnant un jour à Rome avec nostre Ambassadeur, où estoit Muret et autres sçavans, je me mis sur le propos de la traduction Françoise de Plutarche, et contre ceux qui l'estimoient beaucoup moins que je ne fais, je maintenois au moins cela: que, où le traducteur a failli le vray sens de Plutarche, il y en a substitué un autre vraisemblable et s'entretenant bien aus choses suivantes et precedentes" (Montaigne, *Journal de voyage*, pp. 113–14).

24 Ibid., pp. 6–7. Cf. Richard Regosin, "Montaigne's Memorable Stories of Gender and Sexuality," *Montaigne Studies* 6/1–2 (1994), 187–201.

25 Ambroise Paré, *Des Monstres et prodiges*, ed. Jean Céard (Geneva: Droz, 1971), pp. 29–30. The case was sufficiently notorious for Jacques Duval to include it in his *Traité des hermaphrodites* (Paris: Isidore Liseux, 1880, reprint of the 1612 Rouen edition), pp. 338–39. He refers to this incident in support of his apology for Marie le Marcis, a celebrated hermaphrodite of Rouen, who, when he/she abandoned female dress, changed his/her name to Marin, announced his/her intention to marry the widow Jeane le Febvre, was charged and condemned to death by burning as a tribad. Marie, now called Marin, supported by his/her wife, appealed the condemnation, and Duval conducted the anatomical examination which led to his/her acquittal. For a retelling of the case, see Stephen Greenblatt, "Fiction and Friction," in *Reconstructing Individualism: Autonomy, Individuality, and the Self in Western Thought*, ed. Thomas C. Heller, Morton Sosna, and David E. Wellbery (Stanford University Press, 1986), pp. 30–52.

26 Ambroise Paré, André du Laurens, and Jacques Ferrand refer to examples of sex changes in women in Antiquity (including Iphis). These references show the extent to which questions of sex change engaged contemporary scientific and popular interest. Montaigne's account echoes the debate in contemporary medical circles over the natural transmutation of the sexes in humans. Literalists made the case for a sex change in women only through an extension of the clitoris. See Jacques Ferrand, *A Treatise on Lovesickness*, trans. and ed. Donald A. Beecher and Massimo Ciavolella. (Syracuse University Press, 1990), p. 382, and *Les Oevvres de Me André du Laurens, traduites de latin en françois par Me Theophile Gelle, revevës, corrigées, et augmentées en cette derniere Edition par G. Savvageon* (Paris: Chez Ian Petit-Pas, 1639), p. 358.

27 Aristotelian physiology presented woman as a deformed male, and reduced her role in procreation to that of prime matter, awaiting the

forming agency of male semen. Galen, on the other hand, was aware of the ovaries and of female "seed." The pseudo-Galenic *De spermate*, which was still considered to be an authoritative text in the sixteenth century, argued that men and women alike produced sperm, and that the gender of a child was the result of a conflict between male and female sperm. Joubert, for instance, has this to say about female ejaculation and the quality of her sperm: "Il ne faut ia douter, que ne soit bien vray ce que i'ay dit, la semance estre indifferante aus deus sexes, mais que nature pretand touiours d'an faire vn masle: comme celuy des conioins & accouplés, qui fournit plus de sperme, & du melheur, a la vertu formatrice, car la semance de la fame est an doute, si elle ha quelque part an cecy" (*Erreurs popvlaires av fait de la medecine et regime de santé, corrigés par M. Laur. Joubert*, Bordeaus [*sic*]: S. Millanges, 1578, p. 165).

28 This was consonant with Renaissance medical science. Thus Jacques Duval reports that history provides numerous examples of women who suddenly become men, but none of men who become women: "d'autant que toutes choses tendent à perfection, et n'ont regret à ce qui est moins parfaict." And since man's nature is more perfect than woman's, in those cases in which men have been reported to become women, the changes "ne sont survenus par nouvelle procréation, ny inversion des parties génitales, mais par ce que celle qui estoit cachée auparavant s'est mise à pleine évidence" (*Traité des hermaphrodites*, p. 322). Similarly, we find the following variant passage in the 1585 edition of Ambroise Paré's *Œuvres*: "aussi nous ne trouvons jamais en histoire veritable que d'homme aucun soit devenu femme, pour-ce que Nature tend tousjours à ce qui est le plus parfaict, et non au contraire faire que ce qui est parfaict devienne imparfaict" (*Monstres et prodiges*, ed. Jean Céard, p. 30). André du Laurens lists a number of examples, beginning with the Ancients, but concludes sceptically: "Certes ie tiens que c'est chose monstrueuse & fort difficile à croire" (*Oevvres*, p. 358).

29 Presumably the six or seven others were never found out.

30 For a study on female autoeroticism and its politico-religious ramifications, see Gregory de Rocher, "Ronsard's Dildo Sonnet: The Scandal of Poissy and Rasse des Nœux," in *Writing the Renaissance*, pp. 149–64. Henri Estienne recounts the story of a girl from Fontaines, a locality between Blois and Romarantin, who disguised herself as a man and married a girl from the region, living with her for two years. "Apres lequel temps estant descouverte la meschan-ceté de laquelle elle usoit pour contrefaire l'office de mari, fut prise, et ayant confessé fut là brulée toute vive." See his *Apologie pour Hérodote*, vol. 1, p. 178.

31 Montaigne seems to be saying that they married themselves during the

Mass in a ceremony of their own device, and not that they were married during a Mass that was said to solemnize their union.

32 James Boswell's translation of this passage is so inaccurate as to cast serious doubt on any conclusions he draws from it: "Roman experts said that since sex between male and female could be legitimate only within marriage, it had seemed equally fair [*juste*] to them to authorize [these] ceremonies and mysteries of the church." *Same-Sex Unions in Premodern Europe* (New York: Vintage Books, 1994), p. 265.

33 Ann Rosalind Jones and Peter Stallybrass state that there was no discourse "that could even *claim* to establish a definitive method by which one distinguished male from female." See their "Fetishizing Gender: Constructing the Hermaphrodite in Renaissance Europe," in *Body Guards: The Cultural Politics of Gender Ambiguity*, ed. Julia Epstein and Kristina Straub (New York and London: Routledge, 1991), p. 80. This indicates that in Renaissance medical and biological writings, the distinction was considered self-evident, and therefore not problematic.

34 The term hermaphrodite, as Claude-Gilbert Dubois reminds us, takes on a symbolic meaning at the close of the sixteenth century, when it comes to signify an ambiguous attitude composed of a mixture of opportunism and Machiavellianism. While a reductionist interpretation of *L'isle des Hermaphrodites* sees it essentially as a pamphlet against Henri III and his "mignons," Dubois reads it as a "composition allégorique, qui associe les indices de masculinité et de féminité, et rassemble les divers attributs de la vanité et de l'esprit mondain." See his edition of the work (Geneva: Droz, 1996), p. 21.

35 *Description de l'isle des Hermaphrodites, nouvellement decouverte . . . Pour servir du Supplement au Journal de Henri III* (Cologne: chez les Héritiers de Herman Demen, 1724), p. 22. Published anonymously, the work has been ascribed to Thomas Artus, sieur d'Embry, as well as to Du Perron. Cf. Poirier, *L'Homosexualité*, pp. 157–59. Kathleen Perry Long's "Hermaphrodites Newly Discovered: The Cultural Monsters of Sixteenth-Century France," in *Monster Theory*, ed. Jeffrey Jerome Cohen (Minneapolis and London: University of Minnesota Press, 1996), pp. 183–201, is concerned especially with the relationship of sign systems and identity formation.

36 "Elégie III," *Œuvres*, p. 116.

37 'Elégie I," ibid., p. 107.

38 In the "Ode to Aphrodite," the only complete poem of Sappho's in existence, it is not clear, because the text at a crucial point is hopelessly garbled, whether the beloved is a woman or a man. The early printed texts gave several different versions, all of which avoided the gender problem. Thus in Henri Estienne's 1554 edition of the text, the first to be printed in verse form and under Sappho's name, the beloved's gender is unspecified. See Margaret Williamson, *Sappho's Immortal Daughters* (Cambridge, MA and London: Harvard University Press,

1995), p. 51; DeJean, *Fictions of Sappho*, p. 30; François Rigolot, "Louise Labé et la redécouverte de Sappho," *Nouvelle Revue du xvie siècle* 1 (1983), 19–31. For a more recent account, see François Rigolot, *Louise Labé Lyonnaise ou la Renaissance au féminin* (Paris: Champion, 1997), pp. 31–67.

39 Stephen Orgel, "Nobody's Perfect: Or Why Did the English Stage Take Boys for Women?," in *Displacing Homophobia: Gay Male Perspectives in Literature and Culture*, ed Ronald R. Butters, John M. Clum, and Michael Moon (Durham NC, and London: Duke University Press, 1989), pp. 7–29.

40 Historians have surprisingly little to say about women on the French Renaissance stage. Germain Bapst asserts merely that "la femme n'apparut d'une façon constante sur un théâtre régulier que la seconde moitié du xvie siècle. On ne connaît guère au xvie siècle que l'existence d'une seule comédienne de profession." *Essai sur l'histoire du théâtre: la mise en scène, le décor, le costume, l'architecture, l'éclairage, l'hygiène* (Paris: Hachette, 1893), p. 177. We know however that royalty participated in Court performances: "La traduction française de la *Sophonisbe* du Trissin fut jouée à Blois à l'occasion des noces de grands personnages. On est peu renseigné sur les décors, beaucoup mieux sur les acteurs, bénévoles et de haut rang, parmi lesquels figuraient entre autres les princesses royales et Marie Stuart . . ." Madeleine Lazard, *Le Théâtre en France au xvie siècle* (Paris: Presses Universitaires de France, 1980), p. 152. Even the more recent and very thorough *French Theatre in the Neo-Classical Era, 1550–1789*, ed. William D. Howarth (Cambridge University Press, 1997) fails to locate any document referring to the presence of women, outside of courtly circles, on the French Renaissance stage.

41 Estienne Pasquier, *Œuvres* (Amsterdam: Compagnie des Libraires Associez, 1723), I.VII, p. 704.

42 In the introduction to his critical edition of Jodelle's *L'Eugène* (University of Exeter, 1987), p. xv, M. J. Freeman writes, but without supporting documentation, that Jodelle himself played the part of Cléopâtre: "Il y a de grandes chances que Jodelle lui-même ait tenu un rôle dans sa propre pièce, puisqu'on sait qu'il tint le rôle de Cléopâtre dans sa tragédie *Cleopatre captive* [*sic*]."

43 Gillian Jondorf, *French Renaissance Tragedy: The Dramatic Word* (Cambridge University Press, 1990). Other recent studies of the literary aspect of the theatre of the day include Enea Balmas, *Un poeta del Rinascimento francese – Etienne Jodelle. La sua vita, il suo tempo* (Florence: Leo S. Olschki, 1962) and Madeleine Lazard, *Le Théâtre en France*. Neither of these deals with practical problems of acting or staging, presumably because of the lack of appropriate documents.

44 Stephen Gosson, *Playes Confuted in Five Actions*, in Arthur F. Kenney, *Markets of Bawdrie: The Dramatic Criticism of Stephen Gosson*, Salzburg Studies in Literature 4 (Salzburg: Institut für Englische Sprache und Literatur, 1974), p. 175.

45 See Laura Levine, *Men in Women's Clothing: Anti-Theatricality and Effeminization, 1579–1642* (Cambridge University Press, 1994), pp. 9–10.

46 Plato, *The Republic*, 10, 3, 605 and 3, 1, 393–5. Fear of this eventuality is prominent in antitheatrical propaganda in Renaissance England, which argued, after Plato, that boys who perform as women risk being transformed into their roles and playing the part in reality. See Jonas Barish, *The Antitheatrical Prejudice* (Berkeley: University of California Press), 1981.

47 In the attention he pays to clothing rather than the wearer, Rabelais anticipates the "Clothes-Philosophy" of Carlyle's Diogenes Teufelsdröckh. Jean Delumeau, writes that "à l'époque d'Elizabeth, qui posséda, dit-on, 6 000 robes et 80 perruques, le vêtement avait acquis une telle place que dans les portraits il importait désormais plus que le visage." *La Civilisation de la Renaissance*, pp. 332–3.

48 François Rabelais, *Gargantua*, ed. Floyd Gray (Paris: Champion, 1995), p. 85. This is an accurate transcription of the way Aristophanes describes the androgyne in Plato's *Symposium*, except for one significant detail: Rabelais turns its two faces *towards* one another.

49 Humor aptly captured by a recent translation: "They walked upright, as we do, in whichever direction they wanted. And when they started to run fast, they were just like people doing cartwheels. They stuck their legs straight out all round, and went bowling along, supported on their eight limbs, and rolling along at high speed." *Symposium of Plato*, trans. Tom Griffith (Berkeley and Los Angeles: University of California Press, 1986), 190 a.

50 Carla Freccero, "The Other and the Same: The Image of the Hermaphrodite in Rabelais," in *Rewriting the Renaissance: The Discourses of Sexual Difference in Early Modern Europe*, ed. Margaret W. Ferguson, Maureen Quilligan, and Nancy J. Vickers (Chicago and London: University of Chicago Press, 1986), p. 152. See also Jerome Schwartz, "Scatology and Eschatology in Gargantua's Androgyne Device," *Etudes Rabelaisiennes* 14 (1977), 265–75, who seeks to reconcile the comic and Christian aspects of the myth.

51 John Calvin, *Commentary on the Epistles of Paul the Apostle to the Corinthians* (Edinburgh: Calvin Translation Society, 1848), vol. 1, p. 423.

52 *Sex* derives from the Latin *sexus*, the substantive form of the verb *seco*: to divide, to cut in two.

53 See Denis O'Brien, *Empedocles' Cosmic Cycle: A Reconstruction from the Fragments and Secondary Sources* (Cambridge University Press, 1969), pp. 227–30.

54 On the other hand, Plato's Aristophanes refers to a third kind of attraction, one drawing masculine halves to one another, a distinction which may have some similarity to Empedocles' theories of how some men are manlier than others, although the arrangement of heads and genitals is probably all due to Plato (*Symposium*, 189 e, 190 a).

55 Any more than Plato's, at least not until after Zeus had separated them into two entities and Apollo had twisted their face and half-neck round towards the cut side (Plato, *Symposium*, 190 e), an eventuality Gargantua's medallion does not foresee.

56 See Lauren Silberman, "Mythographic Transformations of Ovid's Hermaphrodite," *Sixteenth Century Journal* 20.4 (1998), 643–52.

57 Paré, *Des Monstres et prodiges*, ed. Céard, p. 94.

58 Lucretius, *De rerum natura libri sex*, ed. William Ellery Leonard and Stanley Barney Smith (Madison: University of Wisconsin Press, 1942), v. 837–9:

> In those days also the telluric world
> Strove to beget the monsters that upsprung
> With their astounding visages and limbs –
> The Man-woman – a thing betwixt the twain,
> Yet neither, and from either sex remote.
>
> (trans. William Ellery Leonard)

59 Agrippa d'Aubigné, *Œuvres*, ed. Henri Weber, Jacques Bailbé, and Marguerite Soulié (Paris: Gallimard, 1969), *Les Tragiques*, II, "Princes," vv. 667–9, p. 69. The reference is to ill-suited princes and kings.

60 See Denis Richet, "Henri III dans l'historiographie et dans la légende," in *Henri III et son temps*, ed. Robert Sauzet (Paris: Vrin, 1992), pp. 13–20. Political satirists presented Henri III as "womanish" because he was unable to produce an heir or provide final victory in the Religious Wars. Cf. Cady, "The 'Masculine Love'," pp. 127–28, 132–33.

61 "On le trouve en ce sens dans les *Cent nouvelles*, comme chez Commynes, et le bourgeois de Paris l'emploie en 1522 dans son *Journal* en relatant la nomination de François Ier d'un bailli." Pierre Chevallier, *Henri III, roi shakespearien* (Paris: Fayard, 1985), p. 418.

62 D'Aubigné, *Sa vie à ses enfants*, in *Œuvres*, p. 398.

63 See Alan Bray, "Homosexuality and Male Friendship," in *Queering the Renaissance*, pp. 42–7.

64 Keith Cameron, *Henri III A Maligned or Malignant King?* (University of Exeter, 1978), shows that upon his ascension to the French throne, Henri quickly became the victim of satirical tracts and prints circulated by the Protestants on the one hand, and the League on the other. Cf. Jacqueline Boucher, *Société et mentalités autour de Henri III* (Paris: Champion, 1981), vol. I, pp. 103–09 and *passim*.

65 J. Quicherat, *Histoire du costume en France depuis les temps les plus reculés jusqu'à la fin du XVIIe siècle* (Paris: Hachette, 1877), pp. 419–20.

66 "Cependant le roi faisait tournois, joutes et ballets et force mascarades où il se trouvoit ordinairement habillé en femme, ouvroit son pourpoint et descouvrait sa gorge, y portant un collier de perles et trois collets de toile, deux à fraize et un renversé, ainsi que lors les portoient les dames de sa cour." Pierre de L'Estoile, *Journal*, p. 142, entry from February 24,

1577. Cf. Jacqueline Boucher, *La Cour de Henri III* (Ouest-France, 1986), p. 25.

67 *Discours sur les couronnels de l'infanterie de France*, in Brantôme, *Œuvres complètes*, ed. Ludovic Lalanne (Paris: Renouard, 1873), vol. 6, p. 28.

68 In their article on "The Hermaphrodite and the Orders of Nature," Lorraine Daston and Katharine Park point out that the authors of vernacular medical works relating to generation hoped to boost sales by appealing to the prurient interests of the growing popular audience for printed books. See *Premodern Sexualities*, ed. Louise Fradenbury and Carla Freccero (New York and London: Routledge, 1996), pp. 117–36. Alison Klairmont Lingo discusses the debate in contemporary medical circles on the appropriateness of providing knowledge about the body and human reproduction in vernacular texts available to any literate person with the means to buy them. See her "Print's Role in the Politics of Women's Health Care in Early Modern France," in *Culture and Identity in Early Modern Europe (1500–1800). Essays in Honor of Natalie Zemon Davis*, ed. Barbara B. Diefendorf and Carla Hesse (Ann Arbor: University of Michigan Press, 1993), pp. 203–21. See also Charles-Adolphe-Ernest Wickersheimer, *Médecine et les médecins en France à l'époque de la Renaissance* (Paris: A. Maloine, 1905), especially the chapter on Joubert, pp. 497–512.

69 Although Brantôme's works were not published until 1665 and in Holland, they remain not only an important source of information on the marginal side of Court life in sixteenth-century France, but also, and more pertinently for present purposes, on the way in which sexual matters were regarded and reported at the close of the century.

70 "Si feray-je encore question, et puis plus, qui, possible, n'a point esté recherchée de tout le monde, ny, possible, songée: à sçavoir-mon [*sic*] si deux dames amoureuses l'une de l'autre, comme il s'est veu et se void souvent aujourd'huy, couchées ensemble, et faisant ce qu'on dit *donna con donna* (en imitant la docte Sapho lesbienne), peuvent commettre adultere, et entre elles faire leurs marys cocus". Brantôme, *Les Dames galantes*, p. 119. French Renaissance culture, to judge from Brantôme and Montaigne, did not display fear of homosexuality. On the other hand, anxiety about the fidelity of women was prevalent, as a logical consequence of concern with questions of property and legitimate heirs.

71 Madeleine Lazard has two chapters on "Le rapport Kinsey du XVIe siècle" in her *Pierre de Bourdeille, seigneur de Brantôme* (Paris: Fayard, 1995), pp. 219–46.

72 Book I, 91 (and not 119, as Brantôme states).

73 *Fricatrices* were thought to be suffering from *furor uterinus* or *nymphotomania*, which is an immoderate burning in the genital area of the female, caused by the surging of hot vapor, bringing about the erection of the clitoris. Because of this burning sensation, women were thought to be driven insane, even dangerously violent. Some threw themselves

into the water to cool their ardor, as Sappho is alleged to have done. See Jacques Ferrand, *A Treatise on Lovesickness*, p. 386.

74 Brantôme, *Les Dames galantes*, pp. 124–5. There is a blank in the manuscript, because either Brantôme or his editor did not want to say how and where "godemichis" were made. Less restrained, Ronsard writes that a "godmicy" is "un gros instrument qui se fait pres d'icy" (*Les Amours diverses*, 1578 edition, sonnet xlv).

75 Translated into French in 1578 under the title *Dialogue de la beauté des femmes* by a certain J. Pallet.

76 Brantôme, *Les Dames galantes*, p. 127.

77 The story of Sappho and Phaon arose most probably in the fourth century. Phaon was a ferryman on the island of Lesbos. Approached by Aphrodite disguised as an old woman, he transported her across the water without asking for payment. In return, she transformed him into a beautiful youth with whom all the women of Lesbos fell in love. At some point, Sappho became identified as one of these women. Spurned by him, according to the legend renewed by Ovid, she is said to have thrown herself off the cliff at Leucas. See Williamson, *Sappho's Immortal Daughters*, pp. 8–12.

78 "J'en cogneus l'encloueure, parce que je sçavois bien qu'elle tenoit cette damoiselle en ses delices à pot et à feu, et la gardoit precieusement pour sa bouche." Brantôme, *Les Dames galantes*, p. 124.

79 Ibid., p. 31. In the dedication, he writes that his book was composed with the duc d'Alençon's interest in "bons mots et contes" in mind (pp. 1–2).

80 Since the 1579 edition was not available to me, I quote from Joubert, *Popular Errors*, trans. de Rocher, p. 6.

81 "Millanges to the Reader [1579]," in Joubert, *Popular Errors*. Gregory de Rocher's translation, p. 277. Examining the subject of his book in his 1579 "Letter to a Friend," Joubert asks whether it is "so lascivious and indecent that proper women could not read it or have it read to them," explaining that the acts his words designate "can only be understood by women who are legitimately allowed (because of holy matrimony) to have a certain knowledge and enjoyment of such things. Girls can learn nothing from this, neither good nor evil, if they have not been instructed in these matters elsewhere, as (unfortunately) most of them have already been, and too well" (p. 8).

82 For its popular success, see the "Letter by Barthélemy Cabrol to Anthoine de Clermont" in Laurent Joubert, *The Second Part of the Popular Errors*, trans. Gregory David de Rocher (Tuscaloosa and London: The University of Alabama Press, 1995), p. 15.

83 In his apologetic letter to Marguerite de Valois, Joubert clearly anticipates public criticism for his outspoken language, especially in the chapter on determining virginity: "Ie craindrois les langues venimeuses des anuieus, malins & mesdisans, qui pourront trouuer mal seant, que

ie propose à V. M. vn tel suiet, duquel ie suis côtraint an quelques
androis tenir des propos, qui samblet [*sic*] trop charnels: côme an
traitant de la concepcion, de la grossesse, de l'Anfantemant, de la
Gessive, & sur tout de la cognoissance du Pucellage." "Ala [*sic*] Tres-
Auguste Reyne de Navarre, Filhe [*sic*], Seur et fame de Roy." Joubert,
Erreurs popvlaires, 1578, p. 572. ("I would fear the evil tongues of the
envious, mean, and malicious who will manage to find it indecent that I
suggest such a subject to Your Majesty, when I am forced in a few
passages to touch upon matters that are too physical, such as when
treating conception, pregnancy, birth, lying-in, and, especially, the
reckoning of virginity." *Popular errors*, trans. De Rocher, p. 278).

84 Louis Dulieu, "Laurent Joubert, chancelier de Montpellier," *Bibliothèque
d'Humanisme et Renaissance* 31.1 (1969), 148–49.

85 This reference to the great cost of reproducing the illustrations is found
in the author's remarks "Au lecteur" in *Les Œuvres de M. Ambroise Paré*
(Paris: Gabriel Buon, 1575), p. 2. While the anatomical illustrations
which André du Laurens includes in his treatise are more serious than
sensational, he is not unaware of their diversionary character: "Plusieurs blasment & reiettent l'inspection des tables & figures, & disent
qu'elle retarde les studieux plus qu'elle ne les auance; pour moy ie tiens
qu'elle n'est point totalement inutile . . . Au reste i'ay commandé de
mettre toutes les figures ensemble au milieu presque de l'oeuvre, afin de
recréer les yeux des Lecteurs" (*Oevvres*, Livre cinquiéme [*sic*], postface, S
iiij).

86 Thus Jean Céard writes in the introduction to his edition of Paré's work
(p. xxxv): "le livre *Des monstres et prodiges*, c'est au fond le livre d'images
d'Ambroise Paré, de splendides illustrations accompagnées de textes
qui mettent en mouvement l'imagination – un voyage au pays du
possible, et comme son repos d'un plus grand travail." See also Marie-
Hélène Huet's opening chapter on "The Renaissance Monster," in
Monstrous Imagination (Cambridge, MA and London: Harvard University
Press, 1993), pp. 13–35. In his remarks on monsters and hermaphrodites, André du Laurens refers to the role of the imagination, even
quoting the story of a woman from near Pisa who gave birth to a
daughter "toute couuerte de poils semblables à ceux d'un chameau
parce qu'elle auoit continuellement une image de Saint Iean Baptiste
deuant ses yeux," while postponing his own opinion on the matter
(*Oevvres*, p. 398).

87 If the text of the charges was published, it has not come down to us.
However, Paré's apology, entitled the *Responce de M. Ambroise Paré, premier
Chirurgien du Roy, aux calomnies d'anciens Médecins et Chirurgiens, touchant ses
oeuvres*, was published in 1575 and reproduced by Le Docteur Le
Paulmier (Claude-Stéphen) *Ambroise Paré, d'après de nouveaux documents
découverts aux Archives Nationales et des papiers de famille* (Paris: Perrin, 1887).
Paré's point by point rebuttal indicates quite clearly that he was

charged with writing about anatomical and sexual matters in the vernacular, that is to say in a nonscientific language, therefore in a nonscientific way, with other intentions in mind. His replies invariably include reference to precedent, e.g. "Pour le second poinct, ou vous m'objectez que telle leçon peut inciter la ieunesse à luxure, Gal. liu. 14 ch. 9. nous en a laissé par escrit les mesmes paroles" ("Mémoire d'Ambroise Paré en réponse aux attaques de la Faculté, à propos de la publication de ses oeuvres," in Le Paulmier, *Ambroise Paré*, p. 224), they fail to counter the vulgarization charge directly, inasmuch as the works of the authors he quotes for justification were written in Greek or Latin.

88 Le Paulmier, *Ambroise Paré*, "Mémoire," p. 232. In his 1558 *Recueil d'arrestz notables des courts sovveraines de France*, Jean Papon describes lesbianism as a crime punishable by death. Since the original was not available, I quote from the 1624 Latin translation: "Duae mulieres inuicem lasciuientes absque masculo, morte puniendae sunt: idque delicti genus damnatus & contra naturam foedissimus coitus est . . ." Ioannes Paponius, *Corpvs ivris francici, sev, absolvtissima collectio arrestorum, siue rerum in svpremis Franciae Tribunalibus & Parlamentis iudicatarum*, Cologne: Sumptibus Samuelis Crispini, 1624, p. 707.

89 See Ferrand, *Treatise*, pp. 33–4.

90 Ferrand, *Treatise*, p. 332.

91 Because of its title, potential readers would have associated it with Antonio Beccadelli's *Hermaphroditus*, a priapic poem published in 1425, which acquired almost instant notoriety. Copies of it were publicly burned in various Italian cities and it was condemned by a number of influential scholars, including Lorenzo Valla and Leonardo Bruni.

92 Jacques Duval, *Traité des hermaphrodites*, 10–11.

CONCLUSION

1 Pornography, "writing about prostitutes," emerged from the literature and imagery that purported to recount the lives of prostitutes, a genre that traced its origins to Lucian's *Dialogue of the Courtesans*. Although the *Trésor de la langue française* dates *pornographe* from Restif de la Bretonne's 1769 treatise entitled *Le Pornographe*, the Bloch and von Wartburg *Dictionnaire étymologique de la langue française* gives 1558 for *pornographie*. In any event, what we now call pornography existed long before, even if not as a distinct concept. With the advent of printing, erotic or obscene texts, which had been limited to the private circulation of manuscripts, entered the public marketplace. The resulting censorship imposed by civil and religious authorities reflects the uneasy transition from a society in which access to forbidden knowledge was restricted to the learned to one that divulged it indiscriminately. See *The Invention of Pornography: Obscenity and the Origins of Modernity, 1500–1800*, ed. Lynn Hunt (New York: Zone Books, 1993), pp. 9–18 and *passim*.

Bibliography

PRIMARY WORKS

Agricola, Rodolphus. *De inventione dialectica libri omnes.* Cologne: I. Gymnicvs, 1539.

Agrippa (de Nettesheim), Henri Corneille (Cornelius). *Discours abrégé sur la noblesse et l'excellence du sexe féminin, de sa prééminence sur l'autre sexe et du sacrement du mariage.* Ed. Marie-Josèphe Dhavernas. Paris: Côté-femmes éditions, 1990.

De nobilitate et praecellentia foeminei sexus. Ed. R. Antonioli. Geneva: Droz, 1990.

Aphthonius. *Ludus literarius or The Grammar Schoole.* Ed. E. T. Campagnac. Liverpool University Press, 1917.

Ariosto, Ludovico. *Lirica.* Ed. Giuseppe Fatini. Bari: Gius. Laterza e figli, 1924.

Aristotle. *The Nicomachean Ethics.* Trans. J. A. K. Thomson. London: Penguin, 1958.

[Artus, Thomas]. *Description de l'isle des Hermaphrodites, nouvellement decouverte . . . Pour servir du Supplement au Journal de Henri III.* Cologne: chez les Héritiers de Herman Demen, 1724.

L'Isle des hermaphrodites. Ed. Claude-Gilbert Dubois. Geneva: Droz, 1996.

Aubigné, Agrippa d'. *Oeuvres.* Ed. Henri Weber, Jacques Bailbé, and Marguerite Soulié. Paris: Gallimard, 1969.

Billon, François de. *Le Fort inexpugnable de l'honneur du sexe Femenin [sic].* Printed in Switzerland: S. R. Publishers Ltd., Johnson Reprint, Mouton, 1970.

Bloch, Oscar and W. von Wartburg. *Dictionnaire étymologique de la langue française.* Paris: Presses Universitaires de France, 1964.

Boccaccio, Giovanni. *De claris mulieribus.* Ed. Herbert G. Wright. London: Oxford University Press, 1943.

Brantôme (Pierre de Bourdeille, Sieur de). *Discours sur les couronnels de l'infanterie de France,* in *Œuvres complètes,* vol. 6. Ed. Ludovic Lalanne. Paris: Renouard, 1873.

Les Dames galantes. Ed. Maurice Rat. Paris: Garnier, 1960.

Briçonnet, Guillaume and Marguerite d'Angoulême. *Correspondance (1521–1524). Années 1521–1522.* Ed. Christine Martineau and Michel Veissière, with Henry Heller. Geneva: Droz, 1975.

Brinsley, John. *Ludus literarius or The Grammar Schoole.* Ed. E. T. Campagnac. Liverpool University Press, 1917.

Calvin, Jean. *Institution de la religion chrestienne.* Paris: Les Belles Lettres, 1961.
    Commentary on the Epistles of Paul the Apostle to the Corinthians. Edinburgh: Calvin Translation Society, 1848, vol. 1.

Cardano, Gerolamo (Cardan, Jérôme). *Ma Vie.* Trans. Jean Dayre. Paris: Champion, 1936.

Catullus. *Carmina.* Ed. Robinson Ellis. Oxford: Clarendon Press, 1911.

Cellini, Benvenuto. *La Vita.* Ed. Lorenzo Bellotto. Parma: Ugo Guanda, 1996.

[Cicero]. *Ad Herennium de ratione dicendi.* Ed. Harry Caplan. Cambridge, MA: Harvard University Press; London: William Heinemann, 1989.

Cicero. *De inventione. De optimo genere oratorum. Topica.* Ed. H. M. Hubbell. Cambridge, MA: Harvard University Press, 1968.

Colletet, Guillaume. *Pierre de Ronsard "ses juges et ses imitateurs."* Ed. Franca Bevilacqua Caldari. Paris: Nizet, 1983.

Cotgrave, Randle. *A Dictionaire of the French and English Tongues.* Reproduced from the first edition, London, 1611, with intro. by William S. Woods. Columbia: University of South Carolina Press, 1950.

Du Bellay, Joachim. *Deffense et Illustration de la langue françoyse.* Ed. Henri Chamard. Paris: Didier, 1948.

Du Guillet, Pernette. *Rymes.* Ed. Victor E. Graham. Geneva: Droz, 1968.

Du Laurens, André. *Les Oevvres. Traduites de latin en françois par Me Theophile Gelée, revevës, corrigées, et augmentées en cette derniere Edition par G. Savvageon.* Paris: Chez Ian Petit-Pas, ruë Sainct Iacques, à l'Escu de Venise, 1639.

Duval, Jacques. *Traité des hermaphrodites.* Reprint of the 1612 Rouen edition. Paris: Isidore Liseux, 1880.

Erasmus, Desiderius. *Opera omnia Desiderii Erasmi Roterodami.* Ed. Jean-Claude Margolin. Amsterdam: North Holland Publishing Co., 1971–2.
    De conscribendis epistolis. In *Opera omnia*, vol. 1, part 2.
    De ratione studii. In *Opera omnia*, vol. 2.
    New Testament Scholarship; Paraphrases on Romans and Galatians. Ed. Robert D. Sider. *Collected Works of Erasmus*, vol. 42. Toronto, Buffalo, London: University of Toronto Press, 1984.

Estienne, Charles. *Paradoxes, ce sont propos contre la commune opinion, debatus, en forme de Declamations forenses pour exerciter les ieunes aduocats, en causes difficiles.* Poitiers: Au Pelican par Ian de Marnef, 1553.

Estienne, Henri. *Apologie pour Hérodote.* Ed. P. Ristelhuber. Paris: Isidore Liseux, 1879.

Ferrand, Jacques. *A Treatise on Lovesickness.* Trans. and ed. Donald A. Beecher and Massimo Ciavolella. Syracuse University Press, 1990.

Flore, Jeanne. *Contes amoureux*, ed. Gabriel-A. Pérouse. Lyon: Presses Universitaires de Lyon, 1980.

Gournay, Marie de. *Le Proumenoir de Monsieur de Montaigne (1594)*. Ed. Patricia Francis Cholakian. Delmar, New York: Scholars' Facsimiles and Reprints, 1985.

"Préface à l'édition des *Essais* de Montaigne (Paris: Abel L'Angelier, 1595)." Ed. François Rigolot. *Montaigne Studies* 1 (1989), 7–60.

Jerome, Saint. *Adversus Jovinianum. Patrologia Latina*, vol. 23. Paris: Vrayet, 1845.

Jodelle, Estienne. *L'Eugène*. Ed. M. J. Freeman. University of Exeter, 1987.

Joubert, Laurent. *Popular Errors*. Trans. Gregory de Rocher. Tuscaloosa and London: University of Alabama Press, 1989.

Erreurs popvlaires av fait de la medecine et regime de santé, corrigés par M. Laur. Joubert. Bordeaus [*sic*]: S. Millanges, 1578.

The Second Part of the Popular Errors. Trans. Gregory David de Rocher. Tuscaloosa and London: University of Alabama Press, 1995.

Labé, Louise. *Œuvres complètes*. Ed. François Rigolot. Paris: Garnier-Flammarion, 1986.

La Boétie, Etienne de. *Œuvres complètes*. Ed. Paul Bonnefon. Geneva: Slatkine Reprints, 1967.

Lamentationes Matheoluli. Ed. Alfred Schmitt. Bonn: Philosophische Fakultät der Universität Bonn, 1974.

Le Fèvre, Jean. *Les Lamentations de Matheolus et le Livre de Leesce*. Ed. A.-G. Van Hamel. Paris: Librairie Emile Bouillan, 1905.

Le Franc, Martin. *Le Champion des dames. Liure plaisant copieux & habondant en sentences. Contenant la deffence des dames, contre malebouche & ses consors, & victoires dicelles*. Paris: Pierre Vidoue, pour Galliot du Pré, 1530.

Lemaire de Belges, Jean. *Les Epîtres de l'Amant vert*. Ed. Jean Frappier. Lille and Geneva: Droz, 1948.

Œuvres. Ed. J. Stecher. Geneva: Slatkine Reprints, 1969.

L'Estoile, Pierre de. *Journal du règne de Henri III, 1574–1589*. Ed. L.-R. Lefèvre. Paris: Gallimard, 1943.

Lipsius, Justus. *Epistolica institutio*. Ed. and trans. R. V. Young and M. Thomas Hester. Carbondale and Edwardsville: Southern Illinois University Press, 1996.

Lorris, Guillaume de and Jean de Meun. *Le Roman de la rose*. Ed. Ernest Langlois. Paris: Firmin-Didot, 1914–24.

Lucretius. *De rerum natura libri sex*. Ed. William Ellery Leonard and Stanley Barney Smith. Madison: University of Wisconsin Press, 1942.

Magny, Olivier de. *Les Odes*. Ed. E. Courbet. Paris: Lemerre, 1876.

Map, Walter. "A Discussion of Valerius to Rufinus the Philosopher, That He Should Not Take a Wife," in *De nugis curialium. Courtiers' Trifles*. Ed. and trans. M. R. James. Revised by C. N. L. Brooke and R. A. B. Mynors. Oxford: Clarendon Press, 1983.

Marconville, Jean de. *De la bonté et mauvaisté des femmes. Préface de Françoise Koehler.* Paris: Côté-femmes, 1991.

Marguerite de Navarre. *L'Heptaméron.* Ed. Michel François. Paris: Garnier Frères, 1964.

   Marguerites de la Marguerite des Princesses. Ed. Ruth Thomas. The Hague: Mouton, 1970.

   Le Miroir de l'âme pécheresse. Ed. Renja Salminen. Helsinki: Suomalainen Tiediakatemia, 1979.

Marguerite de Valois. *Mémoires et autres écrits.* Ed. Yves Cazaux. Paris: Mercure de France, 1986.

Marmontel, Jean-François. *Elémens de littérature,* in *Œuvres complètes.* Geneva: Slatkine Reprints, vol. 4, 1968.

Marot, Clément. *Œuvres poétiques.* Ed. Gérard Defaux. Paris: Garnier, vol. 1, 1990; vol. 2, 1993.

Martial. *Epigrams.* Trans. Walter C. A. Ker. London: William Heinemann and New York: G. P. Putnam, 1919–20.

Molinet, Jean. *Les Faictz et dictz.* Ed. Noël Dupire. Paris: Société des Anciens Textes Français, 1937.

Montaigne, Michel de. *Essais.* Paris: chez la veufve Dallin, 1625.

   Essais. Reproduction en phototypie. Paris: Hachette, 1906–1931.

   Journal de voyage. Ed. François Rigolot. Paris: Presses Universitaires de France, 1992.

   Les Essais de Michel, Seigneur de Montaigne. Edition nouvelle. Paris: Jean Camusat, 1635.

   Les Essais. Ed. Pierre Villey and V. L. Saulnier. Paris: Presses Universitaires de France, 1965.

Nevizzano, Giovanni. *Sylvae nuptialis libri sex.* Lyons: A. de Harsy, 1572.

Ovid. *The Art of Love and Other Poems.* Ed. J. H. Mozley. London: William Heinemann, 1929.

   The Heroides. Ed. Grant Showerman. London: William Heinemann and New York: G. P. Putnam, 1931.

   Metamorphoses. Ed. Frank Justus Miller. Cambridge, MA: Harvard University Press, and London: William Heinemann, 1984.

Paponius, Ioannes. *Corpvs ivris francici, sev, absolvtissima collectio arrestorum, siue rerum in svpremis Franciae Tribunalibus & Parlamentis iudicatarum.* Colonia Allobrogum: Sumptibus Samuelis Crispini, 1624.

Paré, Ambroise. *Deux livres de chirurgie.* Paris: André Wechel, 1573.

   Les Oeuvres de M. Ambroise Paré. Paris: Gabriel Buon, 1575.

   Des Monstres et prodiges. Ed. Jean Céard. Geneva: Droz, 1971.

Pasquier, Estienne. *Œuvres.* Amsterdam: Compagnie des Libraires Associez, 1723.

Pizan or Pisan, Christine de. *Livre de la Cité des dames.* Ed. Eric Hicks and Thérèse Moreau. Paris: Stock, 1986.

Plato. *Symposium.* Trans. Tom Griffith. Berkeley and Los Angeles, University of California Press, 1986.

Pont-Aymery, Alexandre de. *Paradoxe apologique, où il est fidellement démonstré que la femme est beaucoup plus parfaite que l'homme en toute action de vertu.* Paris: A. L'Angelier, 1594.

Quintilian. *Institutio oratoria.* Ed. H. E. Butler. London: William Heinemann; Cambridge, MA: Harvard University Press, 1963.

Rabelais, François. *Gargantua.* Ed. Floyd Gray. Paris: Champion, 1995.

Oeuvres complètes. Ed. Pierre Jourda. Paris: Garnier, 1991.

Pantagruel. Ed. Floyd Gray. Paris: Champion, 1997.

Tiers Livre. Ed. Abel Lefranc. Paris: Champion, 1931.

Tiers Livre. Ed. Michael Screech. Geneva: Droz; Paris: Minard, 1964.

Rainolde, Richard. *The Foundacion of Rhetorike.* New York: Scholars' Facsimiles & Reprints, 1945.

Rimbaud, Arthur. *Œuvres complètes. Correspondance.* Lausanne: Henri Kaeser, 1948.

Robert, Paul. *Dictionnaire historique de la langue française.* Paris: Le Robert, 1992.

Scève, Maurice. *Délie.* Ed. I. D. McFarlane. Cambridge University Press, 1966.

Second, Jean. *Les Baisers.* Ed. Maurice Rat. Paris: Garnier, 1938.

Tyard, Pontus de. *Solitaire premier ou Discours des Muses, et de la fureur Poëtique.* Ed. Silvio F. Baridon. Geneva: Droz, 1950.

SECONDARY WORKS

Albistur, Maïté and Daniel Armogathe. *Histoire du féminisme français du moyen âge à nos jours.* Paris: Editions des femmes, 1977.

Angenot, Marc. *Les Champions des femmes: Examen du discours sur la supériorité des femmes 1400–1800.* Montréal: Presses de l'Université du Québec, 1977.

Antonioli, Roland. *Rabelais et la médecine.* Geneva: Droz, 1976.

Armstrong, Elizabeth. *Before Copyright: The French Book-Privilege System 1498–1526.* Cambridge University Press, 1990.

Ascoli, Georges. "Bibliographie pour servir à l'histoire des idées féministes depuis le milieu du xvi^c jusqu'à la fin du xviii^c siècle," *Revue de Synthèse Historique* 13 (1906), 99–106.

"Essai sur l'histoire des idées féministes en France du xvi^c siècle à la Révolution." *Revue de Synthèse Historique* 13 (1906), 25–57.

Baird, Joseph L. and John R. Kane. *La Querelle de la Rose: Letters and Documents.* Chapel Hill: North Carolina Studies in the Romance Languages and Literatures, 1978.

Baker, Deborah Lesko. *The Subject of Desire: Petrarchan Poetics and the Female Voice in Louise Labé.* West Lafayette: Purdue University Press, 1996.

Balmas, Enea. *Un poeta del Rinascimento francese – Etienne Jodelle. La sua vita, il suo tempo.* Florence: Leo S. Olschki, 1962.

Bapst, Germain. *Essai sur l'histoire du théâtre: la mise en scène, le décor, le costume, l'architecture, l'éclairage, l'hygiène.* Paris: Hachette, 1893.

Barish, Jonas. *The Antitheatrical Prejudice*. Berkeley: University of California Press, 1981.

Bauschatz, Cathleen M. " 'L'oeil et la main': Gender and Revision in Marie de Gournay's 'Préface de 1595'." *Montaigne Studies* 7 (1995), 89–102.

"Marie de Gournay's 'Préface de 1595': A Critical Evaluation." *Bulletin de la Société des Amis de Montaigne* 7/3–4 (1986), 73–82.

Beck, William John. "Montaigne face à l'homosexualité." *Bulletin de la Société des Amis de Montaigne* 6/9–10 (1982), 41–50.

Berriot-Salvadore, Evelyne. *Les Femmes dans la société française de la Renaissance*. Geneva: Droz, 1990.

Un Corps, un destin: la Femme dans la médecine de la Renaissance. Paris: Champion, 1993.

Bertreux, H. "Les ascendances et les hérédités juives de Montaigne." *Revue Hebdomadaire* 12 (February 1938), 220–8.

Binford, Roberta Kay. "The *Comptes amoureux* of Jeanne Flore: A Critical Study." Diss. University of Iowa, 1972.

Blamires, Alcuin, Karen Pratt, and C. W. Marx. *Woman Defamed and Woman Defended: An Anthology of Medieval Texts*. Oxford: Clarendon Press, 1992.

Blum, Claude. "Marie de Gournay éditrice des *Essais*." *Bulletin de la Société des Amis de Montaigne* 7/1–3 (1996), 25–37.

Bonnefon, Paul. *Montaigne et ses amis*. Paris: Armand Colin, 1898.

Montaigne: l'homme et l'œuvre. Bordeaux: G. Gounouilhou; Paris: J. Rouam, 1893.

"Une Supercherie de Mlle de Gournay." *Revue d'Histoire Littéraire de la France* 3 (1896), 71–89.

Boswell, John. *Same-Sex Unions in Premodern Europe*. New York: Vintage Books, 1995.

Boucher, Jacqueline. *Société et mentalités autour de Henri III*. Paris: Champion, 1981.

La Cour de Henri III. Ouest-France, 1986.

Bray, Alan. *Homosexuality in Renaissance England*. London: Gay Men's Press, 1982.

"Homosexuality and Male Friendship," in *Queering the Renaissance*, ed. Goldberg, pp. 42–7.

Brenkman, John. "Narcissus in the Text." *Georgia Review* 30 (1976), 293–327.

Brown, Cynthia J. *Poets, Patrons, and Printers: Crisis of Authority in Late Medieval France*. Ithaca and London: Cornell University Press, 1995.

Buche, Joseph. "Pernette du Guillet et la 'Délie' de Maurice Scève," in *Mélanges de philologie offerts à Ferdinand Brunot*. Paris: Société nouvelle de Librairie et d'Edition, 1904, pp. 33–9.

Cady, Joseph. " 'Masculine Love,' Renaissance Writing, and the 'New Invention of Homosexuality,' " in *Homosexuality in Renaissance and Enlightenment England: Literary Representations in Historical Context*. Ed. Claude J.

Summers. New York: Harworth Press, Harrington Park Press, 1992, pp. 9–40.

"The 'Masculine Love' of the 'Princes of Sodom.' 'Practising the Art of Ganymede' at Henri III's Court: The Homosexuality of Henri III and His *Mignons* in Pierre de L'Estoile's *Mémoires-Journaux*," in *Desire and Discipline: Sex and Sexuality in the Premodern West*. Ed. Jacqueline Murray and Konrad Eisenbichler. Toronto, Buffalo, London: University of Toronto Press, 1996, pp. 123–54.

Cameron, Keith. *Henri III: A Maligned or Malignant King?* University of Exeter, 1978.

Louise Labé: Renaissance Poet and Feminist. New York, Oxford, Munich: Berg, 1990.

Cartier, Alfred and Adolphe Chenevière. "Antoine Du Moulin: valet de chambre de la reine de Navarre." *Revue d'Histoire Littéraire de la France* 2 (1895), 469–90; 3 (1896), 90–106.

Castor, Grahame. *Pléiade Poetics: A Study in Sixteenth-Century Thought and Terminology*. Cambridge University Press, 1964.

Cave, Terence. *The Cornucopian Text: Problems of Writing in the French Renaissance*. Oxford: Clarendon Press, 1979.

Champion, Pierre. "La Légende des mignons." *Bibliothèque d'Humanisme et Renaissance* 6 (1939), 494–528.

Charpentier, Françoise. "L'absente des *Essais*: quelques questions autour de l'Essai II-8, 'de l'affection des pères aux enfans'." *Bulletin de la Société des Amis de Montaigne* 17–18 (1984), 7–16.

Chartier, Roger (ed.). *The Culture of Print: Power and the Uses of Print in Early Modern Europe*. Oxford: Polity Press, 1989.

Chatelain, Dr. Review of Richard von Krafft-Ebing, *Psychopathia sexualis mit besonderer Berücksichtigung conträren Sexualempfindung*, Stuttgart, 1886, in *Annales Médico-Psychologiques* 14 (Sept.-Oct. 1891), 330–1.

Chevallier, Pierre. *Henri III, roi shakespearien*. Paris: Fayard, 1985.

Cholakian, Patricia. *Rape and Writing in the Heptaméron of Marguerite de Navarre*. Carbondale and Edwardsville: Southern Illinois University Press, 1991.

Clark, Donald Lemen. "The Rise and Fall of Progymnasmata in Sixteenth and Seventeenth Century Grammar Schools," *Speech Monographs* 19 (1952), 259–63.

Colie, Rosalie. *Paradoxia epidemica: The Renaissance Tradition of Paradox*. Princeton University Press, 1966.

Cottrell, Robert. "Pernette Du Guillet and the Logic of Aggressivity," in *Writing the Renaissance: Essays on Sixteenth-Century French Literature in Honor of Floyd Gray*. Ed. Raymond C. La Charité. Lexington: French Forum, 1992, pp. 93–113.

Sexuality/Textuality: A Study of the Fabric of Montaigne's Essais. Columbus: Ohio University Press, 1981.

Crane, William G. *Wit and Rhetoric in the Renaissance: The Formal Basis of Elizabethan Prose Style.* Gloucester, MA: Peter Smith, 1964.

Culler, Jonathan. *On Deconstruction: Theory and Criticism after Structuralism.* Ithaca: Cornell University Press, 1982.

Curtius, Ernst Robert. *European Literature and the Latin Middle Ages.* New York: Harper and Row, 1953.

Daston, Lorraine and Katharine Park. "The Hermaphrodite and the Orders of Nature," in *Premodern Sexualities.* Ed. Louise Fradenbury and Carla Freccero. New York and London: Routledge, 1996, pp. 117–36.

Davis, Natalie Zemon. "Boundaries and the Sense of Self," in *Constructing Individualism: Autonomy, Individuality, and the Self in Western Thought.* Ed. Thomas C. Heller, Morton Sonsa, and David E. Wellbery. Stanford University Press, 1986, pp. 53–63

"Protestantism and the Printing Workers of Lyons: A Study in the Problem of Religion and Social Class During the Reformation." Diss., University of Michigan, 1959.

De Rocher, Gregory. "Ronsard's Dildo Sonnet: The Scandal of Poissy and Rasse des Nœux," in *Writing the Renaissance: Essays on Sixteenth-Century French Literature in Honor of Floyd Gray.* Ed. Raymond C. La Charité. Lexington: French Forum, 1992, pp. 149–64.

DeJean, Joan. *Fictions of Sappho 1546–1937.* Chicago and London: University of Chicago Press, 1989.

Dejob, Charles. *Marc-Antoine Muret: un professeur français en Italie dans la seconde moitié du XVIe siècle.* Paris, Ernest Thorin, 1881.

Delumeau, Jean. *La Civilisation de la Renaissance.* Paris: Arthaud, 1967.

Devaux, Jean. *Jean Molinet indiciaire bourguignon.* Paris: Champion, 1996.

Dezon-Jones, Elyane. *Fragments d'un discours féminin.* Paris: Corti, 1988.

Doumic, René. "Le féminisme au temps de la Renaissance." *Revue des Deux Mondes* 149 (1898), 921–32.

Dulieu, Louis. "Laurent Joubert, chancelier de Montpellier." *Bibliothèque d'Humanisme et Renaissance* 31 (1969), 139–63.

Duviard, Ferdinand. "A la trace du vrai Montaigne: Montaigne en ménage." *Revue des Sciences Humaines* Fasc. 81 (1956), 5–18.

Febvre, Lucien. *Autour de l'Heptaméron: Amour sacré, amour profane.* Paris: Gallimard, 1944.

Freccero, Carla. "Rape's Disfiguring Figures: Marguerite de Navarre's *Heptaméron,* Day I: 10," in *Rape and Representation.* Ed. Lynn A. Higgins and Brenda R. Silver. New York: Columbia University Press, 1991, pp. 227–47.

"The Other and the Same: The Image of the Hermaphrodite in Rabelais," in *Rewriting the Renaissance: The Discourses of Sexual Difference in Early Modern Europe.* Ed. Margaret W. Ferguson, Maureen Quilligan, and Nancy J. Vickers. Chicago and London: University of Chicago Press, 1986, pp. 145–58.

Garin, Eugenio, Paolo Rossi, and Cesare Vasoli. *Testi umanistici su la retorica.* Rome and Milan: Fratelli Bocca, 1953.

Goldberg, Jonathan. "Colin to Hobbinol: Spencer's Familiar Letters," in *Displacing Homophobia: Gay Male Perspectives in Literature and Culture.* Ed. Ronald R. Butters, John M. Clum and Michael Moon. Durham, NC and London: Duke University Press, 1989, pp. 107–26.

Goldberg, Jonathan (ed.). *Queering the Renaissance.* Durham, NC and London: Duke University Press, 1994.

Goyet, Francis. *Le Sublime du "lieu commun": L'invention rhétorique dans l'Antiquité et à la Renaissance.* Paris: Champion, 1996.

Gray, Floyd. *La Balance de Montaigne: exagium/essai.* Paris: Nizet, 1982.

Montaigne bilingue: le latin des Essais. Paris: Champion, 1991.

Greenblatt, Stephen. "Fiction and Friction," in *Reconstructing Individualism: Autonomy, Individuality, and the Self in Western Thought.* Ed. Thomas C. Heller, Morton Sosna, and David E. Wellbery. Stanford University Press, 1986, pp. 30–52.

Guillerm-Curutchet, Luce, Jean-Pierre Guillerm, Laurence Hordoir-Louppe and Marie-Françoise Piéjus (ed.), *La Femme dans la littérature française et les traductions en français du XVIe siècle.* Lille: Publication de l'Université de Lille III, 1971.

Howarth, William D. *French Theatre in the Neo-Classical Era, 1550–1789,* Cambridge University Press, 1997.

Huet, Marie-Hélène. *Monstrous Imagination.* Cambridge, MA and London: Harvard University Press, 1993.

Hunt, Lynn. *The Invention of Pornography: Obscenity and the Origins of Modernity, 1500–1800.* New York: Zone Books, 1993.

Hyatte, Reginald. *Laughter for the Devil: The Trials of Gilles de Rais, Companion-in-arms of Joan of Arc (1440).* Introduction and translation from Latin and French. London and Toronto: Associated University Presses, 1984.

Jondorf, Gillian. *French Renaissance Tragedy: The Dramatic Word.* Cambridge University Press, 1990.

Jones, Ann Rosalind. "Assimilation with a Difference: Renaissance Women Poets and Literary Influence." *Yale French Studies* 62 (1981), 135–53.

The Currency of Eros: Women's Love Lyric in Europe, 1540–1620. Bloomington and Indianapolis: Indiana University Press, 1990.

Jones, Ann Rosalind and Peter Stallybrass. "Fetishizing Gender: Constructing the Hermaphrodite in Renaissance Europe," in *Body Guards: The Cultural Politics of Gender Ambiguity.* Ed. Julia Epstein and Kristina Straub. New York and London: Routledge, 1991, pp. 80–111.

Jordan, Constance. *Renaissance Feminism: Literary Texts and Political Models.* Ithaca: Cornell University Press, 1990.

Kelly, F. Douglas. "Reflections on the Role of Christine de Pisan as a Feminist Writer." *Sub-Stance* 2 (1972), 63–71.

Kelly, Joan. "Did Women Have a Renaissance?" in *Women, History and Theory.* Chicago: The University of Chicago Press, 1984, pp. 65–109.

"Early Feminist Theory and the *Querelle des Femmes, 1400–1789.*" *Signs: Journal of Women in Culture and Society* 8 (1982), 4–28.

Kelso, Ruth. *Doctrine for the Lady of the Renaissance.* Urbana: University of Illinois Press, 1956.

Kennedy, William J. *Authorizing Petrarch.* Ithaca and London: Cornell University Press, 1994.

  Rhetorical Norms in Renaissance Literature. New Haven and London: Yale University Press, 1978.

Kenney, Arthur F. *Markets of Bawdrie: The Dramatic Criticism of Stephen Gosson.* Salzburg Studies in Literature 4. Salzburg: Institut für Englische Sprache und Literatur, 1974.

Knox, Dilwyn. *Ironia: Medieval and Renaissance Ideas on Irony.* Leiden: Brill, 1989.

Kotler, Eliane. "Syntaxe et narration. Le rôle des relatives dans les passages narratifs de l'*Heptaméron*," in *Colloque Marguerite de Navarre 15–16 février 1992.* Université de Nice-Sophia Antipolis: Faculté des Lettres, Arts et Sciences humaines, 1998.

Kritzman, Lawrence D. *The Rhetoric of Sexuality and the Literature of the French Renaissance.* Cambridge University Press, 1991.

La Clavière, R. de Maulde. *La Femme de la Renaissance.* Paris: Perrin, 1898.

La Garanderie, M.-M. de (ed.). *Mercure à la Renaissance. Actes des Journées d'Etude des 4–5 octobre 1984, Lille.* Poitiers: P. Oudin, 1988.

Larsen, Anne R. "'Un honneste passetems': Strategies of Legitimation in French Renaissance Women's Prefaces." *L'Esprit Créateur* 30.4 (1990), 11–22.

Lauvergnat-Gagnière, Christiane. "La Rhétorique dans *Le Débat de Folie et d'Amour*," in *Louise Labé: les voix du lyrisme.* Ed. Guy Demerson. Paris: Editions du CNRS, 1990.

Lazard, Madeleine. *Images littéraires de la femme à la Renaissance.* Paris: Presses Universitaires de France, 1985.

  Le Théâtre en France au XVIᵉ siècle. Paris: Presses Universitaires de France, 1980.

  Pierre de Bourdeille, seigneur de Brantôme. Paris: Fayard, 1995.

Le Paulmier, Le Docteur (Claude-Stéphen). *Ambroise Paré, d'après de nouveaux documents découverts aux Archives Nationales et des papiers de famille.* Paris: Perrin, 1887.

Lecointe, Jean. *L'Idéal et la différence: la perception de la personnalité littéraire à la Renaissance.* Geneva: Droz, 1993.

Levine, Laura. *Men in Women's Clothing: Anti-Theatricality and Effeminization, 1579–1642.* Cambridge University Press, 1994.

Lingo, Alison Klairmont. "Print's Role in the Politics of Women's Health Care in Early Modern France," in *Culture and Identity in Early Modern Europe (1500–1800). Essays in Honor of Natalie Zemon Davis.* Ed. Barbara B. Diefendorf and Carla Hesse. Ann Arbor: University of Michigan Press, 1993, pp. 203–21.

Long, Kathleen Perry. "Hermaphrodites Newly Discovered: The Cultural Monsters of Sixteenth-Century France," in *Monster Theory*. Ed. Jeffrey Jerome Cohen. Minneapolis and London: University of Minnesota Press, 1996, pp. 183–201.

Longeon, Claude. "Du nouveau sur les *Comptes Amoureux* de Madame Jeanne Flore," in *Hommes et Livres de la Renaissance*. Université Jean-Monnet Saint-Etienne: Institut Claude Longeon, 1990, pp. 259–67.

Lorian, Alexandre. *Tendances stylistiques dans la prose narrative française au XVIe siècle*. Paris: Klincksieck, 1973.

McKinley, Mary. "An Editorial Revival: Gournay's 1617 Preface to the *Essais*." *Montaigne Studies* 8 (1966), 193–201.

Mack, Peter. *Renaissance Argument: Valla and Agricola in the Traditions of Rhetoric and Dialectic*. Leiden and New York: Brill, 1993.

Malvezin, Thomas. *Michel de Montaigne: son origine, sa famille*. Bordeaux: Charles Lefebvre, 1875.

Marboutin, J. R. "La librairie de Michel de Montaigne léguée à un Vicaire Général d'Auch." *Revue de Gascogne*, Nouvelle Série 21 (1926), 60–6.

Maskell, David. "Quel est le dernier état authentique des *Essais* de Montaigne?" *Bibliothèque d'Humanisme et Renaissance* 40 (1978), 85–103.

Mathieu-Castellani, Gisèle. *La Conversation conteuse: Les Nouvelles de Marguerite de Navarre*. Paris: Presses Universitaires de France, 1992.

"La parole chétive: les *Rymes* de Pernette du Guillet." *Littérature* 73 (1989), 46–60.

"Parole d'Echo? Pernette au miroir des *Rymes*." *L'Esprit Créateur* 30.4 (1990), 61–71.

La Quenouille et la lyre. Paris: José Corti, 1998.

Menut, Albert D. "Montaigne and the 'Nicomachean Ethics'." *Modern Philology* 31 (1934), 225–42.

Meyer, Paul. "Plaidoyer en faveur des femmes." *Romania* 6 (1877), 499–503.

Millet, Olivier. *La Première Réception des Essais de Montaigne (1580–1640)*. Paris: Champion, 1995.

Murphy, James J. *Renaissance Eloquence: Studies in the Theory and Practice of Renaissance Rhetoric*. Berkeley, Los Angeles, London: University of California Press, 1983.

Nadeau, Ray. "The Progymnasmata of Aphthonius." *Speech Monographs* 19 (1952), pp. 280–83.

O'Brien, Denis. *Empedocles' Cosmic Cycle: A Reconstruction from the Fragments and Secondary Sources*. Cambridge University Press, 1969.

Orgel, Stephen. "Nobody's Perfect: Or Why Did the English Stage Take Boys for Women?," in *Displacing Homophobia: Gay Male Perspectives in Literature and Culture*. Ed. Ronald R. Butters, John M. Clum, and Michael Moon. Durham, NC and London: Duke University Press, 1989, pp. 7–29.

Oulmont, Charles. "Gratian du Pont sieur de Drusac et les femmes." *Revue des Etudes Rabelaisiennes* 4 (1905), 22–23.

Panofsky, Erwin. *Essais d'iconologie.* Paris: Gallimard, 1967.

Parker, Patricia. "Virile Style," in *Premodern Sexualities.* Ed. Louise Fradenbury and Carla Freccero. New York and London: Routledge, 1996, pp. 201–22.

Patillon, Michel. *La Théorie du discours chez Hermogène le rhéteur: Essais sur les structures linguistiques de la rhétorique ancienne.* Paris: Les Belles Lettres, 1988.

Pérouse, Gabriel-André. *Nouvelles françaises du XVIe siècle. Images de la vue du temps.* Geneva: Droz, 1977.

" 'Cette autre licence grecque . . .': Montaigne et le Pausanias du *Banquet de Platon,*" in *Montaigne et l'histoire des Hellènes. Actes du Colloque de Lesbos.* Ed. Kyriaki Christodoulou. Paris: Klincksieck, 1994, pp. 184–94.

Piaget, Arthur. *Martin Le Franc Prévot de Lausanne.* Lausanne: F. Payot, 1888.

Plantin, Christian. *Lieux communs: topoï, stéréotypes, clichés.* Paris: Editions Kimé, 1993.

Poirier, Guy. *L'Homosexualité dans l'imaginaire de la Renaissance.* Paris: Champion, 1996.

Poel, Marc van der. *Cornelius Agrippa, The Humanist Theologian and his Declamations.* Leiden, New York, Cologne: Brill, 1997.

Quicherat, Jules Etienne Joseph. *Histoire du costume en France depuis les temps les plus reculés jusqu'à la fin du XVIIIe siècle.* Paris: Hachette, 1877.

Rabil, Albert. *Renaissance Humanism: Foundations, Forms and Legacy,* vol. 3, *Humanism and the Disciplines.* Philadelphia: University of Pennsylvania Press, 1988.

Rat, Maurice. "Le ménage de Montaigne." *Bulletin de la Société des Amis de Montaigne* 2/15 (1949–52), 14–23.

Read, Kirk D. "Bibliography." *L'Esprit Créateur* 30.4 (1990), 106–111.

Rebhorn, Wayne A. *The Emperor of Men's Minds: Literature and the Renaissance Discourse of Rhetoric.* Ithaca and London: Cornell University Press, 1995.

Regosin, Richard L. "Rhétorique de la femme: 'de farder le fard'." in *Montaigne et la rhétorique. Actes du Colloque de St Andrews 28–31 mars 1992,* ed. John O'Brien, Malcolm Quainton, and James Supple. Paris: Champion, 1995, pp. 228–9.

Montaigne's Unruly Brood: Textual Engendering and the Challenge to Paternal Authority. Berkeley, Los Angeles, London: University of California Press, 1996.

"Montaigne's Memorable Stories of Gender and Sexuality." *Montaigne Studies* 6/1–2 (1994), 187–201.

Reynolds-Cornell, Régine. "Madame Jeanne Flore and the *Contes amoureux*: A Pseudondym [*sic*] and a Paradox." *Bibliothèque d'Humanisme et Renaissance* 51 (1989), 123–33.

Richet, Denis. "Henri III dans l'historiographie et dans la légende," in *Henri III et son temps.* Ed. Robert Sauzet. Paris: Vrin, 1992, pp. 13–20.

Richou, Gabriel. *Inventaire de la collection des ouvrages et documents réunis par J.-F. Payen et J.-B. Bastide sur Michel de Montagne [sic].* Paris: Téchener, 1878.

Rigolot, François. "L'amitié intertextuelle: Etienne de La Boétie et Marie de Gournay," in *L'Esprit et la Lettre: Mélanges offerts à Jules Brody.* Ed. Louis van Delft. Tübingen: Günter Narr, 1991, pp. 57–66.

"Louise Labé et la redécouverte de Sappho." *Nouvelle Revue du XVIe siècle* 1 (1983), 19–31.

Louise Labé Lyonnaise ou la Renaissance au féminin. Paris: Champion, 1997.

"Quel 'genre' d'amour pour Louise Labé?." *Poétique* 55 (1983), 303–17.

Ruggiero, Guido. *The Boundaries of Eros: Sex Crime and Sexuality in Renaissance Venice.* New York and Oxford: Oxford University Press, 1985.

Rousset, Jean. "La Querelle de la métaphore," in *L'Intérieur et l'extérieur: Essais sur la poésie et sur le théâtre au XVIIe siècle.* Paris: Corti, 1968, pp. 57–71.

Rummel, Erika. *The Humanist–Scholastic Debate in the Renaissance and Reformation.* Cambridge, MA: Harvard University Press, 1995.

Ruwet, Nicolas. "Un sonnet de Louise Labé," in *Langage, Musique, Poésie.* Paris: Seuil, 1972, pp. 176–99.

Sankovitch, Tilde A. *French Women Writers and the Book: Myths of Access and Desire.* Syracuse University Press, 1988.

Saulnier, V.-L. "Etudes sur Pernette du Guillet et ses *Rymes.*" *Bibliothèque d'Humanisme et Renaissance* 4 (1944), 7–119.

Sayce, R. A. and David Maskell. *A Descriptive Bibliography of Montaigne's Essais 1580–1700.* London: Oxford University Press, 1983.

Schmidt, Albert-Marie. *Poètes du XVIe siècle.* Paris: Gallimard, 1953.

Schulze-Witzenrath, Elizabeth. *Die Originalität der Louise Labé: Studien zum weiblichen Petrarkismus.* Munich: Wilhelm Fink, 1974.

Schwartz, Jerome. "Scatology and Eschatology in Gargantua's Androgyne Device." *Etudes Rabelaisiennes* 14 (1977), 265–75.

Screech, M. A. "Rabelais, De Billon and Erasmus (A re-examination of Rabelais's attitude to women)." *Bibliothèque d'Humanisme et Renaissance* 13 (1951), 241–65.

The Rabelaisian Marriage: Aspects of Rabelais's Religion, Ethics, and Comic Philosophy. London: Edward Arnold, 1958.

Rabelais. London: Duckworth, 1979.

Silberman, Lauren. "Mythographic Transformations of Ovid's Hermaphrodite. *Sixteenth Century Journal* 20.4 (1998), 643–52.

Siraisi, Nancy G. *Medieval and Early Renaissance Medicine: An Introduction to Knowledge and Practice.* Chicago and London: The University of Chicago Press, 1990.

Sloane, Thomas O. *On the Contrary: The Protocol of Traditional Rhetoric.* Washington: Catholic University of America Press, 1997.

Solterer, Helen."Christine's Way: The *Querelle du Roman de la rose* and the Ethics of a Political Response?" in *The Master and Minerva: Disputing Women in French Medieval Culture.* Berkeley, Los Angeles, London: University of California Press, 1995, pp. 151–75.

Stanton, Domna C. "Woman as Object and Subject of Exchange: Marie de Gournay's *Le Proumenoir* (1594)." *L'Esprit Créateur* 23.2 (1983), 9–25.

"Autogynography: The Case of Marie de Gournay's 'Apologie pour celle qui escrit'," in *Autobiography in French Literature*, French Literature Series 12. Columbia, SC, 1985, pp. 18–31.

Stevens, Forest Tyler. "Erasmus's 'Tigress': The Language of Friendship, Pleasure, and the Renaissance Letter," in *Queering the Renaissance*, ed. Jonathan Goldberg, pp. 124–40.

Swearingen, C. Jan. *Rhetoric and Irony: Western Literacy and Western Lies*. New York: Oxford University Press, 1991.

Telle, Emile V. *Erasme de Rotterdam et le septième sacrement*. Geneva: Droz, 1954.

L'Œuvre de Marguerite d'Angoulême, reine de Navarre, et la querelle des femmes. Toulouse: Lion, 1937.

Tetel, Marcel. *Marguerite de Navarre's Heptaméron: Themes, Language and Structures*. Durham, NC: Duke University Press, 1973.

"Une réévaluation de la dixième Nouvelle de l'*Heptaméron*," *Neuphilologische Mitteilungen* 72 (1971), 563–69.

Thibaudet, Albert. "Portrait français de Montaigne." *Nouvelle Revue Française* 40 (1933), 646–53.

Montaigne, ed. Floyd Gray. Paris: Gallimard, 1963. Reprint, Les Cahiers de la NRF, 1997.

Traverso, Edilia. *Montaigne e Aristotele*. Florence: Felice Le Monnier, 1974.

Trinquet, Roger. *La Jeunesse de Montaigne: ses origines familiales, son enfance et ses études*. Paris: Nizet, 1972.

"Recherches chronologiques sur la jeunesse de Marc-Antoine Muret." *Bibliothèque d'Humanisme et Renaissance* 27 (1965), 278–81.

"Sur un texte obscur des *Essais* éclairé par une lettre de Madame de Montaigne." *Bulletin de l'Association des Amis de Montaigne* 17 (1955), 45–48.

Vernay, Henri. *Les Divers Sens du mot raison autour de l'œuvre de Marguerite d'Angoulême reine de Navarre (1492–1549)*. Heidelberg: Carl Winter, 1962.

Villey, Pierre. *Les Sources et l'évolution des Essais de Montaigne*. Paris: Hachette, 1908.

Vinge, Louis. *The Narcissus Theme in Western European Literature up to the Early 19th Century*. Lund: Skånska Centraltryckeriet, 1967.

Weinberg, Bernard. *Critical Prefaces of the French Renaissance*. Evanston: Northwestern University Press, 1950.

Wickersheimer, Charles-Adolphe-Ernest. *Médecine et les médecins en France à l'époque de la Renaissance*. Paris: A. Maloine, 1905.

Williamson, Margaret. *Sappho's Immortal Daughters*. Cambridge, MA and London: Harvard University Press, 1995.

Wilson, Thomas. "An Epistle to Persuade a Young Gentleman to Marriage, Devised by Erasmus in the Behalf of His Friend," in *The Arte of*

Rhetorique (1560). Ed. Peter E. Medine. University Park: Pennsylvania State University Press, 1994, pp. 79–100.

Woodbridge, Linda. *Women and the English Renaissance: Literature and the Nature of Womankind, 1540–1620*. Urbana and Chicago: University of Illinois Press, 1984.

Zumthor, Paul. *Anthologie des Grands Rhétoriqueurs*. Paris: Union Générale d'Editions, 1978.

Index

Agrippa, Henri Corneille, 12, 19
amplification, 23, 24, 37, 42, 43
anachronism, 2, 26, 29, 63
  twentieth-century expectations, 14, 15, 46, 47
  "I," 65
  invention, 64–5
  rhetoric, 165
  right reading, 60, 68
  sexual orientation, 135
androgyne
  metamorphosis, 155
  Rabelais, 149–52
  sexual practices of, 161
  see also hermaphrodite
anonymity, 62–5
antifeminism, 11–18, 21, 27, 29, 134
  see also feminism, misogyny
antimatrimonial discourse, 12, 13, 14, 15, 16, 17, 30, 40
  see also misogamy
Apththonius, 6, 9, 22–3
Aretino, Pietro, 159
Ariosto, Ludovico, 145
Aristophanes, 16, 149, 150, 151
Aristotle, 18, 15, 141, 196n.6. 199n.27
Arthus Thomas, 145
Aubigné, Agrippa d', 107, 153, 154
autobiography 63, 73, 86, 87, 107, 108, 121, 126

Billon, François de, 21
blason, 36, 68, 97
Boccaccio, Giovanni, 32, 48, 104
boy actors, 148–9
Brantôme, Pierre de Bourdeille, Sieur de, 155
  cuckoldry, 157
  lesbianism, 156–59
  sexual exploitation, 159
  Sappho, 158
Cato, 9, 23

Catullus, 101, 102, 117, 145
censors and censorship, 127, 129,161, 162, 168, 208 n.1
Cicero, 8, 9, 22, 117, 126, 139
commonplaces, 8, 98, 99
  see also topos
context, 1, 2, 4, 5, 6, 13, 28, 34, 140
  cultural, 19, 134, 135
  decontexualized, 29
  homosexual, 140
  humanist, 14
  limits, 138
  masculine, 18
  print, 21
copy books, 7, 9
cross-dressing, 144–9
cuckoldry, 26, 158

dildos, 143, 157–8
distance, 30, 38, 46, 60, 72, 73
Du Bellay, Joachim, 10, 103, 166
Du Guillet, Pernette
  imitation, 77
  knowledge, 82–3
  myth of Acteon, 81–2
  Scève, 77–8, 81, 82, 83, 84, 85, 86
  word-play, 78, 79, 80, 81, 85
du Laurens, André, 199n.26
du Moulin, Antoine 77, 83, 84, 104
Duval, Jacques, 156, 199n.26, 200n.28

enargeia, 37
encomium, 13, 14, 23, 68, 89
epideixis, 13, 68
Erasmus
  homosexuality, 137–8
  marriage, 23–4
  pedagogy, 91–2
etymology, 17, 19, 38, 55, 59, 68, 94, 150

female voice, 83–4
  audience, 103
feminism, feminist, 13, 14, 20, 21, 27, 28, 29,
    164, 169n.1
  arguments, 164
  Flore, 31, 32, 44, 46
  language of love, 76
  Labé, 91, 94
  Marguerite de Navarre, 53
  Montaigne, 120
  see also antifeminism
Ferrand, Jacques, 162
Flore, Jeanne
  devisantes, 33, 44–5
  Echo and Narcissus, 42–5
  identity of, 177 n.2
  irony, 38–9
  narration, 35
  portrait and dress, 36–8
  reading public, 46
  rewriting sources, 35
  women, 61
furor poeticus, 92

gender
  and reading, 31–2, 47, 131–2
  and text, 146
Gournay, Marie de
  autonomy, 129–31
  as editor 125, 126
  editorial tinkering, 123–5
  and Montaigne's praise, 122–3, 125
  and Montaignes self-portrait, 128
  and Montaignes style, 127–8
  Promounoir, 126–7

hermaphrodite
  Lucretius, 152
  Ovid, 151
  Paré, 151
  Henri III, 152–4
  see also androgyne
homosexuality
  as concept, 134–5
  as condition, 135–6
  Erasmus, 137
  Montaigne, 138–44, 140–1
  print, 133–4
  same-sex marriage, 143–44
  see also lesbianism
husbands, 36, 37, 40, 41, 116
hypothesis and thesis, 22

imitation and invention
  Flore, 37–38, 64–5

mimêsis, 7
  perfunctory, 166
  Pernette, 77–8
  Plato, 148
  Labé, 88
  self-conscious, 10
intertext and intertextuality, 7, 28, 38, , 89,
    96, 98
irony, 30, 34–5, 38–9, 40
  as commentary, 88
  Gournay, 124
  Labé, 95–98
  Marguerite de Navarre, 54
  Montaigne, 144
  Pernette, 35, 38–9, 40

Jodelle, Eugène, 146–8
Joubert, Laurent, 159–60

La Boétie, Etienne de, 122, 131, 138–9
Labé, Louise
  Calvin, 145–6
  Débat de Folie et d'Amour, 89–93, 104
  Du Bellay, 103, 166
  Elégies, 94–7
  Erasmus, 91–2
  female logic, 102–3
  feminism, 92
  memory, 95–6
  rhetorical code, 93, 94, 97, 101
  sonnets, 97–104
Le Fevre, Jean, 17
Lefranc, Abel, 14, 15, 28
Le Franc, Martin, 19
Lemaire de Belges, Jean, 69–73, 78, 80
lesbianism, 136, 156–9, 161–2
  see also homosexuality
Lipsius, Justus, 127, 129
Lorris, Guillaume, 16, 17, 20
Lucretius, 116, 117, 118, 152

margins and marginalizing, 19–20, 62, 63,
    72, 74, 86, 87, 108, 164–5, 166, 167
Marguerite de Navarre
  devisantes, 50, 51, 58–9, 61
  objectivity, 52, 58, 60
  originality, 51
  rape, 53–4
  repos, 54–5
  rhetoric, 53–4, 55
  textual reality, 56–8, 60
  virtue, 59
Marot, Clément, 73–6
  and Villon, 73
Martial, 117, 140, 157, 159

Meun, Jean de, 16, 17, 20
misogamy, 12, 14, 16, 30, 40
    see also antimatrimonial discourse
misogyny, 3, 6, 11, 14, 15, 16, 17, 18, 20, 21, 30,
    61, 116, 120, 164
    see also antifeminism
Molinet, Jean, 66–9
Montaigne, Michel de
    autobiography, 108
    biography, 109, 120
    daughter, 112–3
    digression, 118
    embrouilleure, 119–20
    father, 110–11
    gendered language, 117–18
    Jewishness, 113–5
    licence grecque, 138–40
    misogyny, 116–17
    the *moi*, 107
    mother, 113, 115
    Journal de voyage, 136, 141–4, 167
    printing, 111
    wife and marriage, 109, 112, 116
Muret, Marc-Antoine, 141

narrator
    anonymous, 49
    dramatized, 75
    female, 34
    objective, 47
    narrative space, 50
Nevizzano, Giovanni, 14, 21, 23

Ovid, 18, 64, 65, 142, 158
    Echo and Narcissus, 42–5
    Hermaphroditus, 151–2

paradox, 12–13, 28, 41, 67, 68
paratext, 62, 67
Paré, Ambroise, 160–2
parody, 13, 31, 32, 78, 94, 165–6
    and irony, 34–5
    and imitation, 37–8
    Labé, 37–8
Petrarch and Petrarchism, 20, 39, 89
    antithesis, 97–8
    female rewriting, 82, 88–9, 121, 132,
        146
    masculine discourse, 31, 76, 92
    parody, 94, 165
    rhetoric, 87, 99–01
Pisan, Christine de, 17–8, 104, 164
Plato and Platonism, 8, 15, 20, 82, 128, 139
    androgyne, 149–52
    dialogue, 52

female rewriting, 31, 39, 87–8, 121, 132,
    146
furor, 64
gynocology, 25
love, 86, 90–1, 102–3
parody, 165
and theatre, 148
play in literature, 10, 15, 31, 168
    differences, 47
pornography
    Brantôme, 159
    definition, 208 n.1
    medical literature, 159–63
    Renaissance, 167–8
print, printing, and print culture
    commercial interest, 3–4, 31, 163, 165
    discourses, 2
    author, 66–7, 75–6, 107
    manuscript, 62, 72–3
    public, 4–5, 105
    reading, 169 n.3
    sexual exploitation, 156, 167
    women, 105, 106, 131–2

Querelle des femmes
    and printing, 19–20
    history, 15
    literary aspects, 14, 18–9
Quintilian, 8, 23

Rabelais, François
    androgyne, 149–52
    misogyny, 21
    medical context, 25
    Panurge and marriage, 22, 24–7
    printing, 105
    Querelle des femmes, 21, 27–9
    Rondibilis, 22, 24–5, 27
reader, 1, 7, 11
    audience, 61, 183 n.18
    humanist, 39
    female, 30
    male, 46
    and Rabelais, 21, 24, 28, 29
regendering, 40, 45, 62–3, 76
    and Labé, 86, 87, 88
    and Pernette du Guillet, 86
res/verbum, 7–9, 9–10
rhetoric
    dialectic, 7–8
    female, 94–7
    history of, 7
    masculine, 97–103
    Renaissance, 7, 8
Rhétoriqueurs, 10, 62, 65–6, 70, 82

Rimbaud, Arthur, 63–4

Sappho, 146, 158
Saulnier V. L., 21, 85, 86
Screech, M. A., 21, 22, 26, 27, 28
sex change, 141–3
sodomy, 135, 137, 195–6 n.5

suasoria or *controversia*, 23

topos, 6, 8, 18, 19, 20, 34, 37, 71, 94, 102, 116, 165
Tournes, Jean de, 4, 89

Virgil, 109, 110, 116, 118, 121

CAMBRIDGE STUDIES IN FRENCH

GENERAL EDITOR: Michael Sheringham (*Royal Holloway, London*)
EDITORIAL BOARD: R. Howard Bloch (*Columbia University*), Malcolm
Bowie (*All Souls College, Oxford*), Terence Cave (*St. John's College, Oxford*), Ross
Chambers (*University of Michigan*), Antoine Compagnon (*Columbia University*),
Peter France (*University of Edinburgh*), Christie McDonald (*Harvard University*),
Toril Moi (*Duke University*), Naomi Schor (*Harvard University*)

1 J. M. Cocking: *Proust: Collected Essays on the Writer and his Art*
2 Leo Bersani: *The Death of Stéphane Mallarmé*
3 Marian Hobson: *The Object of Art: The Theory of Illusion in Eighteenth-Century France*
4 Leo Spitzer, translated and edited by David Bellow: *Essays on Seventeenth-Century French Literature*
5 Norman Bryson: *Tradition and Desire: From David to Delacroix*
6 Ann Moss: *Poetry and Fable: Studies in Mythological Narrative in Sixteenth-Century France*
7 Rhiannon Goldthorpe: *Sartre: Literature and Theory*
8 Diana Knight: *Flaubert's Characters: The Language of Illusion*
9 Andrew Martin: *The Knowledge of Ignorance: From Genesis to Jules Verne*
10 Geoffrey Bennington: *Sententiousness and the Novel: Laying down the Law in Eighteenth-Century French Fiction*
11 Penny Florence: *Mallarmé, Manet and Redon: Visual and Aural Signs and the Generation of Meaning*
12 Christopher Prendergast: *The Order of Mimesis: Balzac, Stendhal, Nerval, and Flaubert*
13 Naomi Segal: *The Unintended Reader: Feminism and Manon Lescaut*
14 Clive Scott: *A Question of Syllables: Essays in Nineteenth-Century French Verse*
15 Stirling Haig: *Flaubert and the Gift of Speech: Dialogue and Discourse in Four 'Modern' Novels*
16 Nathaniel Wing: *The Limits of Narrative: Essays on Baudelaire, Flaubert, Rimbaud and Mallarmé*
17 Mitchell Greenberg: *Corneille, Classicism and the Ruses of Symmetry*
18 Howard Davies: *Sartre and 'Les Temps Modernes'*
19 Robert Greer Cohn: *Mallarmé's Prose Poems: A Critical Study*
20 Celia Britton: *Claude Simon: Writing the Visible*
21 David Scott: *Pictorialist Poetics: Poetry and the Visual Arts in Nineteenth-Century France*
22 Ann Jefferson: *Reading Realism in Stendhal*
23 Dalia Judovitz: *Subjectivity and Representation in Descartes: The Origins of Modernity*
24 Richard D. E. Burton: *Baudelaire in 1859*

25 Michael Moriarty: *Taste and Ideology in Seventeenth-Century France*
26 John Forrester: *The Seductions of Psychoanalysis: Freud, Lacan and Derrida*
27 Jerome Schwartz: *Irony and Ideology in Rabelais: Structures of Subversion*
28 David Baguley: *Naturalist Fiction: The Entropic Vision*
29 Leslie Hill: *Beckett's Fiction: In Different Worlds*
30 F. W. Leakey: *Baudelaire: Collected Essays, 1953–1988*
31 Sarah Kay: *Subjectivity in Troubadour Poetry*
32 Gillian Jondorf: *French Renaissance Tragedy: The Dramatic Word*
33 Lawrence D. Kritzman: *The Rhetoric of Sexuality and the Literature of the French Renaissance*
34 Jerry C. Nash: *The Love Aesthetics of Maurice Scève: Poetry and Struggle*
35 Peter France: *Politeness and its Discontents: Problems in French Classical Culture*
36 Mitchell Greenberg: *Subjectivity and Subjugation in Seventeenth-Century Drama and Prose: The Family Romance of French Classicism*
37 Tom Conley: *The Graphic Unconscious in Early Modern French Writing*
38 Margery Evans: *Baudelaire and Intertextuality: Poetry at the Crossroads*
39 Judith Still: *Justice and Difference in the Works of Rousseau: 'bienfaisance' and 'pudeur'*
40 Christopher Johnson: *System and Writing in the Philosophy of Jacques Derrida*
41 Carol A. Mossman: *Politics and Narratives of Birth: Gynocolonization from Rousseau to Zola*
42 Daniel Brewer: *The Discourse of Enlightenment in Eighteenth-Century France: Diderot and the Art of Philosophizing*
43 Roberta L. Krueger: *Women Readers and the Ideology of Gender in Old French Verse Romance*
44 James H. Reid: *Narration and Description in the French Realist Novel: The Temporality of Lying and Forgetting*
45 Eugene W. Holland: *Baudelaire and Schizoanalysis: The Sociopoetics of Modernism*
46 Hugh M. Davidson: *Pascal and the Arts of the Mind*
47 David J. Denby: *Sentimental Narrative and the Social Order in France, 1760–1820: A Politics of Tears*
48 Claire Addison: *Where Flaubert Lies: Chronology, Mythology and History*
49 John Claiborne Isbell: *The Birth of European Romanticism: Staël's 'De l'Allemagne'*
50 Michael Sprinker: *History and Ideology in Proust: 'A la recherche du temps perdu' and the Third French Republic*
51 Dee Reynolds: *Symbolist Aesthetics and Early Abstract Art: Sites of Imaginary Space*
52 David B. Allison, Mark S. Roberts and Allen S. Weiss: *Sade and the Narrative of Transgression*
53 Simon Gaunt: *Gender and Genre in Medieval French Literature*
54 Jeffrey Mehlman: *Genealogies of the Test: Literature, Psychoanalysis, and Politics in Modern France*

55 Lewis C. Seifert: *Fairy Tales, Sexuality and Gender in France 1690–1715: Nostalgic Utopias*

56 Elza Adamowicz: *Surrealist Collage in Text and Image: Dissecting the Exquisite Corpse*

57 Nicholas White: *The Family in Crisis in Late Nineteenth-Century French Fiction*

58 Paul Gifford and Brian Stimpson: *Reading Paul Valéry: Universe in Mind*

59 Michael R. Finn: *Proust, the Body and Literary Form*

60 Julie Candler Hayes: *Reading the French Enlightenment: System and Subversion*

61 Ursula Tidd: *Simone de Beauvoir, Gender and Testimony*

62 Ann Jefferson: *Nathalie Sarraute, Fiction and Theory: Questions of Difference*

63 Floyd Gray: *Gender, Rhetoric, and Print Culture in French Renaissance Writing*

Lightning Source UK Ltd.
Milton Keynes UK
UKOW03f1804020614

232728UK00001B/48/A